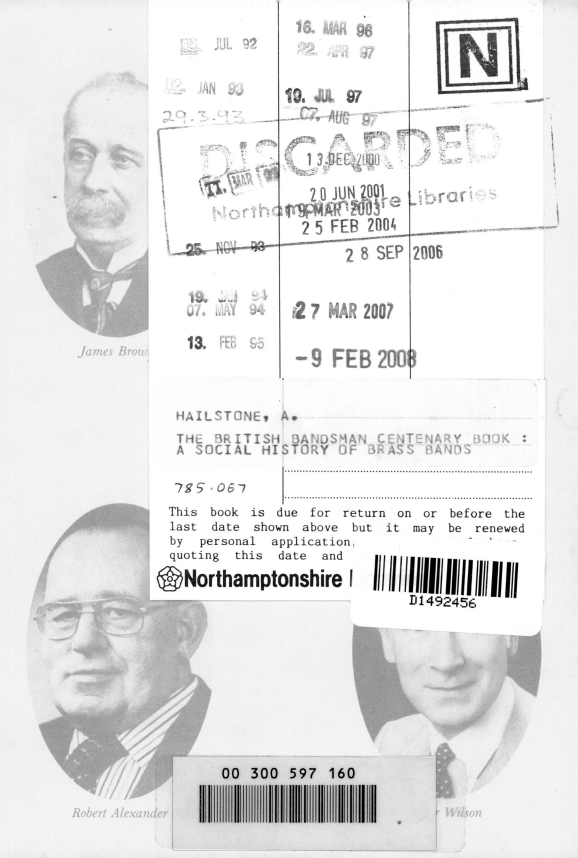

08. JUL 92

16. MAR 96
22 APR 97

N

02. JAN 93
29.3.93

10. JUL 97
07. AUG 97

DISCARDED

11. MAR

13. DEC 2000
Northamptonshire Libraries

20 JUN 2001
09 MAR 2003
25 FEB 2004

25. NOV 93

2 8 SEP 2006

19. JUN 94
07. MAY 94

27 MAR 2007

13. FEB 95

-9 FEB 2008

James Brown

Robert Alexander

Wilson

HAILSTONE, A.

THE BRITISH BANDSMAN CENTENARY BOOK :
A SOCIAL HISTORY OF BRASS BANDS

785.067

This book is due for return on or before the
last date shown above but it may be renewed
by personal application,
quoting this date and

Northamptonshire

D1492456

00 300 597 160

THE BRITISH BANDSMAN

CENTENARY BOOK

CENTENARY
BOOK

— a social history of
BRASS BANDS

by ALF HAILSTONE

EGON PUBLISHERS LTD.

Park Drive, Baldock, Hertfordshire SG7 6EW, England

Northamptonshire
Libraries

785·067

Published in 1987
by Egon Publishers Ltd.
Park Drive, Baldock, Hertfordshire SG7 6EW

Copyright © Alf Hailstone and Egon Publishers Ltd.

ISBN 0 905858 39 5

Designed and printed by
Streetsprinters, Park Drive, Baldock, Hertfordshire SG7 6EW, England

Bound by Staples Printers Rochester Limited

All rights reserved. No part of this book may be
reproduced or transmitted in any form or by any
means, electronic or mechanical, including photo-
copying, recording or by any information storage or
retrieval system without permission in writing from
the publisher.

Contents

Foreword

by Harry Mortimer

One of the pleasures (or penalties!) of long service in the band movement is the number of requests one receives to open bandrooms, present cups and prizes, and to write forewords for the work of colleagues who have embarked on the hard task of writing a book.

In the latter category comes this from Alf Hailstone, who with infinite patience and diligence has delved into the past history of the brass band movement. It is, indeed, an approach by one who is looking at the band scene not as player, conductor, adjudicator or composer, but as an interested enthusiast who is also an independent writer.

It is in no way a book of reference, but there are many events, bands and personalities referred to which you may not have heard of before – I certainly found several. For instance, one illustration on Page 81 is an example of the period when we all rehearsed and played at contests on a square bandstand, with the conductor standing in the centre – that was over 60 years ago, and is only one of countless recollections of the early days.

In fact, on reading this book I believe you will be surprised to find how difficult the past three years were and what wonderful progress our brass band movement has made. I hope you will enjoy reading it!

Harry Mortimer

Acknowledgements

The writing of history is the tribute every age pays to humanity in previous generations. We can know the nature of the ground on which we stand only if we know how we came to occupy it.

This book sets out to be a chronicle but sometimes I try to interpret the past to show decline from high principles or movement, progress or purpose in the course of events. It has been written, in the main, from one primary source, *The British Bandsman*. In a work of this nature access must, of necessity, be had to many and varied sources of information and here I wish to express my gratitude to the former editors, Eric Ball, Alfred Mackler and Geoffrey Brand, for their help and encouragement. Thanks are also due to Margaret Ogborn for her ability to prepare the book from my manuscript and, in particular, to the present editor, Peter Wilson, for his unstinting help. I am indebted to Charles Hailstone and John Diplock for the initial copy-editing.

I have also had the privilege of talking to bandsmen and other contemporaries now in their eighties who have memories of the past which were given to them by others long since departed.

Finally, I must acknowledge my indebtedness to the authors, past and present, of those books which I consulted, to the National Newspaper Library and the archivist of British Coal.

AGH

Flackwell Heath, 1986.

1 *Before publication*

In the mid-nineteenth century, the life of the working man was dull and hard. He worked six days a week, often twelve or more hours a day and, in many cases, alongside his wife and all his family, including the very young. Unions were struggling for recognition, and squalor and vice, crime and brutality were commonplace in the unplanned, overcrowded outer areas of the large industrial towns.

It seemed a life from which there was no escape. The disease-ridden atmosphere of the inadequately lit, unsafe and ill-ventilated mill or factory could be, perhaps, forgotten by drunkenness, singing hymns, joining seditious groups or herding together in recreational activities. It is remarkable how quickly brass bands were formed in these days for probably the same reason.

Men, often with less than five years' education, quickly mastered their instruments, learned the basics of musical notation and progressed through practice to playing in a band. Many towns, villages, manufacturing concerns and mines had either brass, reed or wind bands kept going by sponsorship or subscription.

Teachers, conductors, adjudicators, composers and administrators soon surfaced with native talent or were imported from regimental bands. Brass bands mushroomed so quickly that the opportunities to make money therefrom attracted all kinds of cheats and charlatans. Sub-standard uniforms, belts, buckles, caps and instruments were sold in their hundreds with absolutely no proper redress.

Badly organised contests were, more often than not, occasions for drinking and irrational behaviour. Much money was pocketed by dishonest treasurers; carters inflated transport charges and, with all the fun of the fair, the contests would attract the inevitable thieves, pickpockets and prostitutes.

Some bands were dedicated to their music and very disciplined in their approach to contesting. These bands were in great demand outside their immediate environment. They competed with similar bands in what were called 'true contests' and they viewed, with growing horror, the rag, tag and bobtail growth of the 'money contests' which tarnished their image.

In the early 1880s these lower contests were getting out of hand and no longer was the music the prime reason for so many people, often more than a thousand, to gather in a field. It was an occasion for men and women to swill ale all day in the beer tents, indulge in fighting and vandalism and to be the prey of pedlars, preachers or orators exhorting them to belittle Queen Victoria.

The news of these contests travelled quickly by word of mouth but it was not of musical prowess. It was of hooliganism, indelicacy, of how 'old so and so' could not hold his ale, fidgeted whilst playing, turned outwards from the square formation of the players and did it 'there and then' to the ribald comments of the women.

Prize money was shared out at the conclusion of the contest but most of it was soon gone into the pockets of breweries, itinerant tradesmen or beguiling women. None was left for

Sidmouth Town Band taken in 1862. Note the 'shako' type military headwear and the, then, fashionable beards worn in the Crimean War, still fresh in their memories. A 10% increase in living standards meant the poor, this year, could at last buy matches, soap and paraffin oil.

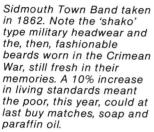

improving the standard of living of the large families they had left behind for the day and, when it came to going home, carters and station masters frequently called the police as brawling bandsmen blasphemed, swore and fought between themselves.

Even among the 'crack' bands, as they were known, dissention occurred at the contests. There was no hierarchy of control, no district, regional or nationally accepted set of rules and, worse, nothing to prevent non-bona fide members from playing in any band. When these bands began to fall out with each other and threats of libel, slander and all sorts of civil action were made, then well-known judges and conductors began to voice their fears that the brass band movement, 20 or so years old, was, in effect, committing suicide.

Sam Cope was privy to these fears. He was already quite famous as a teacher, conductor, composer and administrator and respected by bandsmen everywhere. He said in later life that the real reason he decided to publish *The British Bandsman* was because he had personally been slighted by a well-known musician. Apparently at a musical soirée which were all the vogue in those days, he had attempted to converse with the 'swell' but the gentleman declined as it was beneath him to talk to a conductor who was dressed in uniform and 'dammit not a military uniform either, infernal cheek!'

Sam Cope, founder and editor of The British Bandsman.

This set Mr. Cope thinking. How could he improve the status of the brass band? He was well equipped to supply the answer. he was the son of a bandmaster in the West Country. He played the piccolo in a pipe band at the age of eight. By the time he was 14 he was playing cornet solos at bazaars, fetes and local concerts. The loss of a finger cut short his career as an organist and he became bandmaster to men old enough to be his father. For a while he abandoned his music in favour of the law but soon returned to his first love.

He talked the problem over with some of his friends and soon conceived the idea of a magazine 'to chronicle events and marshal opinion' which might well provide the answer. Already there was in existence a newspaper which catered for brass bands but he envisaged a more personal approach, more technical and friendly. This would include teaching, musical philosophy and editorial comment.

All through 1887 he sought opinion, made financial sacrifices, gathered his friends around him and finally 'with fingers crossed and a prayer' decided to go ahead and in September 1887 the magazine was launched. There were to be two editors for the first year, he and James Waterson, but from then on Mr. Cope was both owner and editor of *The British Bandsman*.

James Waterson who edited The British Bandsman *with Sam Cope in its first year. (Photo: Royal College of Music).*

2 The first five years

It had a long title: *The British Bandsman. A monthly magazine for Bandmasters and Members of Military and Brass Bands*. Sam Cope was asked some time later why he called it *The British Bandsman*? It seems that in the embryo stage of planning, London had many German Bands busking in the streets so he decided to call it 'British' to avoid any identification 'with these foreign gentlemen'. Maybe an apocryphal story because another theory is that he toyed with the idea of calling his magazine *The British Army Bandsman* but this contradicted with his aim of reaching the civilian. In the end he compromised. You have to take your pick for there are other theories around.

The new magazine was sold by newsagents, on railway station bookstalls and, as was the custom in those days, from ticket agencies. the initial price was 2d. but, every three months, a music supplement complemented the magazine and the price was increased to 3d. In his first editorial, Mr. Cope wrote: 'We feel confident we can take with us the hearty and unanimous wish of all, that *The British Bandsman* may have a calm sea and a prosperous voyage'.

A calm sea? A bit of a problem in 1887. On the one hand many had celebrated, in all sincerity, the Golden Jubilee of Queen Victoria but on the other the Federation of Social Democrats had their meeting in Trafalgar Square, London, brutally broken up by the police and soldiers. This was known as Bloody Sunday and for years people remembered the looting of shops and houses in Pall Mall, Piccadilly and St. James's. Within a few months of its first issue more anxieties beset the authorities. On 10 February, London was enveloped in dense black fog and rumour gained credence that over 50,000 desperate men from the riverside suburbs were gathering, prior to an organised attempt to seize control of the city. The attack never materialised but this

atmosphere of apprehension prompted Cope to hope for a calm sea as his life savings were at stake.

Brighouse and Rastrick Brass Band, taken in 1885, the time of 'the Great Depression' which lasted to 1896.

From the beginning he never minced words and was forthright in his condemnation of what he called 'sly practice'. An opportunity to 'have a go' soon presented itself. There had been a long running dispute between military bandsmen and their officers who had prevented the various regimental bands from playing at engagements outside their particular military district. Consequently the weekly pay packet of the military bandsmen was seriously affected, performances suffered and morale became very low. Mr. Cope sprang to the defence of the bandsmen and blamed 'the whole vulgar row on a few parliamentary busybodies'.

For most of its first year *The British Bandsman* attracted little advertising and that which did appear seemed somewhat incongruous. One such advertiser only sold banjos. Its sixteen pages were filled with news which was mostly about regimental bands. Its first professional advertisement read: *W. H. Dowdhall, Late Bandmaster Oxfordshire Light Infantry. Available for musical contests of every description strictly adjudicated, or bands carefully prepared for same.*

Cope's main task was to try and settle the vexed question of band rules which varied considerably between bands. Few bands could agree on rules for contesting which, mainly, were agreed to be a show of hands on the day of the contests. It is not difficult to understand why so many contests broke up in acrimony. He therefore decided, within a very short while, to offer a prize for 'A Model Set of Rules'.

The early editions of the paper were completely sold out. How many we do not know and in his time as editor and owner he never revealed the true circulation figures. From readers' letters it seems many copies were purchased by the ordinary amateur bandsmen, most of whom could read music better than the written word. What they made of such articles as *Research into the songs of Schubert* and other erudite articles, blatantly reprinted from *The Musical Times* and *The Musical Society* is anyone's guess. A whole column was devoted to wind instruments whilst others described the science of music in terms which were hardly suitable for the layman.

Apart from this it was quite chatty. 'Fancy,' he wrote, 'I have just seen a lady cornetist but I am not surprised for you can see ladies now dressed in surplices and velvet caps and singing in church choirs'. There was also a column for humour, superfluous really for the news was quite unconsciously funny. He reported where, at a funeral of a bandsman, the band played so well at the moment of interment, that the mourners turned to applaud.

He appointed a chain of correspondents; ten in London, 66 in the rest of England, six in Wales and one in Scotland. Through devotion to journalistic duty one could progress to County Representative and eventually to Provincial General Representative. The Saltaire correspondent was immediately very active and seemed to want to progress, not that money was the spur for they were all unpaid. All these contributors had pseudonymns and just as well as it helped them to publish and be damned.

The Saltaire man wrote that *The Yorkshire Post* had written in no uncertain manner that the Saltaire contest officers should 'abandon the utter farce of band contests' in view of the disgraceful scenes at Saltaire in 1887. Research shows that a judge was severely jostled and subjected to unprintable abuse, after sitting for six long hours shivering in a wretched little tent on a miserable, wet, cold and windy day, hardly able to hold the pencil.

Another of his items included: 'The members of the Saltaire Brass Band were thrown out of the Tombstone coach whilst returning home from Liverpool. It is a matter of surprise that, pitched as they were from the coach, they should have escaped with their lives. Bandmaster Lewis had a narrow escape. He was thrown amongst the horses but was instantly pulled out by a bystander.'

Within six months letters were arriving at the rate of ten a day, the majority from orchestral players and, as a direct consequence of this, the title was changed in June 1888 to *The British Bandsman and Orchestral Times* and sub-titled 'A monthly illustrated magazine for wind instrumentalists'. It contained a gossip column — about who had attended concerts and where, who had accompanied them and how many carriages were used.

Articles about Meyerbeer, Wagner, Rossini and others proliferated and letters debated and argued over the most obscure and ancient musical terms. Military bandsmen participated in these often spirited exchanges but there is no evidence of the brass bandsmen being concerned or even any letters or complaint being received.

Regimental bandmasters began to report their own concerts although over pseudonymns. Writing in the third person they reported not only the items played and how they were received but ended inevitably with 'the band, under the able conductorship of the very talented bandmaster Mr. —, played magnificently before 1,500 people'. In the end so many of these reports were received, each vying with each other in self glorification, that they could only be published by reducing the size of print.

In *The British Bandsman's* second year the daily papers were full of Zululand being annexed by Great Britain and the many strikes, including the Great London Women's Matchmaking strike, although one item which was to have far reaching consequences seemed sadly neglected, but not by Sam Cope. Mr. Edison had invented the phonograph. *The British Bandsman* said: 'It is now quite feasible for hundreds of people to hear over the four quarters of the globe a man singing "Father O'Flynn" or "The Vicar of Bray". It is not for a brass band as every instrument would require a tube'.

He viewed this sensational development with great concern and over the weeks argued it was a backward step and the death knell for live performances. This did not, however, deter him from accepting advertisements for the machine.

The magazine grew to 24 pages, a few of which he devoted to brass band news. He was scathing in his comment about the hooliganism, drunkenness and 'rough usage of the judges' at the Belle Vue contest of 1888 held at Manchester and horrified to think 'the constabulary had to enter the hall'. He campaigned for an organisation on the lines of the Jockey Club to be set up nationally and to have an agreed set of rules, and a controller independent of the sponsor.

But it all came to nothing. It was a great disappointment to him and he could see no future in the brass band contesting scene. He made his magazine much more of an outlet for the orchestra. Reviews of classical concerts were published together with piano and classical music supplements. One can even notice the use of Latin phrases.

This did cause complaints and the editor reverted to a more balanced identity, but he did not relent. He wrote: 'For all our sakes copy your continental colleagues and stop the earpiercing, tormenting tutti. Consider, please, amongst other things, counterpoint, fugue, imitation, etc. and not the monstrous ta-ta-tha-ra-ta-ta'. Yet in the same issue he wrote that loud playing was not to be injurious to health. 'Incontestable medical authorities have proved exactly the contrary to the case. It develops the chest, strengthens the respiratory organs. Wind instrumentalists are invariably men of good constitution'.

Some of these instrumentalists became quite rich by making what were called 'brass appearances' in town squares. Mr. Cope said they were nothing but self styled artists and a positive disgrace to the arts. This led him into the controversy of 1888 (and it seems for ever more). 'What is an amateur?' he asked. To him it was simple: 'An amateur is a Lover. They mostly come from the Upper Classes'.

He was not at all averse to blowing his own trumpet and frequently reprinted news items from overseas periodicals which said what a fine fellow he was: '*The British Bandsman* possesses an Editor who has a fluent and graceful style. It is the essence of wisdom and good feeling. What would we do without Mr. Cope?' and 'I am a better bandsman and a better breadwinner because I am reading Mr. Cope's honest feelings and his love of music'.

Towards the end of 1888 brass bandsmen began complaining that they were fed up with the Editor's love of military bands. One said 'Who wants to read the full programme of the Kneller Hall concerts or to know how many officers were there and what medals they got?'. There was a spin-off from this and correspondence flowed in regarding the ideal programme. The Editor said whatever the programme the 'first piece should not be too light not too heavy but interesting'. This was backing it both ways but, nevertheless, a reader wrote thanking him for his wisdom.

In 1889, Messrs. Heywood & Co., Ludgate Hill, became the publishers of the magazine. At the same time Mr. Cope relinquished all his responsibilities other than editor and contributor. A structure evolved consisting of sub-editors, office administrators and accountants. A business manager was appointed. All this left the editor with much more time to become involved in the issues of the day.

Sabbatarians were active, campaigning for a total ban on Sunday music concerts. He was absolutely against this and he wrote how pleased he was 'to see the Lieutenant Governor of Portsmouth stop these Sabbatarians with excessive politeness. They were given the right about face without much palaver'. The Governor was on safe ground. He knew military band concerts were to be given on a Sunday at Windsor Castle 'for the comfort of Her Majesty the Queen'.

During this year the readers were told the circulation had doubled and all was set fair. Yet within a few weeks of this announcement the economy became quite depressed and work was hard to find, money was scarce and the Greater London Dock Strike took its toll on the availability of food. In the personal columns of the magazine one could read such advertisements as:

'Instrument player seeks position in Factory band. Not afraid of hard work such as porter, messenger, time keeper, or any place of trust, fair scholar, married, total abstainer'.

And another:

'I am a fair player, honest & sober, can turn to anything. Married with a large family but can attend practice regularly. Must be factory near Bradford'.

Now the magazine was on a sound footing Sam Cope wrote and wrote. Article after article appeared. One began: 'I can tell you the story of *Fra Diavolo* in a few words as the plot is simple' but it did not end until he had written one thousand words. He had though, from time to time, to come back to the muddy waters of contesting. Far too many bands were now applying to participate in the better contests because the money was good. Over 513 bands were now jostling for places in the top contests but, of course, many failed to make it. From the pages of *The British Bandsman* it is easy to see why. No more than 20 bands could knock off the coconuts.

The B.B., as it had now come to be called, published a list of ideal rules. Rule II read:

'Contest managers reserve the power to limit the number of competing bands. Should more bands enter (i.e. turn up) than is required, the entrance fee will be returned to those who entered last'.

On the face of it a proper democratic and necessary rule, but rarely used. If a band was told it was unlucky it would often move to the street or track and play loudly to disrupt the contest until other contesting bandsmen threw stones at them or moved them away by physical force.

In January 1891 the title was again changed to *The Orchestral Times and Bandsman*. The word 'British' was dropped because it was intended to reach the colonies and dominions overseas. The editor wanted the magazine to be an exhaustive encyclopaedia of music but not to rival Grove. It became, in modern parlance, very up-market and incorporated the *British Musician*. Nearly all of the issues were taken up with articles and comments about string and woodwind instruments, orchestral societies, choirs and sacred music. Articles on banjo and accordion playing ceased and the harp and French horn took their place.

Other articles were on Chinese music and the art of bowing. Advertisements were carried such as for Whiteland's Cremona Amber Oil Varnish for Violins, etc. The 'wanted' column was for bassoon, oboe, piano players and the like. Cope wrote: 'If you want your orchestral concerts to be mentioned and reviewed just send me the tickets'.

In 1891 *The British Bandsman* title and commercial rights were sold to F. Howard Doulton & Co. Sam Cope now felt free to reveal the circulation figure. 'We are selling at 5,000 and increasing by 100 each month'. No balance sheets have survived from these early days but from the money supply statistics, meagre as they are of the early 1890s, there is no doubt that at its price the magazine was making a healthy profit. Certainly the profit came from its interest to the orchestral player and the dilletante. There was now no news from brass band correspondents and the hierarchy was abandoned. Editorial comment ceased and letters dwindled away. In an issue of 26 pages only two were devoted to brass bands and this was mostly trivia such as:
'CLEANLINESS IN THE BAND ROOM
Provide waste paper baskets, make sure chairs are to be sat on and not used as leg rests. No smoking, as this poisons the air'.

In its fifth year, Mr. J. A. Browne, formerly Bandmaster of the Royal Artillery (Mounted) and one time editor of the *Surrey Musical Journal*, was appointed joint editor with Mr. Cope, by the new proprietors. The first five years ended with brass bands hardly tolerated. *The British Bandsman* had lost its identity.

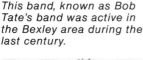

This band, known as Bob Tate's band was active in the Bexley area during the last century.

3 Resurgence

During the last decade of the nineteenth century the proprietors of *The British Bandsman* were always looking for ways in which they could increase circulation. It was obvious from the returns that there was insufficient interest from brass bands to sustain a magazine mostly printed for their benefit. It was decided to broaden the scope of its appeal and for most of the 1890s the magazine was called *The British Musician.*

This is not to say brass bands were totally ignored but interest shown by the editor was lukewarm, to say the least. By 1897 the unruly and scandalous scenes at many contests were beginning to affect the number of bandsmen in a band. Full instrumentation could not be provided because some players said enough was enough. Bands, like other organised groups, reflected all kinds of personal feeling, some were teetotal, others shy or extrovert, some committed Christians and good family men. No wonder a few withdrew and left the band short of players. Such was the aggravation that some bands ceased contesting altogether.

The editor wrote: 'The contesting field is dying because of the riotous assemblies. The military bandmasters are looking at us with utter contempt'. Judges were refusing to adjudicate and complained bitterly to the editor of the appalling conduct to which they were often subjected. They were upset at the stringent lengths to which promoters went to safeguard security. Some were blindfolded as soon as they left the railway station and were taken by wagon to the field. Some had to be in the tent an hour or so before the bands arrived.

The editor reported one ugly incident in which an entire band, not in the money, physically assaulted the judge, swearing, blaspheming and hissing as the bruised man stood dazed and trembling. The band then encircled him and played the *Dead March* from Handel's *Saul.*

It is certainly not too harsh to say that 1897 saw the beginning of disillusionment of the general public to contesting, from which the movement has never fully recovered. A few desultory measures were taken to introduce some control. The British Amateur Band Association did exercise a limited authority but inevitably lost the battle with the several beer tents which were always pitched temptingly around the field.

The British Musician asked, through Sam Cope, if contesting was necessary any more, because brass 'bands are now beyond the pale'. He complained of the betting, quarrelling and fighting, not only between bands and supporters, but between bandsmen themselves if they thought the 'pot of gold' the band had won had not been shared out properly. So it continued. Contests became fewer and fewer, concerts were rarely promoted and rehearsals withered away. From the comment later made by Sam Cope, apart from the 'crack bands' the movement had disintegrated and lost all credence and the proprietors of *The British Musician* were on the verge of abandoning the brass band altogether.

Suddenly a glorious sound rose up from the cities, towns, villages and even hamlets. Brass bands, dormant for some time and completely forgotten, reformed in their hundreds to take their place, completely swamping the 'crack bands', military

The Veryan Band taken around 1895. They are dressed in their best clothes which reveals the lack of ironing facilities in what was then a very remote part of Cornwall.

bands and other combinations, at the head of the processions to celebrate the Diamond Jubilee of Queen Victoria. National newspapers and the music world as a whole were astounded at this unsuspected and, hitherto, unidentified grass roots base for brass.

One of these bandsmen is reported as saying: 'My jacket fair bust with pride as we marched full of sparsey spirit past the Mayor. I never see him before and he doffed his high hat to us'. One interesting fact emerged from the research of the activities of these brass bands on the day of the Jubilee celebration. Apparently in a large town there were up to four processions. The one which had the fire brigade marching behind the band drew by far the largest crowd. A commentator of the time said: 'They love to see the gladitorial helmets and can get so worked up at the sight of the gold gleaming in the sunshine that they would have all willingly laid down their lives there and then for Her Majesty, should she have been in peril'.

The editor was quick to exploit this bubbling emotion. He published a special Diamond Jubilee song: 'Cheer! for the soldier boy on land. Cheer! for the lads at sea. Brave Volunteers! March hand in hand, To Keep Old England Free!'

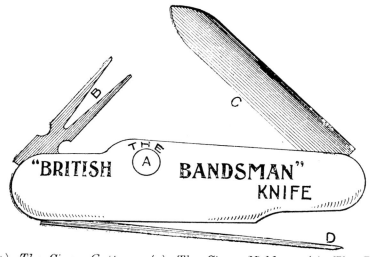

(A) *The Cigar Cutter.* (B) *The Cigar Holder.* (C) *The Pen Knife.* (D) *Pipe Cleaner.*

The first commercial give away 1901, worth 25p but sold to 'B.B.' readers at 3p.

News and comment of brass bands flooded back into the magazine as local correspondents stirred themselves and got caught up in the patriotic fervour. For a while brass bands dominated *The British Musician* but, alas, it was a nine days' wonder. Brass bandsmen were not buying the magazine. Its title repelled rather than attracted these men and so it remained until a colossus appeared when John Henry Iles strode onto the scene.

It is not difficult to assess the impact he has had on brass bands. The Bible says that without the vision the people will perish and this was probably true of the loosely knit brass band scene of the day. Mr. Iles did not deliberately set out to knock on the door and it was only by sheer chance that he found what Beethoven had called 'the unquenchable fire'.

But what kind of man was this who had the vision to influence bands and mould their world into what we see today? At the age of 15 years, shortly after leaving college, he was appointed organist and choirmaster at a Methodist church and studied singing under the world-famous Clara Butt. Soon he was showing considerable ability in organising concerts, was controlling a magazine called *The Organist and Choirmaster*, and had a journalistic interest in several musical periodicals of the 1890s.

In 1898 he was 27 years old with 12 years involvement with the commercial life of the City of London. His contempories were somewhat in awe of this young risk-taker. He had a fertile mind, a restless spirit and a flair for making money, a man to be reckoned with by the City Fathers – a Victorian whizz kid!

During this year he was in Manchester on business and, finding time on his hands, discovered there was a brass band contest being held at the Belle Vue gardens. He sat enthralled for hours 'thunder struck and thrilled at the sound'. Believing the players to be men with military band or orchestral experience, he said he found the truth 'a humbling experience'. He had never heard a brass band before!

He went back to his office but try as he might to immerse himself in the money market, he could not rid himself of this indelible experience. The picture of these bandsmen, playing beautiful music, sometimes delicately and sometimes with full power, haunted him. By his standards the players had little or no education, came from the grim industrial areas, where money was scarce and the masters held sway, yet made truly wonderful music.

Some unkind persons might see his vision as one prompted by a greedy desire to take the bands by the scruff of the neck and shake them unmercifully for profit. Others as a desire to bring brass bands to the notice of the musical world. The truth is, from all the evidence, that he found a hobby to help counteract the pressures of business.

With characteristic directness he contacted Sam Cope and laid his cards on the table. It was a simple message: 'I want to help'. From the very beginning they were firm friends and within 12 months Mr. Iles had purchased *The British Bandsman* and its stable companion, the brass music publishing house of R. Smith & Co.

On 1 January, 1899 the title reverted to *The British Bandsman* and sub-titled *An Illustrated Monthly Magazine devoted to the interests of Brass, Reed and String Bandsmen and the Trade*. At long last it had found its niche and thereafter only flirted from time to time with the classical music world. In August that year a magazine from

The British Bandsman.

An Illustrated Monthly Magazine devoted to the interests of Brass, Reed, and String Bandsmen, and the Trade.

VOL. XII.   No. 136.   January 1st, 1899.   PRICE THREEPENCE.

Below: The masthead of the 1899 'British Bandsman', with its rather awkward sub-title.

the same publishing house, called *The Contest Field* was published simultaneously with *The British Bandsman* and, under its editor, J. Ord Hume, it became compulsory reading for all contestants and reached a circulation figure of over 10,000.

It was whilst playing the cornet with the Brighton Aquarium Band, following his departure from the band of The Royal Scots Greys, that Ord-Hume met Sam Cope and a life long friendship began. He had a thorough knowledge of all aspects of music and was a teacher and adjudicator. To bandsmen he is known as a prolific composer of marches, one of the most famous of which is

Southampton Elementary Schools Band 1899 and one of the first in the country. Soon to be followed by orphanage and schools for the crippled bands.

the often played *B.B. and C.F.* which he composed for the magazine, the initials standing for *British Bandsman and Contest Field*.

The entrepreneurial flair of Henry Iles, as he liked to be called, soon showed itself. The magazine now cost 3d., had 28 pages and attracted substantial advertising. It offered free music, free accessories and, subject to certain conditions, free instruments to

The 'B.B.' grand prize list for military and brass bands which collected most money for the Boer War Fund 1899, showing yet again the close relationship between brass and military bands.

those readers who enrolled an agreed number of readers. Letters and professional advertisements reappeared. As the Boer War claimed its first casualties, *The British Bandsman* became one of the foremost organisations in the raising of money for dependants. In co-operation with the *Daily Mail* it began The British Bandsman War Fund.

A whole front page was devoted to this worthwhile effort. Readers were asked to imagine a railway station where a husband was entraining for war: 'A young mother with a child in her arms.

The last kiss. The last handshake. The last glance, perhaps for ever. Does this not touch your heart, bandsmen? While you are reading these words our soldiers are shedding their blood and the poor souls are crying at home with the little bairns around them wondering what is the matter with mother'.

Money came rolling in and an event occurred about which some of the older bandsmen can remember their parents telling

The advertisement for the great inaugural contest at the Crystal Palace – The 'National'. No agency work. Designed by the editor.

them. *The British Bandsman* organised a simple plan of campaign. It obtained the exclusive right to publish Sir Arthur Sullivan's stirring setting to Rudyard Kipling's great patriotic poem *The Absent Minded Beggar*. At the same time Messrs Boosey & Company gave *The British Bandsman* exclusive rights to all arrangements of this music as a quick march. J. Ord Hume agreed to do the musical adaptation and it sold at 6s. 4d for military bands and 4s. 4d. for brass bands. Thousands upon thousands were sold.

A unique 'Don't look at the camera' photograph of German bandmasters and John Rogan of H.M. Coldstream Guards taken in 1899 as an example of the Musical Entente Cordiale.

Opposite: An advertisement of the same year showing the eagerness of brass bandsmen to identify with the military.

The *Daily Mail* offered a list of magnificent prizes worth £300 to the bands which collected most money for the fund. *The British Bandsman* said, 'Let us prove Music and Love are akin'. With others, Henry Iles organised a great band festival in January 1900 at the Royal Albert Hall. Eleven bands took part including the world famous bands of Besses o' th' Barn and Black Dyke, with Dame Clara Butt as guest artiste.

Initially the ticket sales were sluggish and caused anxiety to the joint promoters. Henry Iles said it was a big headache. (Oddly enough this was the year aspirin was marketed). He used *The British Bandsman* in an all out assault to persuade his readers to buy tickets for the concert. Slowly the sales increased but a fiasco seemed imminent. Then, almost overnight, his persistent campaign succeeded and 2,000 tickets at 2s. 6d. each were purchased by bandsmen and the general public soon snapped up the others.

Over this period *The British Bandsman* was in the van of the fund raising activities. Henry Iles promised the monies of the fund, over £510,000, would not be hoarded or invested but distributed

Mallett, Porter & Dowd,

GOVERNMENT CONTRACTORS.

Telephone:
No. 662, KING'S CROSS.

BAND OUTFITTERS.

Telegrams:
"MALPORT, LONDON."

465, CALEDONIAN ROAD, LONDON, N.

Great Improvements for this Season.

High-Class Uniforms at prices within the reach of every Band.

ILLUSTRATED PRICE LIST SENT ON APPLICATION.

In writing please mention British Bandsman.

The Perseverence Temperance Brass Band 1900 with its home made banner for the 'B.B.' Boer War Fund.

The complicated points table of the early nationals.

immediately 'to those poor souls who, through the breadwinne having been called away, are left unprovided for'. This dramati statement created administrative difficulties and criticism mounte (somewhat like the recent Falkland's Fund) but statesman as h was, Henry Iles succeeded in his aim. There were in fact 5,77 British casualties suffered in the Boer War.

CRYSTAL PALACE CHAMPIONSHIP CONTEST

SEPTEMBER 28TH, 1901.

Table of Points gained by each Band.

Name of Band.	No. Drawn.	En-semble	Style.	Into-nation.	Sop. Cor.	Solo Cor.	Horns.	Barits.	Tromb.	Euph.	Basses.	Total.
Irwell Bank	1	12	12	10	8	6	6	6	6	8	8	82
Nantlle Vale	2	18	18	16	8	8	8	6	6	10	10	108
Lee Mount	3	20	20	20	9	10	10	8	10	10	10	127
Wingates Temperance	4	20	11	18	8	8	10	8	8	9	10	110
Kingston Mills	5	18	16	18	7	10	10	10	8	8	10	115
Batley Old	6	18	18	16	6	7	8	10	8	8	10	104
Crooke	7	16	14	16	4	8	6	4	6	7	10	91
Besses 'o th Barn	8	18	18	16	7	8	8	6	7	8	10	106
Hartlepool Operatic	9	18	18	16	7	8	8	5	7	8	10	105
Ferndale	10	16	16	16	6	8	7	4	8	8	10	99
Luton Red Cross	11	16	16	20	8	8	9	6	8	10	10	111
Kettering Rifles	12	19	19	18	11	8	10	10	8	8	10	121
Arael Griffin	13	16	16	15	6	8	8	4	6	9	8	96
Wyke	14	16	14	15	7	9	9	8	6	10	8	102
Irwell Springs	15	20	20	20	8	9	10	8	10	10	10	125
Northfield	16	16	15	14	7	9	9	8	7	9	9	103
Denton Original	17	20	20	18	8	11	9	9	9	10	10	123
Tillery Collieries	18	16	16	15	8	12	9	8	8	8	8	107
Rochdale Public	19	20	20	18	8	10	8	8	7	8	8	118
Dannemora	20	16	16	14	8	10	8	6	8	8	8	102
Kettering Town	21	20	20	20	8	8	10	8	8	8	10	120
Linthwaite	22	16	12	14	7	8	8	6	8	7	8	94
Rushden Temperance	23	18	15	15	8	7	8	6	8	7	10	102
Hucknall Temperance	24	16	12	12	8	8	8	6	8	6	8	92
Pendleton Old	25	16	15	16	7	7	7	7	8	4	8	95
Lindley	26	20	18	16	8	10	8	8	10	11	10	119
Rotherham Borough	27	18	12	12	8	8	8	7	7	9	10	99

The One Thousand Guinea Challenge Trophy competed for by brass bands from 1900 until World War II. It was acquired by John Henry Iles from the organisers of The Great Handel Contests of the late nineteenth century. Made in 'solid' gold and silver and richly jewelled, it is now a priceless piece in the hands of The Folk Museum of Wales.

A new century saw the introduction of the saxophone into ome brass bands and a new march called *The British Bandsman* ritten by the joint editor, J. A. Browne and scored, among other struments, for piccolo, oboe, clarinet and bombardon. A aracter also appeared writing under the pseudonym of 'Billy ounder', a kind of 'Private Eye' reporter. A terrible chap by all counts. Nothing was sacred and bands at functions, rehearsals d contests would say, 'look out, look out, Bounder's about'. metimes this contributor wrote in verse and signed himself

William Bounder, Poet, Prophet, Scribe to The British Bandsman and *Contest Field*. How he escaped prosecution for libel is a mystery.

Soon *The British Bandsman* began to publish letters which were quite abusive, yet all in good fun. The various denunciations of machiavellianism and sly practice by bands, the arguments and vilification, always ended in time with the protagonists pledging eternal friendship. Anyone could have a go, no one signed their names or revealed their bands. In one issue alone pseudonyms included 'The Owl', 'XYZ', 'Acorn', 'Well Wisher', 'Novitiate', 'Electra', 'Lover of Fair Play all Round' and 'Bumpetty Bum'. In all cases the writers were inviting each other to eat humble pie.

Remarks of the judges were now published of the many contests adjudicated. One such judge at Belle Vue wrote, 'Opening good', 'Band good', '*ff* attack good', '*ff* good', 'Allegretto good', '9-8 all good', 'Acceleration good', 'Molto good'. 'Should be in the prizes'. Well, at least Wingates (W. Rimmer) knew beyond all reasonable doubt that they were 'good'.

4 A gamble pays off

On 8 March, 1902 *The British Bandsman* became a penny weekly and sub-titled *A newspaper devoted to Brass Bands*. The economics of the publishing trade meant that half of the penny would be swallowed up in wages, administration and overheads and the other half by printing and distribution. Henry Iles had to underwrite the initial losses and said in his own editorial: 'Only by selling a huge number of copies can an undertaking of this nature be maintained'.

He gave his readers good value for money and the early issues were completely sold out. It now included numerous prepaid advertisements, eight full page advertisements and many displays. It carried an average of 70 news items relating to brass bands and a very extensive coverage of contests. The correspondents were instructed to write in a 'pithy, short and racy style' of which these examples were typical: 'Wot Ho: Here am the bird again. I have just been having a look around, and, my conscience, What Do I See? Things going with a large BIFF all over the show.'

'How to march in step. Start on the right foot and listen to the drum, drum, drum. Head up, not too high and never look down, down, down'. It ended upon a note of mystery, 'Remember Knaresboro!'.

'Goodness Gracious! Another year gone by and the Palace here again. It seems like only yesterday your humble was recounting his experience. Well, I was on duty and, my word, everything was trimmed with gild edge sparks and jewelled in four holes. Old Dick Wagner's piece was the Battle.'

Advertisements were becoming associated with the brass band and bandsmen allegedly endorsed products through unsolicited letters':

'I drink Doctor Tibbles' Vi-cocoa because it is favoured by the hospitals of Great Britain. Coffee clogs the stomach'.

'I used to have a cupboard full of pills. Then I discovered Page Woodcock Pills and after years of suffering I am no longer party to chronic indigestion, constipation [a wide spread worry in those days] stomach pains, hangover, liver troubles, nervousness and the wind'.

'I have had indigestion for years culminating in an ulcerated stomach and burst blood vessels but I tried your Mother Seigel's Syrup and am now completely cured for only 11½d a bottle'.

Henry Iles' vigorous projection of the magazine now attracted advertisements of all kinds, for prams, polish, pianos, bicycles, books, banjos: custard powder, wheelchairs, gramophones, stationery, acetylene lamps and one which read: 'An overcoat which you can wear with your uniform or work clothes'.

These advertisements must have had a fair response because they ran and ran. Henry Iles was now in profit. Yet money in the economy of the country was in very short supply. Bands were finding it almost impossible to find the money to enable them to contest at the Palace. 'Find a sponsor' urged Henry Iles. 'Call on the publican and ask him to donate a barrel of double X as a raffle prize. Call on the butcher for a whole sheep, BUT DO NOT FORGET to print a list of the prize winners or Mr. Policeman will

Full page advertisements. A much needed form of revenue. The words of the easy payment scheme for watches practically unchanged after 87 years.

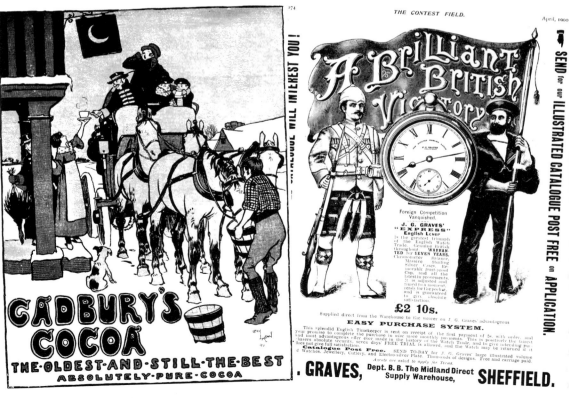

ave some doubts'. Would you believe, several publicans and
utchers did supply as Mr. Iles suggested.

Despite 'Uniform Funds', many bandsmen had to wear their
unday best when contesting as the cost of uniforms was too
igh. In some bands, some were in uniform, others were not. *The
ritish Bandsman* said: 'It is no use some wearing military style
eak caps and the others in trilbys, bowlers and boaters – much
etter, gentlemen, for all to wear nice flat caps.'.

The 'Uniform Fund' was always the first to be plundered and
ne editor reminded secretaries of the forthcoming coronation of
ing Edward VII and not to use the Uniform Fund for excursions
> contests, of which in this year alone, according to *The British
andsman*, over 150 took place. 'No', he wrote, 'use the fund for
plendent uniforms to parade yourselves in tribute to His
ajesty.'

VICTORIA – 1819-1901.

The Queen is dead : our Queen has passed away,
To all her lands the message sad did say.
From all imperial cares, she free, doth sleep,
And peoples, nations, all the earth doth weep.

The Queen is dead : Victoria well-beloved,
Rests from her labours.   Deeply moved
Her people mourn for her, who home has gone,
For heaven above has welcomed back its own.

The Queen is dead : Victoria's labours o'er.
She calmly rests on yonder blessed shore.
A glorious crown on earth to her was given,
A grander far, she now doth wear in heaven.

The Queen but sleeps : Victoria the Great
Lives in our hearts, and we must quietly wait,
And ever striving to be like her, rise
To brighter, fairer, mansions in the skies.

The Queen but sleeps : and takes her well-earned rest,
Her son, Royal Edward, reigns by her request,
And loyal to him, our homage give and sing,
And pray to God above—God save the King.

A sincere tribute to the late Queen Victoria in the poetic style of the time. Probably the work of one of the Editor's literary friends.

There is no doubt that contesting was now a way of life for
ands and for some reason, difficult to discover, *The British
andsman* had the cast-iron copyright of all the adjudicators'
marks and woe betide anybody who used them without
ermission. They were pursued relentlessly. The tenor of the
djudicators' remarks was beginning to cause *The British Bandsman*

33

some concern. It had already chided the judge on the 'Wingates' performance but now the remarks were so caustic that some bands were a little apprehensive of contesting in case their dignity was offended. 'No intelligence here. Why did they come? Better if stranded in the fog. Is the conductor ill?'

The British Bandsman asked judges to be a little kinder, perhaps to generalise and to enthuse rather than destroy. This resulted in the other extreme: 'It will be much better not to criticise this performance in detail. The band has evidently much to learn but it has done as well as it could. The performance was not great but the heart of the band was, and that heart, will if fostered by the warm blood of kindness, will one day assuredly beat high for praise.'

Privately the judge said the performance was abominable. Still this was the stuff the bands wanted to hear and it renewed dedication in the bandroom, although the poor judges were never out of trouble. In a reply to a letter, the editor wrote, 'Dear Disappointed. You confess to being disappointed but you have no reason to impute dishonest or offensive motives to the judge. Without absolute proof you have no right to say the judge cooked the contest.'

To keep the circulation of *The British Bandsman* up to the mark, the owner sometimes stooped to a little cloaked blackmail. To celebrate the coronation, a Prize March Fund was started and Iles announced the special commission of *The Coronation March*, copies of which could be obtained at advantageous prices. After a slow start he inferred that those bands which were not purchasing the music were unpatriotic. This had some effect and by 17 May, 1902, 502 copies had been sold but the overall target was 10,000 with half that number apparently being the break-even figure. He wrote: 'If you want to take part, your band will be included in a beautifully bound book for presentation to His Majesty the King. If you take part it will be proof of your loyalty. Do not delay, be in the swim. YOU CANNOT AFFORD FOR YOUR NAME TO BE LEFT OUT OF THE LIST'

The Coronation number of 28 June, 1902, with is imperial red cover, was a sell out, the build up to which had begun weeks before. Every scrap of band preparation was published. Correspondents were quick to point out that many councils and organisations were disappointed because there were not enough bands to head the forthcoming processions. Brass, Reed, Voluntary Military, Boys Brigades, Bugle and Salvation Army bands, even Concertina bands were all fully booked. One can understand why one councillor was on record as saying, 'With no band we might as well be celebrating a funeral'.

Henry Iles reminded the civic authorities that it was no use expecting brass bands to play for nothing and no use appealing to patriotism alone. The editor observed: 'The bands will only say Hey Ho! and Hey Up! to this and councils should remember they will lose a day's pay and will not be satisfied with just a cup of tea'.

Right up to the last minute *The British Bandsman* implored bandsmen to watch 'the intake of ale' and exhorted bands to rehearse their marching technique. The propaganda exercise to sell the *Coronation March* continued. *The British Bandsman* wrote: 'Not long to go now, my friends. Is your band on the list? A few bands have yet to purchase'.

But it was a lot longer than *The British Bandsman* could have imagined. Due to the illness of the King, the coronation and all the events in the country were cancelled. 'Rarely,' said the editor, 'has the Nation suffered such a crushing disappointment.' And so for that matter did *The British Bandsman*, the trade and bandsmen everywhere, as there was wholesale cancelling of orders and arrangements. Anticipating record attendances at coronation concerts, brass bands had paid deposits on halls and had, in fact, purchased various goods, barrels of beer and refreshment. Most of this could not be returned and they found themselves out of pocket.

Some bands were threatened with court proceedings and instruments were sold to raise the necessary cash. *The British Bandsman* could only offer sympathy. It too suffered a set back. Henry Iles had reprinted *The Coronation March* but was now left with quite a stock on his hands. He cut his losses and issued it as a free supplement.

The coronation eventually took place on Saturday 9 August, 1902, but by then *The British Bandsman* had completely exhausted its resources and allowed the local correspondents to do all the running. It was quite an anti-climax until, out of the blue, the editor discovered the Kings Cross Brass Band had been invited to play before the King. He hastily descended to his knees and wrote:

'First, our Noble King whom we have all been watching anxiously for so many weeks fighting for His life and strength, has triumphed over all. The universal prayers of His people and their aspirations have been granted. The King, God Bless Him, is now crowned, not only on His head but in the hearts of His People. We are sure the King has no more faithful and enthusiastic subjects than bandsmen.'

The Halifax Kings Cross Band was invited to play before King Edward VII in 1902.
This was, in those days, an astonishing achievement for a brass band. The brass bands could scarcely believe it.

After the Kings Cross Band had played he wrote: 'Henceforth all brass bandsmen will feel a few inches taller, so to speak, when they play in public. MAY THE KING LIVE FOR EVER.'

The King expressed absolute astonishment that a brass band could produce 'such superb renditions'. He ordered a special meal for the entire band and its officers in the luxurious surrounding of the Great Hall of the Household at Buckingham Palace. Henry Iles seized the opportunity of furthering the Royal interest and wrote to Lord Knollys asking if permission could be granted by His Gracious Majesty for a brass band to play the *National Anthem* outside the Palace one Sunday morning. He added: 'They are all working men, and not withstanding this, play wonderfully well. They are very respectable'. He might as well have said 'hard working men' as most were toiling for 13 or 14 hours a day. Lord Knollys promised to do his best.

5 Conduct unbecoming

The national press, which was now presenting grand trophies to be won at the Crystal Palace, increased its interest in brass bands and the resulting publicity brought a surge of goodwill to the whole movement. It also brought fierce competition between the instrument makers as brass bands found themselves appreciated more and more at concerts and the money began to roll in.

Credit terms were made easier and various promotional inducements offered. Messrs Hawkes & Co., Boosey, Besson and Alfred Hays all vied with each other. Prices were cut, profits were dangerously low and the firms became touchy. *The British Bandsman* reported a specific make of instrument had been played at a contest. John Dixon of Boosey wrote to the editor: 'You have got it all wrong! The Hemshore Band could not have purchased this instrument from Besson's because WE ARE THE ONLY manufacturers of the patent compensating basses in the country!'

The interest of Buckingham Palace brought the brass band out of its specialist bond. Letters and news items regarding their activities were published in newspapers and their achievements became table talk in the orchestral world. It became the 'in thing' for classical music-lovers to attend a brass band concert in the park and occasionally a well known music critic would comment. George Bernard Shaw and Sir Henry Wood often stopped by to listen awhile. Carriages and fours lined up in the park and the concerts from the bandstand became a social occasion for all classes to mix.

It was not infrequent for a conductor to be called out by an aide or servant of some Member of Parliament or aristocrat, to be received by the important person and to accept the gracious comments with suitable servility. Bands became more ambitious in their programmes and asked *The British Bandsman* for its advice on the ideal content for a park concert. The editor gave what he called 'a well received programme': 1. March; 2. Heavy Selection; 3. Solo; 4. Standard Overture; 5. Novelty; 6. Light Selection; 7. Suite; 8. National Fantasia.

The suite requires an explanation. The editor is referring to a new idea very fashionable at the time. It was in essence a succession of three short dances, a gavotte, an intermezzo and, maybe, a waltz and they had all kinds of names, *Village Fête*, *Rural Scenes* and *Rustic Views*. One such suite which might have raised an eyebrow or two included items which followed each other. *Joys of Youth*, *In the Woods* and *Twilight Reverie*.

The Grand Coronation Band Festival at the Crystal Palace was given top priority by Henry Iles and Sam Cope. *The British Bandsman* said this was to be the year brass bands became fully accepted by the country and would be on a par with the great symphony orchestras. The run-up to the 'Great Day' was a nervous time because bands were slow to apply. *The British Bandsman* cried: 'If you have not the money to go, VISIT THE PAWNBROKER and fulfil your desire'. The Festival was, in the end, fully patronised.

Forward publicity by *The British Bandsman* had been on a grand scale. Railway companies announced special cheap day excursions to London and all the trade concessions at Crystal Palace had been oversubscribed. The editor wrote: 'Thousands of loaves have been baked for this army of occupation'. From the early hours trains arrived at the principal termini disgorging hundreds and hundreds of people all besieging the various types of transports to take them to 'the Glasshouse'. Many bandsmen were in uniform and those who had been soldiers wore their medals.

Various accents filled the air and, naturally, those from different parts of the country went around in groups and there was a lot of good humoured bandinage especially between Yorkshire and everywhere else. For most of this exciting day, supporters of the bands and the general public with its families thoroughly enjoyed this brilliantly organised and properly run contest. The London Press Corps which was out in full congratulated Henry Iles and *The British Bandsman* on a magnificent day.

Then came the bombshell. The evening was different. After the first results had been announced the Festival became such a shambles that men could remember it in all its damning detail for years later. The press were quick to call it 'Hooligan Saturday.' *The British Bandsman* could not contain itself, exclaiming: 'Blackguardedly ruffianism', 'Unholy Savages', 'Despicable Orgies'. The editor wrote: 'Officials (which included Henry Iles and Sam

Cope) and their Ladies were subjected to uncomplimentary and ribald epithets. It was a slur and a disgrace upon the whole movement. Such behaviour will repel decent people. The language directed to the Judges was absolutely foul'.

Drunken bandsmen and women sang obscene songs, impromptu indecent dancing took place, fighting was uncontrollable and people left the scene as quickly as they could, averting the eyes of the ladies and children from the quite open debauchery.

Sam Cope said it was like Sodom and Gomorrah. (My father was there and despite my pleas to be allowed to go in the early 1930s I was expressly forbidden and was weaned on the Feltham Band in Richmond Park). From the pages in subsequent issues of *The British Bandsman* it seems reasonable to assume this Festival destroyed the comfortable image of working men making music for the enjoyment of others and, as a consequence, the public with no interest in banding except to listen for pleasure, began to desert contests in droves, leaving them to the participants and supporters.

How would it fare next year? There is no evidence of the various interested bodies, police, associations, caterers, amusement concessionaires or the Crystal Palace authorities getting together to plan ahead. Henry Iles, wounded by press criticism of himself, could only counsel bandsmen through his columns and much he had to say. He began early in the next year: 'DO NOT by your behaviour give anyone the slightest chance to say anything derogatory about these brass bands. No rowdyism of any kind.'

Stronger and stronger condemnation of such conduct as was witnessed the previous year was kept going to the end. There was a certain nervousness apparent throughout the day of the 1903 contest. It was crowded with more from the North than Londoners out for the day. More police were in evidence as the mass of people milled around. Ale tents and bars were open, the men drank beer and the women, milk stout. Queues formed up to enjoy *The Topsy Turvy Railway, the Eighth Wonder of the World.*

As the excitement built up to the announcement of the winners, drunken people were hustled away by their friends anxious to avoid any threat of 'hard labour' which had been meted out to some last time. Others looked over their shoulders apprehensively, whilst the police gathered in groups. But nothing happened. The results were generally accepted as 'true'. The crowd heard a collective sigh of relief. The very next issue of *The British Bandsman* carried the headline: 'Thanks Gentlemen.

"THE GOOD OLD DAYS."

A writer in a contemporary says that "Judges who give unpopular decisions should be driven off the field." Our friend may rest assured that respectable bandsmen have no desire to return to the ways of "The Good Old Days."

Thanks.' The national press seemed disappointed and only gave the contest a few lines.

Henry Iles was a showman. To attract the crowds to the Crystal Palace he thought up a gimmick and, although of the utmost simplicity, it succeeded beyond his wildest dreams. *The British Bandsman* was used unmercifully to promote it. A man, whose identity was only known to Mr. Iles, would part with a crisp white fiver if he was accosted by anyone at the Palace and who had a copy of *The British Bandsman*. All he had to say to the mystery man was: 'Have you got that five pound note.'

The competition was a lot of fun and the issue was completely sold out. At the end of contest, people waited for the unknown man to be identified and to be told how many fivers had been handed over. The awful truth was that none had. No one had even approached him. The committee suggested Mr. Iles should, with a nudge and a wink, ask one of his trusted friends to claim one but he would have none of that and decided to tell the vast audience the truth. There was no backlash because the crowd was so big and packed like sardines that by the time his announcement had reached the back of the hall by word of mouth (there was, of course, no PA system) it had been turned upside down and inside out and many people left thinking it had cost Mr. Iles quite a considerable sum of money.

Opposite: Only slightly exaggerated by the cartoonist. Many judges could show their bruises (1911).

6 *The British Bandsman becomes the 'bible'*

The next year saw a battle of a different kind, and, for a while, *Th British Bandsman* sat on the fence. It was known as 'The Year of th Saxophone'. Although the owner wanted the advertising revenu from the instrument makers, comment was muted to say th least. Many brass bands were now including the saxophone i their instrumentations and the marketing managers of the bi four manufacturers and distributors went to town. Again it wa Hawkes, Boosey, Besson and Hayes who trumped each other claims with advertising blurbs like 'Exquisite Tone', 'Marvellou workmanship' or 'We supply 31 Military Bands'.

The demand for saxophones slackened after the immediat impact and *The British Bandsman* abandoned its neutral stance. I came out in favour of saxophones, apparently to keep th advertisements going. It said: 'Brass Bands lack variety as far a tone colour is concerned. The Saxophone is an instrument'. Th campaign lasted six months. The instrument did not catch on. I was finally abandoned by brass bands and found its place i military bands. One uncharitable comment from the secretary o Goodison Mission Band was: 'It is too easy an instrument fo brass bandsmen to play; Regimental bands will love it'.

Gradually letters came from people who could remember th first Crystal Palace concert in 1863. Almost the last letter said 'There were 1388 performers including Distin's Big Gong Drun which needed two people, one to hold it and one to labour it. Letters still arrived, most of them anonymous, all exposin scandals, corruption and malpractices, to seize the escalatin prize money. The Pontypridd contest of 1903 offered '£20(SOLID CASH' as its main attraction.

The majority of these unsigned letters went into waste paper baskets but the canny editor, Sam Cope, filed some away and if a scandal did break he was able to refer to these letters and report much background material in such time honoured phrases as, 'I understand, etc.' or, 'I have learned from reliable sources.'

Henry Iles and Sam Cope, although always tied by an umbilical cord to *The British Bandsman*, began to go their separate ways. Mr. Iles became less and less involved with editorial policy and gave more of his time to his impressario actvities. These were, however, always fully reported in *The British Bandsman*, even when he became unstuck. There was the occasion when he organised a tour of England by the New Zealand Band under its conductor, Lieutenant Herd, which left him £500 out of pocket. Nevertheless the experience gained stood him in good stead for the never-to-be-forgotten tours he was to arrange in the golden era just around the corner.

Mr. Cope was emerging as the acknowledged expert in brass band matters and his advice on controversial matters was constantly sought. One of his most famous pronouncements in *The British Bandsman* concerned the use of drums by Besses o' th' Barn, whose long run of success had prompted other crack bands to query this addition to brass band music. It was thought this made Besses a military band and therefore debarred them from contesting. He was asked to give his definition of a military band. He wrote: 'A military band is not necessarily an army or Regimental Band, nor conversely, is a Regimental Band as a matter of course, a Military Band. It is the instrumentation that classifies bands. Brass Bands with clarinets, and piccolo are Reed and Brass Bands. If oboes, bassoons and french horns are added, is then a military band. There is nothing to prevent a Brass Band having a drum major!'

As a direct result of this, bands began to introduce drums. The editor became very enthusiastic. Bass, kettle, any drum, he praised it and wrote that all bands worthy of the name should have at least one. It was after an article he wrote under 'DRUMS ARE GOING GREAT GUNS' that he had to refute suggestions he had a financial interest in drum-making firms. He did answer one recurring request from drummers who wished to know the best way of harnessing these sometimes large instruments to their bodies to ease discomfort on the march. With tongue in cheek it seems, he drew attention to bandmasters to the method adopted in Serbia:

'The Regimental Big Drum is placed on a small two-wheeled cart drawn by a dog trained to keep its place throughout the longest and most tedious and marches. The drummer takes up

his position behind the cart and performs on the instrument
the animal pulls it along.'

Believe it or not but several experiments were tried.

Whatever the bands thought of the contribution of the dru[m]
to the aesthetic quality of their music, there is no doubt t[hat]
public welcomed it and sometimes the conductor had to bri[ng]

*Advertisement for the 'A1'
acetylene lamp. Some of
these lamps gave off evil
smelling odours and were
dangerous but the 'A1' was
a great advance and sold
well.*

the drummer forward to take a bow. When these brass ban[ds]
played in the parks, large crowds turned up to listen to the cla[sh]
of cymbals, the deep beat of the 'big 'un' and the dramatic dru[m]
rolls by dexterous drummers. This martial ground base appear[ed]
to satisfy some primitive desire. As one reader wrote: 'It brin[gs]
me over all goosey pimples'.

This increasing support by the public for open-air concerts l[ed]
to formation of a society called *The Professional Musicians of Londo[n]*

aim was to persuade the London County Council that only
ofessionals should be allowed to play in any of the parks under
control. These professionals played in orchestras almost
ways dominated by brass instruments. They were very worried
eir fees would be 'mightily reduced' as a result of this growing
nateur competition. The publicity department of this society
s much better organised than the fragmented brass band
ternity which had no means to defend itself in strength from
e fierce press attack mounted against them. 'Brass Bands are
l of Blacklegs' headlined one paper, whilst another said: 'The
fish brass bands are ruining their better trained musicians'.
Band secretaries appealed in their hundreds to the editor to
swer back and he wrote: 'Have nothing to do with this society.
is composed of certain officials paid to run it. A small
rcentage are bona fide professionals but largely they are
RADE UNION sympathisers who know nothing about music
t only give inflammatory speeches'.

However, it did become serious and brass bands found
emselves edged out of the lucrative engagements. He went on
say that, despite his pleas for a National League of Brass Bands,
was disappointed at the response. 'Let us,' he wrote, 'make a
mbined effort and be united in our task to defeat this monster.
ontact me and I will form the National League'. All in vain. No
e bothered.

In the first few years of the 1900s *The British Bandsman* began to
ceive letters from Salvation Army musicians who joined the

*The Great Western Silver
Band (Pontypridd) 1903.
The year they headed the
Pontypridd and Rhondda
District Miners
Demonstration. A march of
four miles. Immediately
afterwards, they caught a
train to Abergwnfi and
walked over the mountain
to Pontycymmer where they
won first prize in a contest.*

Christmas carols outside The Plough at West Wycombe in 1895 with the West Wycombe Band.

debates regarding such things as drums, saxophones, tuning an
marching. The editor realised The Salvation Army was a neglecte
market for readership and the associated business it woul
create. He set out deliberately to woo these musicians to *T*
British Bandsman.

So *The British Bandsman* began a long column headed *Salvatio
Army Notes* and the first salvo read:

'Anyone with a sensitive ear would not have gone willing
within a mile of a Salvation Army band but I can now assure n
readers that there are several that one may listen to wi
pleasure.'

For several weeks he praised Salvation Army bands and the
went straight for the jugular:

'Do you know that 7,000 Salvation Army Bandsmen will pla
instruments worth £100,000 at the Great Congress to be held i
London from 24 June to 14 July, 1904? And do you know ther
are over 17,000 bandsmen in the Salvation Army? IF ONLY eac
bought a copy of *The British Bandsman.*'

It had some effect. He invited all Salvation Army musiciar
attending the Congress to visit him in the offices of *The Briti*
Bandsman which was opposite the Congress Hall and, speaking i
many tongues, they did. Hundreds besieged the office waiting t
shake the hands of Henry Iles, J. A. Browne, and especially Sar
Cope. He was now internationally known as a band traine
composer, arranger, conductor, adjudicator, journalist an

EEVER'S, HUDDERSFIELD. THE NATIONAL BAND CONTEST
HE OLDEST AND LARGEST
AKERS OF BAND UNIFORMS.
CRYSTAL PALACE. 1903.

A typical trade stand at the Crystal Palace, 1903, advertising the 'B.B.' publicity ploy.

hilosopher. Perhaps this list should include 'Master circulation anager' because after the congress he wrote: 'The performances t the recent congress were a real eye opener to the HUNDREDS ho had always sneered at anything like music coming from a alvation Army Band.'

Within a month, he was boasting that more and more *British andsman's* were being sold 'in their hundreds every week'. The ctual figure was never mentioned and to his advertisers he never eally separated readers from buyers. One effect of the influx of alvation Army readers was a swing towards the more learned ype of article, often by contributors with the academic qualifications f Mus. Bac. and F.R.C.O. As a result of this new market Henry es was able to afford 26 large pages, 11 of which were given to ull page advertisements.

Outside bands lapped up the activities of these Salvation rmy bands and were overawed by their discipline and dedication. One news item observed: 'When Bristol II SA visited Yatton, nost of the men missed the train, but undaunted, formed up and alked the 16 miles in the the broiling sun.'

The involvement of Salvation Army bands with *The British andsman* enabled the editor of *The War Cry* to solve some niggling problems, the most important being what had become known as 'the right to be heard'. When a brass band held the town square for a Saturday and a Sunday it was not unusual for the Salvation Army band to march around causing both bands to play louder and louder. In one reported case, the Salvation Army band drew up just yards away from the brass band and held their meeting whereupon the brass players 'blew unseemly notes upon their instruments'. Vulgarity and the threat of disorderly conduct was never far away and the editor of *The War Cry* said:

'I advise all Salvation Army bands to show true Christian spirit and stop playing when they are in earshot of the band holding the pitch.'

The support of the quite large crowds who listened was fickle and the town band generally won. It was just a matter of pure theatre against the faith. The Salvation Army bandmaster conducted in a precise, no-nonsense manner whereas the town bandmaster threw himself all over the place and was consequently much more exciting to watch. *The British Bandsman* records one such incident where the conductor of a band in Derby dislocated his shoulder. The editor, learning of this news from the editor of *The War Cry* wrote:

'Sir Edward Elgar agrees a conductor should aim at absolute purity of a rendering without humbug. Some people think that the more a conductor jumps about the more successful the music.'

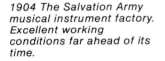

1904 The Salvation Army musical instrument factory. Excellent working conditions far ahead of its time.

A Saddleworth band in its 'Sunday Best' with King Edward VII bowlers and boots.

With little excitement in their lives, anecdotal evidence at the turn of the century does show that as soon as the strains of music were heard in the streets even if it were only a barrel-organ, people would flock out of their 'back to backs', sing and dance and lose themselves for an hour. 'These are the places to play', advised the editor, 'You will always find a penny from a poor pocket'. As these street concerts took place on Sunday morning and were played at full blast and drum of martial music, criticism was received at the *The British Bandsman* from the secretary to the Dean of St. Paul's Cathedral, London, as some bands played within distance of the many well-packed churches. The editor, a true Christian and churchgoer, hastily wrote an editorial which included:

'People come out of the public houses and strut about behind you and this does offend. Be intelligent. No one will complain if these people strut to the strains of *Brightly Gleams Our Banner* or *Lead us Heavenly Father*.

He had several letters to ask where one obtained the music of the former. This audience participation with brass bands soon spread to contests. Every time a player had his solo spot in the test piece the crowd would applaud with shouts of encouragement – 'Go on Tom, good lad' or, worse, the ringing of handbells after the style of football supporters. 'This must stop' the editor wrote, and his icy blasts soon put a stop to this. But no matter how he tried editorially he was quite unable to control the hooliganism park concerts attracted. For a while he countered press criticism by saying it was 'only high spirited lads and lasses enjoying themselves' but when *The Pall Mall Gazette* wrote on 20 August, 1904: 'Audiences are very rough at Brass Band Concerts in the park. They show their disapproval in a most ungentlemanly manner', he changed his mind.

About this time *The Professional Musicians of London* abandoned their campaign to ban brass bands and soon these had the monopoly of the park concession although military bands were flexing their muscles to get into the act. Sam Cope wrote: 'Now you have got over this hurdle, what do I see?' What he saw was people leaving the park early because of notorious behaviour, or some hooligans marching in and out of the band playing imaginary instruments or trying to hit the big drum with stones or clods of earth.

The *The British Bandsman* reported where a bandsman had dropped his instrument and fought with 'one wild youth'. The bandsman was reprimanded and suspended and, although an amateur, lost his perks such as inflated travel expenses, refreshment allowance and anything else that could be legitimately milked from the funds, in itself a valuable source of income. The youth who was arrested came off much better. He was bound over to keep the peace for 12 months.

All this comment was a run up to the usual pleas to be of good behaviour at the 'National'. It was only by hammering home, year after year, this message that Henry Iles and Sam Cope could protect their investment . . . and sometimes to protect the morals of the visiting bands. Sam cope said: 'I say to those bandsmen who come from the villages and towns in other parts of our Fair Isle NOT to stray into those lower parts of London which have a business-like manner towards the money in bandsmens' pockets'.

7 *The early peaks and troughs*

The history of Besses o' th' Barn band has already been written but mention must be made of *The British Bandsman's* involvement with this historic band and, in particular, Henry Iles without whom the band's undoubted musical ability would never have received world-wide acclaim.

Welded together as a virtuoso band by Alexander Owen this band was already a household name in the industrial cities of Lancashire and Yorkshire and Henry Iles brought it south. The band took London by storm and played before audiences of 30,000 with superb results both musically and financially. *The British Bandsman* became its publicity machine and reported this southern tour in some detail, including the complete menu in French of the farewell dinner held in its honour at the Hotel Cecil, London. To make quite sure his readers grasped the magnificence of the regal repast, *The British Bandsman* mentioned the 'many bottles of champagne' and the 'shilling cigars'.

Who knows what these bandsmen made of 'Brunoise a l'orge' and 'Poires a l'Imperatrice'? They coped because, as one reads and follows their progress in some detail, they had not only pride in their band but pride in themselves and, more importantly, pride in their country for which they were to prove very worthwhile ambassadors.

The British Bandsman was always conscious that these men had been thrown into the deep end of a world totally unknown to them. It gave all of them solid support. The London tour could not have taken place without the help and co-operation of London bands and Sam Cope once again urged this brotherly love could be turned into a 'National League'. He became quite dramatic. 'Step forward and be applauded Greenwich Boro', East Ham Military, Southwark, London Prize, Ealing Town,

Uxbridge and Hillingdon, North London Excelsior, Enfield Foresters and Stoke Newington Military'.

Naturally these bands and others basked in the reflected glory of the extraordinary display of affection and appreciation towards Besses at such diverse places as the People's Palace in the East End of London and the Queen's Hall, London, to which the 'carriage set' went. Of course, some payment had to be agreed for these bandsmen but *The British Bandsman* made sure the large amount of money the tour made did not line the pockets of the bandsmen. It printed in full how much went to charity; for example, the Fresh Air Fund for the Slum Children of London received £406 5s. 1½d.

The question of dispersal of concert takings was always a sore point with bandsmen and of great interest to the editor. Bandsmen were often bamboozled by an accountancy system which allowed for several funds to be administered by a small committee, usually no more than the officers. These funds were always a little dubious and went under such titles as 'Bank Holiday Fund', 'Visitors' Fund' and one upon which the editor seized, 'Mr. Addison's Favour Fund.' he wrote: 'It is no use saying concert takings barely cover travelling expenses. Bandsmen have a right to know. Paying at the door leaves the door wide open for misunderstanding' and he published a specimen balance sheet.

Officials of the Scottish Central Amateur Brass Band Association posed in 1904 to a stately home backcloth.

This is not to say there were no honest treasurers and secretaries. Indeed many of them were trying their hardest to come to grips with the money problems caused by success. Give or take a little dishonesty, it was comparatively rare to hear of a really scandalous state of affairs. If one was reported, it not only meant a prison sentence with hard labour but the whole family being totally ostracised in what was, more often than not, a closely knit community.

An interesting case was reported which nowadays would not have wasted the court's time. A bandsman purposely left a window ajar so he could come back later and take the band gramophone home for the weekend. Devious, but with no intent to deprive the owner thereof. He was nabbed when he returned it. He was sent to prison for six months, never played in a band again and never found employment. The editor counselled: 'never even borrow then, because the police have a good record of sending people to prison for this'. Not the magistrates, you will notice, but the police, because in those days people equated the police with the judgment of the court.

A word about 'band gramophones'. The Gramophone & Typewriter Company advertised extensively in *The British Bandsman* using the full front page of alternate issues. This advertising was an extremely good source of revenue and *The British Bandsman* constantly praised the usefulness of this 'miracle machine'. It printed 'you can listen to the finest bands in the world from Russia, Germany, Italy, France, America, Spain, Sweden, Portugal and Japan'. Japan?

This caused a few letters of enquiry as to what sort of music a Japanaese brass band or orchestra played because, as far as some readers were concerned, Japan might as well have been in outer space.

Some crack bands were sufficiently affluent to afford the new *Triplephone*. This extraordinary gramophone played three of the

The much sought after Triplephone of 1904 and used by the more affluent bands at gramophone concerts.

53

same records at the same time on synchronised turntables. It was, the editor saw, a must for brass bands and if it could not be afforded then 'Get Mr. Owen in and it will not be long before the cash comes rolling in'. (Mr Owen being a famous brass band conductor and teacher). That is if they ever received the cash.

Many cases were drawn to the attention of *The British Bandsman* where bands were finding it difficult to claim the prize money due to them. They were urged to take the promoters to court but even that did not always succeed. At Oldham County Court on 16 June 1904, several bands were told that the defendant had no property upon which to distrain, and they went away empty handed.

Listening to the gramophone records of foreign bands provoked much comment from readers who complained of the staleness of the same old sound of the British brass band. One asked: 'Whoever wants a cornet when a clarinet is better at the caper?'. Amazingly the editor was inclined to agree but realised if this were to happen then the traditional sound would be lost for ever. He sounded out the opinion of his friends (mostly military men) and wrote: 'The limit of what a Brass Band can be expected to do has been reached'. This did not please Henry Iles and he and the editor huffed and puffed in print over the problem. Finally Sam Cope wrote:

'The interest in the present sound [of the brass band] is beginning to wane. I challenge Henry Iles to allow me to present a band at the Crystal Palace Band Festival Concert in October 1904 with the following instrumentation. I will add to the present sound 4 flugel horns, 2 french horns, trumpets, 4 saxophones and tympani.'

The offer was graciously declined. One reader wrote: 'We do not want any of these flash instruments'. Others said: 'You talk of trumpets, these are easier to play than cornets'. He replied: 'Oh no they are not!' and he let the somewhat libellous replies which attacked his integrity go on for a few weeks.

As was usual prior to the October Crystal Palace contest, the lights burned night and day in the offices of *The British Bandsman*, particularly this year as Henry Iles was thinking of a tour by a brass band 'to that great continent of Europe'. The discussions narrowed down to one demanding problem, expense. Finally Mr. Iles decided to promote it solely by himself and he used *The British Bandsman* without any embarrassment to obtain the maximum publicity. He chose Besses o' th' Barn band to 'show their brothers in France what the working men of Britain can do in the way of instrumentral music'.

This flair, this entrepreneurial expertise of Henry Iles, enabled him to make money on peripheral matters concerning the Crystal Palace contest. Again he used *The British Bandsman*. It was he who gave the railway traffic managers the estimated number of passengers the trains might be expected to carry and grateful companies accepted his underwriting to the figures and he received a commission. Not all that much of a gamble as he had precedents upon which he could act. He wrote: 'The Great Central offers rapid travel in Luxury. There are now new Express Dining Trains on the Sheffield to London route'. He told bands the way to raise money was to go from house to house and leave a little note to say how grateful the band would be if they could give a little to help in 'this educational project'.

Educational? Well maybe. But often only the so-called entertainment which acted as a magnet to many bandsmen in the 'whore-lanes of Pimlico' after the contest was over, all recounted with great gusto and exaggeration back in the all-male preserve of the band room.

The British Bandsman had extended itself almost too far. It was a myth that the greater the circulation the more profit was made. It could be true today with instant financial figures and consequent control but not then and the coffers were half empty, but the only answer Henry Iles had was to increase sales. Week after week it titillated its readers with what they might expect from a forthcoming serial to be published 'Only In Your *British Bandsman*', 'A Publishing Scoop' by a 'Great Internationally Known Acclaimed Novelist', 'A Story of our Time', etc.

Below and overleaf: The Crystal Palace at the turn of the century 'An eighth and ninth wonder of the world' said the King.

It was called 'Intrigue and Passion'. Henry Iles and Sam Cope must have thought their readers a bloodthirsty lot, for within the first few lines they read 'Oh! It's a glorious time for the army when the Nation is smelling Blood!' and in the second instalment 'It's War! War! To the Knife and the Bitter End. Hurrah! War!!' No wonder, perhaps, that for the Crystal Palace concert, Messrs. Boosey & Co. supplied a 12 foot high big drum for the battle scene in the fantasia *A Soldier's Life*.

The serial did not boost circulation and was an expensive flop with readers' letters saying it was a waste of time. Not to worry, Cope told the office staff, we have another card up our sleeves. But this, too, nearly went wrong. Big cash prizes were offered to readers who could place the first 20 bands in order at the Crystal Palace contest. Almost as soon as the issue hit the streets, readers were asking if '20' was a printing error because the odds of getting even the first ten in order of merit was astronomical. Hastily it was altered to the first seven. In the end just over 2,000 entries were received. The first prize went to the man who could only forecast correctly 2nd, 3rd and 4th. The second prize for forecasting only two in correct order and a mere pittance to 300 others who had only one in its right place.

The reason for this was the sensational result of the contest. It completely stunned the 60,000 crowd. The bands of Besses, Black Dyke and Wyke were nowhere and this was the talking point for the rest of the day leaving no time to knock the place or each other about. This, in turn, denied the press corps of any so-called good copy so it queried the unbelievable placings and did in fact, call into account the propriety of it all. Henry Iles had to defend the judges against a ground swell of protest. He wrote: 'As regards the comments that generally have been made on the Championship result amongst bandsmen and THE PRESS, perhaps the least said soonest mended'. It was widely believed that an unfortunate mistake had been made with regard to the first prize but as the judges, after careful investigation, stated emphatically that they were conscious of no such thing, there remained no other alternative but to accept the decision announced as correct as far as their opinion was concerned.

Crack bands were disappointed. Little bands were gleeful. The winning band, Hebburn Colliery, remained detached and dignified even after Sam Cope blamed the result on enthusiastic conducting which always commanded the greater applause. He wrote:

'Conducting is the influence of soul over soul, done now by the eyes, now by a meaning glance, now by a burst of excitement, all shown in the face NOT by flourishing a stick or by gymnastics.'

He referred to one conductor at the contest as 'Mr St. Vitus'.

The 1904 contesting scene was generally 'one of absolute disgrace and you bandsmen should be thoroughly ashamed of yourselves' the editor thundered. He blamed the sale of beer. He wrote of drunken players playing instruments in a wild musical manner, of them being pulled off the platform or from the field to lie down and sleep it off. 'Years ago,' he said, 'it had been so different. At the Crystal Palace concert thousand upon thousand of you removed your caps to the hymn *The Last Wish* and stood with tears in your eyes.'

This year saw *The British Bandsman* incorporate a column headed *The Scottish Bandsman's Weekly Chronicle*. It also included a column for the Bands of Wales written entirely in the Welsh language. This provoked the Yorkshire correspondent to write in the Yorkshire language: 'That beats all I ivver saw. I telled missen an ah'd just getten started off yamwards when I nooaticed a magpie'. Great fun.

8   *Let's have a quarrel*

One can see that through the letters in *The British Bandsma*
everybody seemed to be having a go at everyone else, mostly ov
the vexed question of borrowed players which had smoulder
on long before the paper was born.

Conspiracy, corruption and deceit would, if the letter-write
were to be believed, be quite natural in the contesting arena. On
band was categorically accused, in 1905, of sacrificing i
principal cornet player to another band in the same contes
Apparently the financial gain to the band from this transactio
was greater than the prize money. Another band went t
pathological lengths to prove a rival band had won with tw
borrowed players and should have been disgraced, disqualifie
and disbanded. The accused band replied and challenge
anyone, anywhere, including the editor, to point a finger at any o
their players who were not bona fide members.

The editor agreed and told bands to check their facts ver
carefully before rushing into print. But there were red faces a
round. The two players concerned, confessed and said they ha
been paid handsomely for their services. Easy to get away wit
primarily because so many bands played in civilian clothes.

After a wintry January and February the bands rubbed the
eyes, and crept from their hibernation to face another contestin
season which, despite pleas from *The British Bandsman*, opene
with much acrimony similar to the previous years. Judges bega
to revert to their old pompous ways. It was now the practice fo
judges to say a few words while the results were checked. On
judge, reported in *The British Bandsman*, said, 'Some wer
moderate, some were bad and some, if there be a place o
torment, will be engaged to play'. The editor told judges to sto
this sarcasm as there was enough of this 'in the PAPERS'.

He was right. The press covered all the big contests, seekin
voraciously any copy which would sell the newspaper, that is

ighting, hooliganism or sensational results. This year, since they ound very little, the reporters lampooned the bandsmen as 'red aced fellows bursting the buttons of their uniforms, puffing out heir cheeks to get the Oom Pah Pah!'. *The British Bandsman* ccused the press of being most unfair and unprofessional. It aid; 'The British Bandsman is not comic or funny. They are hard working men employed in real work during long hours of the day nd give up night after night to practice'.

The more serious newspapers took note of all this (and it is ere that one notices the tremendous news value brass bands vere acquiring). *The Times* blamed these so-called 'word pictures' of brass bandsmen on the numerous German bands now playing up and down the country in their fancy dress. Nevertheless the aricature of a red faced perspiring bass player playing the overworked Oom Pah Pah struck a chord with the public and ven now is revived by reporters who should know better.

Brass bands were niggled about this trend but the celebrated Doctor of Music, Sir Frederick Bridge, came to the rescue. At the Annual General Meeting of the illustrious Incorporated Society of Musicians he said: 'The Brass Band is like a mother-in-law, the ontinual butt of the comic newspapers but their performances completely put to shame many of those in the Orchestral ociety'. For some bands this was not enough and to escape the idicule added piccolo, E flat and B flat clarinets, alto and tenor axophones, drums and restyled themselves 'Military Bands'.

The British Bandsman did not pursue this too far, mainly because Henry Iles and Sam Cope were now so busy that the magazine ppeared a bit ragged round the edges. Iles was at meetings all day and night it seems. At weekends he was at festivals, contests, oncerts and dinners. Cope was writing for most of the magazines of the day which were remotely concerned with music. He eldom had a day off or a holiday. Whether the punishing chedule adopted by these two giants was for the love of brass ands or only brass, we shall never know. We do know from *The British Bandsman* that the contesting season was, yet again, in the doldrums and this was a worry for all those with a finger in the pie - *The British Bandsman*, *The Champion Journal* and all the rest of the rade.

It seems to have been due to a lack of presentation by the ands, and Henry Iles suggested that contests should be part and parcel of flower or horticultural shows. Some bands took this up nd *The British Bandsman* was soon reporting contests held in partnership with rabbit, pigeon and poultry shows. There was a mall increase in the interest but it took all the expertise of the editor to keep it going. His comments told the story: 'Have a

large tent in case it rains', 'Organise a comic singing contest f
the audience', 'Allow the audience to dance if the test piece i
quadrille or a valse'. Nothing was left out; firework displa
funfairs, clowns and comedians and for a while it worked b
eventually the contest music became background music and
was back to the drawing board.

If this were not enough, the Sabbatarians became active aga
with more fire in their bellies. The clergy everywhere, of
denominations, began preaching strongly against the brass ba
concerts in the parks on Sundays.

This opposition was best put by the church leaders in Darwe
Lancs, who wrote to *The British Bandsman*:

'These concerts lend to the desecration of the Lord's Day ar
injuriously affect the best interest of the people and milita
against the work of highly beneficial religious organisations.

Some bands whose sponsors, subscribers and indeed playe
were pillars of the church, withdrew. Others compromised a
began and finished with a hymn and prayers. It took courage
make a stand against this onslaught, especially as the pre
appeared to support the need to observe the Lord's Day qui
strictly, but make a stand *The British Bandsman* did. Aft
explaining his and Henry Iles' staunch adherence to the 'Christi
Principle', Sam Cope wrote an editorial under the bann
Pharisaism in Music (these days we would probably use *S
Righteousness* or even *Hypocrisy*). His message was that it is absolu
nonsense to think only music in churches can be productive
spiritual or moral good and even greater nonsense to say bra
band music is not capable of giving any intellectual enjoyment
the masses 'It is', he said, 'religious intolerance. We buried it
years ago and we do not want it raised again'.

Brave words! In the late nineteenth century and early twentie
century the Christian religion was perhaps enjoying one of i
greatest periods of success, if by that we mean the growth of i
institutions and outward observances, its spread in Asia ar
Africa and the respect generally accorded to it. But he kept up h
spirited support: 'Do these people not know there is mo
sacredness in attending Sunday concerts than taking out girls f
walks on warm Sunday nights.'

The clergy of Leeds demanded an end to his support becau
park keepers could not keep order or control the licentiousne
Brass band concerts, they said, support sin! However, they wou
allow these concerts but only on two conditions: 1. The Lee
Police attended in large numbers and 2. a collection f
missionaries, and not the band, be made. Then there w
another worry. Secular attacks on Sunday concerts began. 5(

eople petitioned the Corporation of Manchester to stop brass
bands playing in Boggart Hole, Clough, as it disturbed the
tranquility and quality and peace found when walking 'through
the glades away from the din, noise and worry of the City'.

The editor toured the country, speaking at many Sunday
concerts to give his point of view. He was often howled down.
Sometimes the police intervened and many an ordained minister
shook his fist at him. An interesting fact revealed itself as he
travelled around. He noticed some of his old acquaintances were
missing from the bands and on enquiry found they could no
longer play as all their teeth had been removed following various
dental complaints. He went back to London and wrote: 'There
are very good false teeth available these days and bands should
start A FALSE TEETH FUND for toothless bandsmen because
the teeth are costly and beyond the pocket of the working man'. A
surgeon-dentist, Mr. Shipley Slipper, quickly spotted the market
and advertised: 'I have had great success in supplying teeth to
those who have lost them playing brass instruments!' The word
soon spread that blowing into a wind instrument ruined the teeth
early on. Time proved this false but it was a fair old scare for a few
months.

9 The lean year of 1905 The poor get poorer

The depression, especially felt in Wales, was emptying the pockets of the working class fast, a major headache for band committees. Footwear, for example, was repaired, patched and swapped until the feet were exposed. Bandsmen in many part only attended rehearsals, contests and concerts if it were dr underfoot.

Tension built up in bands. Jealousy flared up over the division of 'the take' at brass band events. *The British Bandsman* reported that one secretary to a band committee put exactly half of the monies received into his own pocket as his expenses and defied a rowdy meeting of the band for anyone to do it cheaper. In thi case his 'take' equalled the week's wages of a collier. Fraudulen practices crept in. A bandsman would have his instrumen owned by the band repaired for £1 but the receipt would be fo £1.10s.0d. the difference being split between repairer and player

Contest money was avidly coveted and led to intense activity away from the contest field. Secretaries were writing in confidence to the chosen judge offering to meet him 'by chance' on the train to offer him 'suitable refreshment'. To their credit the judges to a man posted these letters off to *The British Bandsman*. Sam Cope never published them but quietly let it be known to the contest promoters.

The effect of the depression extended to judges and a free-for all developed with everyone undercutting everyone else. The usual fee of £3.10s.0d. dropped within weeks to 15s.0d. Some judges came for nothing but took a fifth of the 'take'. It also extended to professional conductors. Many bandsmen had gained vast experience in playing, of the theory of music and it science and had advertised themselves as conductors. A M Chas. Pavey, who had placed an advertisement for a professiona onductor for his band, wrote to the editor and said he had received over 50 replies, yet three years ago he had received only even.

Despite the need to watch every penny, the brass band aternity, loosely knit as it was, stood firm. In July 1905 an xplosion occurred underground at Wattstown National Colliery d many families were instantly deprived of any money. Those cky enough to receive relief could not manage as it was far too adequate to live on properly. The Ynyshir and District Brass and appealed through *The British Bandsman* for help and andsmen all over the country contributed generously to the lief fund.

As the year progressed, economic conditions worsened and any bandsmen took to busking outside public houses. Other andsmen considered this professionalism and wrote to *The ritish Bandsman* demanding they be banned from the band om. The editor, realising that busking kept starvation at bay, rote that this sort of thing was all right 'if one does not derive the rincipal part of his income from playing. That is to say one hose vocation is other than playing an instrument'. It was a ictum that stood the test of time. There were one or two bright ots in this terrible year. Bandsmen everywhere followed the iumphal tour of France by Besses o' th' Barn with great interest.

Besses o' th' Barn leaving Paddington Station for Windsor to play before H.M. The King.

The souvenir copy of *The British Bandsman* issued on 22 July ran to 36 pages and was immediately sold out. Henry Iles ordered a reprint and this was quickly sold out as well. A set of 17 postcards of the tour were on sale at 2d. each and these too disappeared from the market very quickly.

Bandsmen marvelled at the ability of Chalk Farm Salvation Army Band to find the money to tour Scotland. It travelled over 2,000 miles and finished up in the West of England. The editor wrote 'They are no different to you. They are mostly working men who provide their own uniform and receive no remuneration what so-ever, but then they do not have to worry about a balance sheet'. It is a bit difficult to know what he meant by this observation.

The British Bandsman watched with great sadness as bands gave up because of the expense. The editor wrote, 'Keep together lads. Trade is slack at the moment but who knows what a prayer and good fellowship might not bring.' This lean year found the solidarity of the workers particularly strong. Bands never failed to provide free concerts. Raunds Temperance Band headed a troop of striking boot-makers and walked many miles to demonstrate outside the War Office in London, playing at towns and villages on the way to defray expenses. The officer in charge of the police, who were on duty to prevent any disorderly conduct, even requested the band to play his favourite march.

Some brass bands, against their better nature but wanting the money, accepted the job of heading the civic dignitaries, the mill, factory and mine owners to the annual mayoral church service. One bandsman wrote to say 'they are full of the high and mighty and set aside from us poor mortals!' Mr. Cope in reply to this wrote, 'When times are bad and wages low and scarce it is our bands who feel the pinch. Bankers do not give credit to employers and workers go without money. Be of good cheer, the great national gathering will soon take place at the Crystal Palace'.

It would be quite wrong to infer that the poor, unwanted bandsman was disillusioned with his country. There were many examples of this. When the King visited Moreton-on-the-Marsh the local Post Office Band took up its position in the square and played the *National Anthem* again and again which *The British Bandsman* said 'was graciously acknowledged by His Royal Majesty'.

The *laissez-faire* policy of the Government did cause a cautious return to work in the autumn and advertisements appeared offering good employment for steady workers who could play a brass instrument and this provided a spur for the mobility of

Opposite: Jackfield (Ironbridge Gorge) Band, probably 250 years old. The village then had numerous pubs, brothels and other distractions. The Evangelists were appalled at the lewd dancing and bawdy songs sung by the workers of both sexes who worked under terrible conditions to manufacture cannons for the Napoleonic Wars. The band, then drums and pipes, led these bacchanal revels until the coming of the railways aided Jackfield's importance as a port. It became known as the Jackfield Brass Band in 1893. This photo was taken in 1905 outside the Rectory with the vicar on the right.

... and the Jackfield Band today. Certainly not so serious as it looked eighty years ago.

labour to increase. For the first time southerners began playing
in northern bands. Yes! even in Yorkshire.

The Crystal Palace contest was affected by this surge in
production. Employers who were not sponsors or enthusiasts
were quite unco-operative and thought twice about releasing
players on a Friday to contest in London. Some of the men who
went before Saturday were sacked on the spot. This made some

bands from the industrial areas slow to apply and Henry Ile
voiced his concern. Sam Cope, the editor, reverted to the usua
ploy of advertising in such circumstances as, in effect, 'Hurr
whilst stocks last' and every week *The British Bandsman* sai
'applications are coming in thick and fast' when they were no
and 'do not delay to avoid disappointment' and similar exhortation
in the end this paid off and in 1905, 113 bands competed.

This time there was no mayhem and the *Sheffield Daily Telegrap*
was convinced this was because of the increasing number o
clergymen accompanying the bands. It said: 'A wholesom
tribute, not merely to the regenerating influence of music o
the working class but also to the widening scope of the clergy'
parochial interest'. This good behaviour did not last and by th
end of the contesting season *The British Bandsman* called for
black list of bands guilty of 'profanity, assault and indecorou
conduct'.

Actually *The British Bandsman* might, with hindsight, be con
sidered a contributory factor to misbehaviour for it allowe
many inches of space for bandsmen to vilify each other in prin
and this time the arguments ended in an invitation to 'fisticuffs a
the writer is not only ignorant but insolent.' Not that it woul
have come to anything. The letter-writers seldom indentifie
themselves. This letter is typical.

If *'Mr. Subscriber' will call on me have no fear that, by the time I hav
finished with him, he will leave my affairs alone. Signed, 'Constant Reader.*

The year closed on yet another disaster for bands. Most of th
national press reported an ugly riot at a contest. *The Britis
Bandsman* said: 'No wonder the press were full of it. A Lady o
Title was insulted. Just fancy. A Lady of Title!

Even a lady is not safe from the blackguardly rowdyism o
some bandsmen. Shame, gentlemen, shame, a thousand time
SHAME. Language was used totally unfit for publication.' Th
cause of the riot? The judge had made the right decision but th
contest promoter had spent all day in the ale tent and gave th
results the wrong way round making the ninth band first.

One can detect a veiled and sustained male chauvinism sinc
The British Bandsman was published. Sam Cope, in particular, wa
always deeply suspicious of lady instrumentalists and printed
what would now arouse a chuckle.: 'We males have a distinc
advantage over the weaker sex in manipulating our large
instruments'. When one of his friends, knowing of his antagonism
told him there was a complete brass band in Walsall 'compose
entirely of women' he made urgent enquiries to 'unearth thi

very worrying news'. It transpired that in a local church outside the town, a group of ladies were responsible for polishing the brass objects and had become known in the parish as the 'brass band'.

10 *Happy for some*

The great Liberal party victory in 1906 also brought into parliament 29 Labour members and the working class in the North asked for immediate reform but up until the outbreak of the First World War, the years were marred by bitter and violent controversies over the dispersal of the national income.

However, some of the Government Bills did pass into law and escaped being thrown out by the Conservative majority in the House of Lords. Trade unions were freed from the anxiety over the law of conspiracy; free meals for necessitous children, old age pensions and a wage-fixing machinery came into being. All this contributed to a greater feeling of comfort for the men in the bands and the poorer people at last felt recognised.

In the same year *The British Bandsman* issued an 80-page Year Book packed with facts. It cost 3d. and was sold out. This enterprise was made possible because *The British Bandsman* was now selling well. It doubled its staff and initiated a promotion structure. Each week it pleaded for more readers: 'If every bandsman read *The British Bandsman* think how easy it would be to track down the miscreants who prey on good natured bandsmen'.

It was referring to what had become known as the wandering minstrel, a breed of confidence trickster with a glib tongue and an ability to play an instrument fairly well. His *modus operandi* was simple. He would travel only half a dozen miles from his home, turn up at a band room and tell the band he was out of work, had a large family and was staying in the 'Spike' for a few nights. Often the band would have a whip round, invite him to sit in and, without checking, lend him an instrument to practise on back at the workhouse. Needless to say it was promptly pawned in the next town. (If anyone comes across a Hawkes Superior Class Cornet No. 17383 perhaps the Hanwell Band would still like to know.)

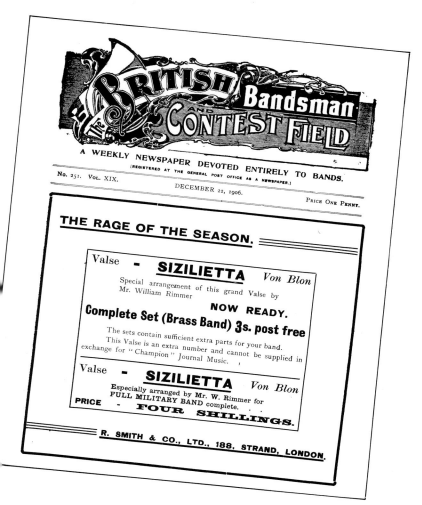

The editor would not get away with this now.

The British Bandsman urged audiences to watch out for pick-pockets and issued advice on how these thieves can easily be spotted: 'Anyone who has not had a drink and does not smell of drink is keeping a steady hand for your pocket'.

In the North, huge, unmanageable crowds gathered. In the 1906 Ilkley contest over 6,000 crammed into the field where there were betting places, fortune tellers, evangelists and thieves, either after 'your money or your soul'. *The British Bandsman* remarked: 'There were also the rosetted Committee members, inflated with importance, prancing up and down, trying to do something worthy of their conspicuousness'.

Southern bands did not have the same dedication. *The British Bandsman* said: 'They see a black cloud in the sky and the contest is called off'. It implored them to match their brothers in the North. The Burnley band, for example, played in squally, windy weather and, although drenched to the skin, bravely completed a two-hour performance. Afterwards they were warmly congratulated by the park keeper, the only spectator.

Because of the disastrous summer of 1906 and no contest news, *The British Bandsman* allocated pages to its army of letter writers. The contents of the letters were never checked and eventually led to threats of court action. As a consequence of these proven and unproven revelations, all bands were on the look out for 'moles'. Players, wives, friends, all were suspect. *The British Bandsman* was receiving copies of confidential minutes and original balance sheets, the subsequent ones being altered for the Annual General Meeting. All good copy for the letter pages but the editor should have exercised greater restraint.

One band, the Victoria Mission, was livid when it read its players were always late for band practice. The Uxbridge band read that one of their cornet players could not really play his instrument, so it would be a complete waste of time for the band

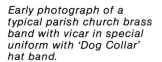

Early photograph of a typical parish church brass band with vicar in special uniform with 'Dog Collar' hat band.

oing to contest at Rosherville (a charming park near Gravesend nd ideal for contesting). The Salvation Army bandsmen joined n: 'Brixton Salvation Army Band are too rough to play anywhere'. One, signing himself *The Spy* wrote: 'Who is it who thinks he is etter than his bandmaster?' and again 'No wonder the *London Opinion* thinks very little of Salvation Army Bands'.

The letters ran on completely out of control until, finally, the Chorlton Band made a stand and demanded of the editor the dentity of the man who signed his letter *Artiste* because this erson was a liar, a terrible accusation to make at this time. Chorlton completely refuted the allegations, the band was not in ow water, the players did not wear tatty uniforms and had new niforms all paid for in cash and purchased from Messrs Evans vho would be pleased to confirm. The band always had about 20 t rehearsals and not nine and, finally, the bandmaster, Mr. J. Vinstanley, was a professional conductor. The editor sat on the

fence and no comment was ever made by him in *The British Bandsman*. He just printed the letter.

The libellous statements worsened. One letter written over a pseudonym called the Nunhead Christian Band 'a funny lot of fellows' but this band had men of the professions amongst the players and legal action was threatened against *The British Bandsman* and its editor for publishing such a libel. (The word 'funny' was construed in the threat as meaning 'insane'). The editor published a fulsome apology and the letters quickly returned to normal; that is to say, to their usual back-biting and carping nature.

If you are wondering how much a professional conductor was paid, Mr. Winstanley received £1 a week. Most conductors received anything between £30 and £60 a year. A conductor of a Mission Band received generous expenses but it was no use applying for the job unless you were 'well and truly saved'. From the bands' activities the average amount received by a bandsman was in the region of £1.1s. a week. If a 'paid player' was engaged to play at a concert, or through the back door, at a contest he was paid about £5. These paid players were not generally liked by bands. One said: 'They were so full of airs and graces that most of us would like to kick them up the you know what'.

Throughout the summer, letters were published at the rate of two dozen a week and covered all aspects of banding amongst which was the concern about the dearth of learners in brass bands. In Bradford the position was so critical, there were over 20 players moving from band to band and, without adverse comment, the practice was accepted to allow contests to continue. Sam Cope, the editor, had his own theory. Learners bypassed the bands and went straight into the Salvation Army because 'of the military feel, the ritual, the flags and the ranks and because they are taught to march properly, and in step and not to play wrong notes when turning corners'. The Salvation Army bands could always guarantee work for players and advertisements read 'Salvationist Boot Repairer required for permanent employment Must be solo cornet' and 'Salvationist required for Dundee II any instrument, must be able to work Litho machine'.

Slack marching always offended *The British Bandsman* and the Miners' Demonstration (now a Gala) at Blackpool was a case in point. The editor said the bands wore dirty uniforms with dirty old instruments and they did not march, they walked, taking two strides to three beats, were careless in playing and every drum 'banged and banged as hard as possible'. He went on: 'This is one of those things which cause people to look upon Brass Bands as something low and beneath the dignity of better class people

Scunthorpe District Total
Abstinence Prize Band.
Some bands such as these
were formed in 1900-1910
as a direct result of
Salvation Army teachings.

Some of the bands were in uniform, some in mufti and some had holes in their shoes'. This was a most unfair comment to make and one can see the hand of Henry Iles behind it as he appeared to want only crack bands to appear in public displays. The lesser ones should know that their place was at contests and village fêtes. In any case some of these bands composed of mineworkers existed on a shoe-string and came together to make music not to seek the 'big time'.

The editor referred to the smartness of the Salvation Army bands; this caused these musicians to preen themselves in print and a lively correspondence followed. Somehow it developed into a debate concerning the very first Salvation Army band. The editor managed to keep the pot boiling for several weeks and created such excitement and sometimes bitterness that 'Mr.' Bramwell Booth stepped in and ordered a special board of enquiry. After lengthy research, it was announced the honour belonged to the Consett Salvation Army Band.

Henry Iles came back in print in *The British Bandsman* with a vengeance as the Crystal Palace contest approached. He said the festival was so important to the music of the world that it ranked equal to 'The Wagner Festival at Bayreuth'. He styled it in *The British Bandsman* as 'The Greatest International Brass Band Festival and Contest for the Championship of the World'. The magazine was used ruthlessly for his propaganda and in 1906, 65,000 people crowded in. All passed off reasonably well but the editor made the point that 'the disgusting habit of spitting on the platform when performing must cease'.

11 *Compulsory reading for MPs*

In 1906, Henry Iles adopted the grand title of 'Controlling Editor and Director General of the British Bandsman' and Herbert Whiteley was appointed editor. He had specialised in teaching harmony by postal tuition and came to London to be musical adviser to Mr. Iles. He held the post until 1930 and was a splendid all-round musician to whom the brass band world of today owes probably more than anyone else for the challenges that were to take place over the next few decades. He was the prime mover in the founding of the National Brass Band Club. He also established a rapport with the editor of its famous contemporary *Brass Band News*, not that the rapport became co-operation. This had to wait many years.

The *Brass Band News* seldom referred to Crystal Palace contests and, if it did, it was often detrimental. On 1 January 1907, for instance, it printed an editorial which said that as far as was known the prizes for the last 'C.P.' had not been paid to the judges, winning bands and the evening concert bands. It told the people to write to the promoters of this concert and, if that failed, to take them to the County Court. It went on: 'DO NOT write to us. Anyway, why go to the Crystal Palace and spend £60 and maybe only win a fiver?'

The winter of 1906/7 was disastrous. Heavy falls of snow and blizzard conditions severely curtailed the lucrative carolling season which, because of its great 'take' started towards the end of November and extended to the 12 days after Christmas. When it was possible to play, all the local bands were hurriedly called together, for there were no weather forecasts of any reliability, and would jockey for the best position. Somewhat surprisingly bands found themselves consulting other bands. This was the first step toward many new associations.

A village band from Stotfold, Bedfordshire braving the elements during the 1906 Christmas carolling season.

Swansea, for example, had four bands all wanting to play in the same place at the same time the Police, the Temperance, the Tramway, and Postal. Some conductors and bandsmen now felt confident enough to arrange some carols to give a more harmonic and stirring sound. Some of these found their way on to the desk of Mr. Cope (now an adviser to the editorial department of *The British Bandsman*) who wrote: 'Some of these arrangements are akin to what a Scottish fisherman knows about the Chinese language'.

The offices of *The British Bandsman*, being in central London, quickly became a clearing house for information. Many military bandmasters would drop in for a chat and therefore it was not surprising when *The British Bandsman* took up the cudgels on their behalf and suggested there were far too many conductors of military bands from 'foreign parts'. The press quickly took this up and trumpeted: 'conductors of our military bands should in future be ALL BRITISH and henceforth no foreigner need apply.' After the retirement of Lieutenant Zavertal (Royal Artillery), there were to be no more. Sam Cope remarked: 'We have stopped British conductors being slighted by the peculiar snobbery of the Officer Class'.

If a British conductor was appointed it took years before he was commissioned. Take the case of Doctor of Music Albert Williams. He joined the Army in 1878 and went to Kneller Hall in 1885, leaving there to become bandmaster to the 10th Hussars. He later transferred to the Royal Marine Artillery Band and following his degree, Mus. Bac., in 1891 he was appointed as bandmaster to the Grenadier Guards band. In 1906 he became

Doctor of Music and it was not until then, 21 years later, that he was selected for commission to second lieutenant.

The letter pages had been quiet for far too long and Mr Whiteley resumed the practice of allowing writers to hide behind a pseudonym. The Kircaldy Trades Band held an inquiry into 'Whoever that is writing to *The British Bandsman* and the local paper with malicious gossip about the band, signing his or herself *Spring Chicken* or *Nanky Poo*'. The band wrote to *The British Bandsman* to say the news item was 'beneath the contempt of Bandsmen of the Kingdom of Fife'. One letter was signed *Always Gay* but only because the atmosphere in the writer's band room was worse than 'Thompson's Funeral Parlour'.

Worse was to come. Letters openly accused bandsmen of 'telling the missus – well I'm off to the band room because it is practice night – but they don't. They end up in a pub or someone else's welcoming arms!' Judging from the follow-up letters this also applied to hand-bell ringers, concertina and reed band players. The editor commented, 'All right. You might get better at other things but you'll never be good players.' Rehearsal suffered through lack of success. Bands relied upon the old faithfuls because no one needed to practice for a park concert when they were going to play *Gems of Mozart*, *Moments with Schubert* and the like. Consequently the lack of preparation showed.

The editor, cast in the same mould as his predecessor, wrote, 'This lack of rehearsal results in indifferent performance, slovenly dress, long intervals and dilatoriness. Beware, I say, because the Sabbatarians will seize on it'. And they did.

This is a selection of letters to the national press in 1907.

Dear Sir, The public parks and open spaces of Manchester are the scene of Sabbath Desecration through these Godless Brass Bands being heard on a Sunday. No wonder filthy literature pours into the city.

Dear Sir, Those who value the English Sabbath and the infinite blessing it has been to the nation must stand firm. Bible classes are opposed to the insidious attempts by brass bands to ruin the sabbath rest.

Dear Sir, As a Minister of the Grace of God, I raise my voice against the flagrant evil of the Brass Bands which are ruthlessly ignoring, scorning and a trampling under foot the fourth commandment. Their Sunday playing encourages immorality.

And lastly,
Dear Sir, The devil must be defeated. As a Churchwarden I can see the playing of brass bands on a Sunday in Leeds as a threat to the Holiness of the Sabbath and the awesome Wrath of God will fall on these base fellows.

The protest gathered pace and many letters were received from individuals and religious societies imploring the editor to intervene before it was too late. One letter said 'Brass Bands will receive The Punishment of the Omnipotent Father in Heaven'. The Editor was careful in his reply and made sure it could not be challenged. He wrote 'How can it prevent people going to church on a Sunday when, according to statistics published by the Church authorities, only FIFTEEN out of EVERY THOUSAND go to church on a Sunday anyway'.

A compromise was eventually reached without a meeting of the two sides. It really started when the Abertillery Silver Band advertised a Sunday concert thus: 'A SACRED concert will be held in the Pavilion in aid of the Hampstead Colliery Fund'. It was a full house and hundreds were turned away. The programme included *Teach me, Oh Lord* to Sam Cope's robust *A Sailor's Life*. So the bands enjoyed the blessing of most sects and every Sunday concert became a sacred one and included the singing of a hymn.

Wales, however, did not take kindly even to this extension and most councils reached their decision by local poll. The Welsh editor never took sides and one wonders why. He was a most forthright commentator on other issues. Dip into any of his columns and one can read. 'Things are not as they should be at Tonyrefail. Mr. Bentley has just about had enough of it'; 'Mr. Murrey has moved back to Ferndale because things at Ynyshir have given him the hump', 'Senghenydd are dead and the instruments up for sale – too many gaffers' and one which was a little enigmatic. 'I regret I cannot yet name the Prima Donnas but if I see C. J. or I. H. E. playing the tantrum instead of the cornet and trombone, then they can expect to be recognised.'

The British Bandsman also became involved with prima donnas and opera, particularly the very successful Gilbert and Sullivan opera *The Mikado*. It printed a news item, harmlessly tucked away, which said it was probable the *The Mikado* would not be played in his country again because of views expressed by our Japanese friends. Within a day of the publication the telephone never stopped ringing. Fleet Street had read it and soon developed the news into a major sensation.

On the 30 April, 1907 every evening paper in London plastered the news stands with inflammatory placards decrying his appalling decision. It reached the House of Commons. Mr. Vincent Kennedy MP, asked the Foreign Secretary if he had been informed of the news item and, if so, had any complaints been received from the Japanese Ambassador protesting against the playing of *The Mikado* and had any steps been taken to forbid its performance in London and would the provinces be affected?

Mr. Runciman replied 'Sir Edward Grey had said no suc[h] objections had been raised by our friends the Japanese but th[e] Lord Chamberlain had withdrawn the licence sanctioning suc[h] performances'. So how, asked the press, pertinently, did th[e] editor of *The British Bandsman* know of this decision. Was he priv[y] to the actions of the Lord Chamberlain? The editor said h[e] would answer the question in the next issue. He made much [of] his media fame and dropped a hint or two about 'high place[s]' and an 'unscrupulous source'. When the magazine came out [it] sold out immediately. Somewhat loftily the editor wrote: 'A plai[n] hint was conveyed from His Majesty the King that a revival of th[e] opera would not be advisable and that on no account should th[e] playing of *The Mikado* take place during the coming visit of Princ[e] Fushima. Naval and Military Bands are not to play selections[.]'

Fleet Street was stunned by the scoop and overawed at the us[e] of *The British Bandsman* to leak a 'Royal Preference' (but, of course[,] it was not. Sam Cope had picked it up as gossip at a soiree). No[t] that he let on. The next week, *The British Bandsman* wrote a[n] amicable mockery which caused the Members of Parliament t[o] disolve in laughter:

'So are we now to understand *Carmen* will not be played for fea[r] it will offend the Spanish, or *Hamlet* offend the Danes, or *Henry* [V] the French. Have we seen the *Merchant of Venice* for the last time[?] Do not sing the touching ballad *Oh Willie we have missed you* whe[n] the Kaiser visits.'

Henry Iles was nervous when he read it and had words with th[e] editor. It was a wonder, he thought, that the editor was not take[n] straight to the Tower. But it did the trick and within a few month[s] the Waterloo Prize Silver Band grasped the nettle and played [a] full selection from *The Mikado* at a concert at the Hippodrome an[d] the Lord Chamberlain turned a blind eye.

For a few years *The British Bandsman* lay, privileged, each wee[k] on the library table in the House of Commons as a testimony o[f] its influence. But influence on what? Some contemporaries saw i[t] as an influence on the working classes, others saw it as a libera[l] influence on conservatism. The ubiquitous Sam Cope said it wa[s] read by MPs to make sure 'they were not caught on the ho[p] again'. Basically it was only an influence on the brass ban[d] movement but, such was its moment of fame, its importanc[e] became grossly exaggerated.

12 *Deceit, drink and devotion*

The British Bandsman soon had another problem with which to cope. An influential school of thought in the North felt that only cups should be contested for and the take divided equally between all participating bands. Further, any prize money put up by the sponsors or promoters should be made available for better facilities, refreshments and travelling expenses and any left over to charity.

Charity was a consuming interest in 1907, as such funds as 'The Relief Fund for the Poor of . . .' were forever being called upon by the destitute for money to enable them to barely survive above subsistence level.

The reason for this proposed radical change was to prevent great anxiety, disappointment, jealousy and disillusionment. When bandsmen said goodbye to their wives and, often, large families, all of them hoped and even prayed, that the husband would come back with money from the prizes to help with food, clothing and coal. The new proposal, it was thought, would help to 'abate the fighting that this disappointment brings'. No contest promoter entertained the idea because the lure of the pot of gold was much too strong.

Many contests were offering quite staggering amounts of money; enough, in some cases, to give all bandsmen who won first prize an amount more than a week's wage. In its wake it brought fierce and sometimes odd reaction from the frustrated losers. 'Why', asked one, 'were the committee on the platform at Slaithwaite when the judge was giving his decision?' The promoter replied: 'The Committee are all gentlemen of high social standing and, was not the Serjeant of police present on the platform watching over the interests of everyone?'

So strong was the desire to win a contest, display the cup and above all pocket the money that judges were put under a great strain. Mr. J. Ord Hume, the well known adjudicator, was returning home from a contest and had to wait at Crewe railway station for a connection. He was eating in the first-class refreshment room when members of a band and its supporters, all the worse for drink, burst in and subjected him to such foul abuse 'that some of the expressions actually made the electric light flicker'. Charges of bribery, cheating and fraud were made 'What is more', Mr. Ord Hume said, 'there were several boys in the band which, when confronted later, roundly denied all this' but Mr. Ord Hume produced several witnesses of some standing.

Worse was the attempted bribery of a judge outside Cardiff railway Station when Mr. James Boner, a noted judge, was offered £5 immediately with more to follow to fix the Aberdare contest. Despite a good description given by Mr. Boner, the contact was never traced. A measure of the frantic desire to get their hands on to any monies due was the appeal by bands for the Parks Committee of Middlesbrough to pay out immediately a performance was over. In the areas where no work really meant no money, brass band players were amongst the privileged who could make purchases 'on the slate'. The editor warned against this practice – 'Beware of the shopkeeper who allows this then takes you to court when he hears you haven't won'.

In 1907 an enlightened Government decided that Working Men's Clubs were a necessity and consequently made them legal institutions. They were bound, however, by regulations strictly enforced by the police. Many brass bands took advantage of this and, to further their social activities, rented or built premises to be used as the band club and institute. It was not to be long before some of these bands were struck off the register mainly because of allowing drunkenness on the premises or, as one summons stated, 'Not being conducted in good faith as a club.'

Despite the tremendous divergence of the aims of these registered clubs it was to be a brass band that was first to test the courts and the legislation. 'The Ferndale Band Club Raid' became a national headline. It excited the interest not only of other band clubs but of every newly formed club and institute in the country. The reason for this was that, apart from the usual drunkenness charge, the vexed question of membership qualification, membership cards, affiliation and gratuitous drinks were also part of the prosecution case.

Hundreds besieged the Porth police court amongst whom were leading figures in the brass band movement and many of the town worthies who were on the premises at the time of the

aid. The editor felt it 'right and proper' to report this case in
detail. What comes over from his and newspaper reports is the
close, intimate relationship between prosecutor and defendant.
The raiding party of the two sergeants and one constable were

The band room at the
Ferndale Band Musical
Institute at the time of the
famous court case.

obviously very well known to all and sundry. It is not without its
humour. Witness: 'When the police invaded, a man called out,
lemonade for the police, barman.'

The editor's interpretation of the evidence and his selectivity
of pertinent points, had the national dailies copying his report
word for word. He made great play of the evidence which agreed
that the premises were excellent in every respect. The brass band,
the police sergeant said, was one of the best, the books were well
kept and the daily alcohol consumption of each member was less
than 2d. per day. The editor wrote 'I say that if it is found against
this band then every brass band club in the country will have to
close'.

Then came the thunderbolt. It was the practice of this club to
give up to six free 'sleevers' (a little over half a pint) to the artists
who came to the smoking concerts to sing, play the piano or act
the fool and also to give two free 'sleevers' to committee men. On
one day the prosecutor, to the utter astonishment of the
magistrates, defendants and the press said that if the Prevention
of Corrupt Practices Act 1907 had been in force at the time of the
raid, the officers of the Ferndale Band Club would have faced
several years in prison. Shock waves reverberated throughout the
cosy world of the Working Men's Club. An element of fear now dwelt
in the minds of the officers facing the magistrates. The police
gave their evidence factually and unemotionally to prove that

excessive drinking could not possibly be necessary to achieve th object of the club, which was 'to promote a knowledge of music

As the case dragged on the editor was confident it would b dismissed. Thirty-three witnesses appeared for the defence bu the prosecution won the day. The editor urged Ferndale t appeal and wrote, 'One touch of adversity makes the whole ban world kin.' So important was this to the club world that the edito printed a 3,000 word summing-up by the magistrate in full an the reasons for the decision to strike the club off the register fo 12 months. Ferndale carried on but on a 'temperance' basis.

One would think brass bandsmen were weaned on ale. At th same time as the Ferndale case, the editor was running a limeric competition to find the last line to this:

There is a musician called Rimmer
Who at contests is always a winner
His experience is wide
And he's quite without side

(and, would you believe, the winning line was)

Let's toast him "good health" with a brimmer. (an overfull pint).

On the other hand, in circles where drink certainly was not problem, this year saw dissent among Salvation Army bandsmer The catalyst was the strict interpretation of a rule which insistec in effect, that Salvation Army bands were NOT to help out an bands and friends outside the Salvation Army. The editor foun out, however, that non-Salvation Army bands were to b encouraged to help in Salvation Army band work. He though this most odd, to say the least, and asked, 'What will the Missio Bands have to say about this?'. Not a lot, apparently, as non protested in print.

The British Bandsman became the focal point for an explosion c dissatisfaction from Salvation Army musicians who quite under standably in the climate of the times wrote under pseudonym: All, however, were properly signed with addresses. Letters pile up signed *Twenty five years faithful, Man in the Street*, or *Robin Hoo* All sorts of accusations were bandied about. 'Did Salvation Arm bandsmen get paid?' – one correspondent 'in the know' knew c one Salvation Army band, the members of which received 2s. 6c per head 'when they play a half day's job outside'. Anothe question was: 'Can Salvation Army bandsmen become teacher and play in outside bands?'

One writer complained that some of these men were using th property of the Salvation Army for this purpose and he coul name many who played regularly for outside bands. When thes men asked if they could use Salvation Army property for teachin purposes they 'were uncomfortably told they could not'. Ye another question caused debate – 'Can Salvation Army bandsmen attend "smokers"?' ('Smokers' were popular social concerts promoted by brass bands). One complained: 'I cannot, but several do'.

Now that *The British Bandsman* had opened its letters column to air this grievances, the issue widened and some of the printed comments included: 'I pay £6 for my uniform', 'I have to put into the cartridge every week what I can afford and pay 1d. for the band league!' 'I have to give to the limit in the collection', 'I have to buy the journals (music) and pay all my expenses for summer outing and visits.' Some complained of being out NIGHT AFTER NIGHT in the 'wet and cold and receiving nout for it'.

If the correspondence flagged *The British Bandsman* refuelled it and rather naughtily wrote, 'I find our Salvation Army bandsmen do not get a free ticket for their Christmas banquet'. Being a good editor he also printed all the letters which pointed out, in effect, the end product of the Salvation Army — and that included the bandsmen — was the number of converts The Salvation Army made to the Christian faith. The editor agreed with these and wrote that it was the Salvation Army band which was the magnet to attract people to the Word.

The debate rumbled on until the editor wrote an open letter to Bramwell Booth, some of the points of which included: 'Take note of the complaints in the letters, issue *The Hallelujah Chorus* and *The Heavens are Telling*, they have much more religious effect. Many Salvation Army bandmasters are swollen-headed and play music too difficult for their bands. Provide teachers and do not be afraid to ask for outside help. Because you tax the bands ten per cent of the money they receive, the bands are at a disadvantage to outside bands.'

His most telling indictment was to draw the Chief of Staff's attention to the arbitrary and unnecessary rules which were much too strictly applied by corps and divisional officers. He asked for more generosity to be shown and wrote: 'I have little hesitation in saying that the band is often the principal part of the corps, therefore, think a little more kindly of them'. The long letter can best be summed up by saying 'Get off their backs'.

13   *1907 and 1908: Two busy years*

The Prevention of Corrupt Practices Act of 1907 went unlargely unnoticed by brass bands but as its importance emerged it resulted in rough justice for some secretaries and committee men.

Since the time brass bands were first formed as we know them today, secret commissions were paid to band secretaries to persuade them to buy instruments from a particular manufacturer. To the salesman and the maker this was considered a perfectly permissible business transaction and, to be fair, the majority of these secretaries reflected the commission in the balance sheets. But to some it was manna from heaven, a goodly sum of money to pocket to pay family debts.

It is on record that quite a few band secretaries were now writing confidentially to all instrument makers seeking a personal commission. One wrote, 'Our band is considering purchasing a new set of instruments. Before making a recommendation to the committee to buy your instruments would you be so kind as to tell me in confidence how much my commission would be?'

It was not restricted to bands. For years it had been the custom of several examining bodies to offer to teachers of music a percentage of the fees based upon the number of pupils sent to them for examination. In several cases this commission had been a strong driving power and because of this some institutions flourished and those who paid poor commissions went to the wall. Brass band teachers found this a very healthy perk.

Because of this Act, almost overnight the word 'commission' became 'bribe' but the practice continued until *The British Bandsman* highlighted the 'greedy and deceitful ways of the band secretaries' and pointed out to them they were nothing more than felons. This caused some bandsman to ponder and questions were asked of their officers. They could remember a holiday or two to the seaside being taken by secretaries which they would otherwise be unable to afford and yet the secretary was on the next machine as them doing the same work for the same money.

Many a kangaroo court was held resulting in total ostracism from the band and the close-knit community in which most bands were formed. It was a very serious business and accounted for at least two suicides. *The British Bandsman* stood on the sidelines appalled at what it was witnessing and implored the bands to examine, very carefully, the evidence upon which they announced the harsh sentence of being 'sent to Coventry' which is much worse than hard labour'.

The publicity did not prevent some unscrupulous officers still asking for a commission and it was never really stamped out. It became more sophisticated with gifts, food hampers from Fortnum and Masons, shoe vouchers and occasionally a paid trip to a big city with all expenses met. It did, however, make the bandsmen more aware of their player power and it was not long before officers were elected by everyone, whereas previously committees had been self-perpetuating (mainly because of band apathy) and the secretaryship had become a matter of 'Buggin's turn!'

There appears to be no evidence of the crack bands being affected by bribery. One of the reasons was that there was always plenty of money to go round. From the columns of *The British Bandsman* this affluence of the elite caused considerable jealousy and there were some wry smiles when it became known that Black Dyke were in grave financial trouble. The tour of America had been a financial disaster with a shortfall of some £3,000. Although it became a temporary setback, it left the band disorganised with the problem of where to find the money. The *Bradford Daily Telegraph* asked if readers could make any suggestions for the removal of this burden which would fall on every bandsman's pocket. *The British Bandsman* echoed this appeal.

Some lower bands were hoping that there might be defections from the band and began sounding out various players. It would not have caused as much as a ripple if some players had moved. In the mid-1900s bandsmen were constantly on the move as they sought better paid employment encouraged by advertisements in *The British Bandsman*. The editor had to be forever cautioning an applicant; to make sure exactly what the terms of employment were, for there was very little scope for redress and, if a worker did query the initial terms, he was promptly sacked. Not easy to swallow once you had moved with your wife and family maybe 100 miles or more.

The British Bandsman reported a case of a bandsman who was offered 5s.0d. per day and signed on, only to find there was in his hand the equal of 3s.6d. per day. 'He was', said *The British Bandsman* 'engaged on heavy work for light pay'. The man argued his case to the pay clerk and the money was forcibly taken from his hand. He was sacked.

As ever, it was engagements which provided the much-needed cash for bandsmen but they found themselves in serious competition with military bands. *The British Bandsman* thought it was a question of repertoire. 'Why not look to the music of Wagner and Tchaikovsky – the Cake Walk is out'. It was considered a mistake to think about playing any music by Beethoven because his music was not understood 'by the masses'. This did not prevent Mr. Cope from writing a full page article and likenesses of the great composer, the next week.

The editor walked a tight rope. His readership had become too diverse. At one end was the unemployed worker who could not afford spectacles to read the small print employed by *The British Bandsman* and was dependent upon someone else to read it to him. At the other end, famous names, some long since forgotten, including internationally known military bandmasters, conductors of the great symphony orchestras, even Sir Henry Wood and the gifted critic, Hannen Swaffer included *The British Bandsman* in their weekly reading.

Sometimes the 'lower orders' complained, 'there is too much swank in the paper' but the editor could not cater just for brass bandsmen as he and Henry Iles had built it up to be a paper of some influence in the whole of the musical world and beyond. It still lay in the Parliament Library each week.

Wherever there was a musical cause the editor took up the cudgels on its behalf. At Leith, Scotland, the puritan desire for no music on the Sabbath led its devotees to threaten the church organ with destruction by axes and hammers and throw it out on to the street and make a bonfire of it. How he got to know of all these peculiar news-items is a mystery but when he did, he let fly, and the Leith business was called 'mischievous cant'.

Whether or not he was becoming provocative on purpose to increase sales is not clear. Certainly *The British Bandsman* was beginning to lose some of its readership in the lower wage bracket. It was now obvious that sales of *The British Bandsman* within a band had slumped to one or two. Financially it did not appear to worry Henry Iles, who was now making his fortune from his entrepreneural activities, but it was his pride which suffered.

Against the advice of his business friends, the staff and his family, he decided upon a major step to improve circulation and it was dramatic. 1908 began with the cost of the magazine being increased by 100 per cent to 2d. Pages were increased from 20 to 36 and the frontispiece was in colour. It was now 'entirely devoted to music'. The extra pages enabled him to print lengthy news about concertina bands, handbell ringers (with photographs), The Salvation Army, choirs, orchestral and string bands and cartoons. The local correspondents were encouraged to scrape the barrel for news items, many of which were two-liners, e.g., 'Fossils are beginning to drop off the whiskers of the Perth City

Horbury Hand Bell Ringers 1907. A feature of the Crystal Palace brass band contest.

Fathers' whatever that might mean. It carried the equivalent of 8 full pages of advertisements and ran competitions.

It was able to report fully the triumphant, major and financially successful world tour of the Besses o' th' Barn band organised and underwritten by Henry Iles, which was read with great interest by bandsman everywhere as they basked in its reflected glory. Brass band news items were often featured on the front pages of the various national and provincial daily newspapers and for a while its contribution to the music scene reached a new peak.

The editor wrote an extremely fulsome appreciation of Mr Iles taking up most of the front page. It was so sycophantic that the editor told his readers that it was his work alone and Mr. Iles had no idea it was written until he had received his copy.

Mr. Iles had many enemies in the brass band fraternity. This addendum by the editor was made to ensure he did not add

Besides being the programme for the Great National Band Festival it was the official programme for the whole complex. If bandsmen wished they could wander through a menagerie for 6d (2½p), have a meal for 12½p, visit an aquarium, go boating on the Great Lake or get wide eyed at the Parisian Pleasure Fair.

It was a wonderland for the people visiting London for the first time. Palms and heads could be read and the future told, various exhibitions very well appointed from Mexico, Egypt, Rome and Spain were always thronged. The children were in awe of the monkey and parrot house, the Natural History Museum and the Zoo.

If you wanted to watch a F.A. football match there was always the Crystal Palace F.C. playing in the grounds on a Saturday afternoon. It was idyllic in the daytime but come evening as the night drew in it was necessary to print prominently and boldly in the programme 'CAUTION – The Crystal Palace Company gives notice that as the grounds are now lighted, persons passing through same after dark do so at their own risk'. Nowadays we call it 'mugging' then it was 'robbery with violence'. And the ladies of the night were invisible except for the light of a cigarette – an enticing glow worm.

further to the feeling that Mr. Iles was a glory-seeker and might have had a hand in the writing of the article. For most of his life Henry Iles had to put up with damaging remarks about having 'his hand in the till', 'talk about commissions, he lives on them' and the like. But without him the movement would have fragmented before the decade was out. The reasons for this jealousy were primarily a feeling that Mr. Iles and Sam Cope were feathering their nests at the expense of the working man. This reaction surfaced every now and then for the rest of their lives.

The paper was extraordinary good value for money and this, in a way, made the readership restless. All the different tastes for which it catered wanted more publicity. Craftily the editor rang the changes. One week brass predominated, the next, handbell ringers and so on. Overseas news was just a waste of space. As one reader remarked 'What possible interest is to us up here (Stockton) to know what is going on in Australia.' The 1900s were the hey day for letter writers, articulate, blunt, provocative but always interesting, revealing in many cases the steps taken by some bandsmen to improve their education.

There was much speculation regarding the status of the Volunteer Bands as the new act forming the Territorial Army redefined the role of the bandsmen, several of whom played in well known brass bands. Hitherto, their role was never spelt out but now they were 'Territorials'. *The British Bandsman* saw that it was in no position to give advice but reading between the lines it hinted that war was well nigh impossible these days. It excited little comment from the bandsmen and those who transferred to the new Army were quite sure, as were most people that, with Mr. Asquith as Prime Minister and Lloyd George as Chancellor, Great Britain was impregnable and its Army and Navy the envy of the world especially as more new 'Dreadnoughts' were being built. Was not the new government already taking steps to put more money in people's pockets? All seemed tranquil and at peace – and yet within six years these men in the territorial bands were among the first to engage the enemy.

The British Bandsman continued in its sedate manner, inventing problems to keep the pot boiling. One such question being asked regarded 'own-choice' contests and were they fair? The editor courted letters by writing! 'The True Contest is a Contest which gives Fair Play all round and which places every band on the same footing'. One Northerner wrote 'Maybe it is but it does not pay us much. People who pay good money to go to a contest don't come to any more when they realise they hear the same old tune over and over again. Own-choice fills pews always'.

Marching contests soon became the fashion and many promoters jumped on the bandwagon only to have their fingers burned. The Lancashire and Cheshire Miners Demonstration (gala) attracted 100,000 onlookers and 33 colliery bands played in the procession. Although a marching contest at the gala had been expensively and extensively advertised it attracted only a handful of bands. One wag thought those who were going to march in the evening contest at the gala must have been colliery temperance bands for how else could they have put one foot in front of the other.

To find more money for either drink or personal finance this year saw a flood of offences for illegal pawning. It was rife through the country and hardly any band escaped. Bandsmen would take their instrument home, pawn it the next day, miss some rehearsals by pleading illness and then retrieve it before being found out. It was a way of life for many hard pressed people and necessary to make both ends meet. However, if the bandsman was exposed — and they often were — it meant a month in prison and worse, to be for ever condemned in the labour market. In those days an E flat bombardon valued at £8.8s.0d. could be pawned for 10s.0d.

These were the years when bands proliferated at a tremendous rate. Every organisation and religious sect seemed to have one. In Band of Hope processions one could hear Salvation Army bands, Primitive Methodists, sometimes Fire Brigade and Postmen's bands, League of the Cross, Mission and Orphanage, tramways, railway and lifeboat bands. There were Red Cross and Samaritan bands Institute and Cottage Homes bands, those of Industrial Schools, of construction firms, manufacturing concerns and even bands formed on a kind of itinerant basis composed of navvies who came and went, with up to 50 members and down to a dozen or so. At the Metropolitan Asylum in Essex a brass band was formed and the unfortunate boys were soon 'restored to sanity, even the most feeble minded'.

No colliery was a colliery unless it had a brass band, no village worth its name could afford to be without one. The new Public Health Act entitled the various councils to provide for a brass band out of its rates and quite a few took advantage of this. It is impossible to know of all the bands of this busy time but from the columns of *The British Bandsman* well over 2,500 are mentioned and some were very well known but who now hears of the Cocoa Works band, the Steam Shed band, the Pollockshaws Burgh band or the Bristol Milk Street Prize Band.

Inevitably the trade cut its throat to increase the share of this burgeoning market. *The British Bandsman* profited with advertisers

The brothers Brown of Milk Street Silver Band, Bristol in 1908. Many bands had several brothers, large families being normal.

queuing up for space. Discounts were becoming larger and larger, credit facilities quite ludicrous and the bribes more valuable.

Equally as predictable was the crash when it came. Bands found themselves unable to meet their financial commitments and were either taken to court or had the payment period extended almost *ad infinitum*. Some of the smaller tailoring and instrument firms ceased trading. *The British Bandsman* always advised on the perils of extended credit but it was seldom accepted.

Henry Iles could see the bubble must burst and became worried that the possibility of insufficient local funds would prevent bands from coming to the Crystal Palace and exhorted them, through *The British Bandsman,* to start the 'going off club' and pay in a small amount each week. Another idea, which helped the fund, was to invite the general public to rehearsals and to charge a small entrance fee. In many areas this paid dividends but, alas, *The British Bandsman* reported the 'failure of some treasurers to know their responsibility'. One converted the sum of £25 to his own use – a large sum at that time.

These years witnessed a bumper crop of contests with good money to be won. It is no wonder stringent measures were taken all the time to ensure the complete isolation of the judges. At an August Bank Holiday contest in Wales, a competing bandsman found a hole in the brailing of the tent, about seven inches from the ground and only an inch in diameter but the committee had to find yards of canvas to cover not only the hole but to wrap round the rest of the brailing as the new canvas was not of the same thickness as the tent canvas. This was not all. The local guardian in an impassioned speech entreating the public not to shout out the names of the band on the field, ended by saying 'Wi Abertillery kindly come on to platform'. And so it will ever be

Advertisements for bandmasters of Welsh brass bands wer among the most unique in the country. The Conway Counc wanted a bandmaster, preferably a cornet player but said 'it wi be part of his duties to inspect Hawkers, Boats and Carriages an know about Warehouses'. The editor cautioned any applicant that there would be little time for banding. He ended these year on what was then a serious topic. Naval bands played th *National Anthem* at a tempo of 100 crotchets to the minute wherea Army bands took it at 65 crotchets. It took a high level conferenc to finally agree it should be 85 crotchets to the minute. When th editor was asked what was the going rate for brass bands, h diplomatically replied that it all depended on the weather!

4 A touchy year

After a quiet start to 1909 the brass band scene became progressively more unstable. It was to witness some frightening scenes at contests where conduct unbecoming was the norm. One such incident was widely reported and it did the movement no good at all.

For some time the relationship between two bands had been worsening to such an extent that it was only a matter of time before they came to blows. At the contest in question, what started out with cat-calling and stone-throwing quickly developed into savage fighting with no quarter asked and none given. Several of the bandsmen were treated in hospital for quite serious injuries. The police were powerless to intervene and the riot did not finish until there was no one left standing. It would, perhaps, be unkind to name the bands except to say they both came from Ireland.

The editor did not believe this could be true, but it was and he and Mr. Iles told bands, in no uncertain manner, that this behaviour would kill the contests for good. They both came down firmly on the side of law and order. Hardly had these words appeared in print when readers began to criticise councils for engaging certain bands to play in the parks. The main thrust was that constabulary brass bands were tendering too cheaply, that the police were taking the bread and butter from the mouths of bandsmen but, more seriously, that they were professional bands. The question was asked: 'Why can the Government pay the wages and allowances of these gentlemen whenever they play AND rehearse'.

This widened very quickly to include the regimental military bands, the musicians of which were cosseted to some extent by the officers. These twin perils to the brass bandsman's pocket caused much grievance and they wrote many letters asking the editor to organise a monster petition to Parliament. It was quite a serious matter as all over the country brass bands were reporting that their lucrative park and promenade concerts were being 'snuffed out' by the councils.

For a while the editor, and particularly Henry Iles, did nothing, anxious not to offend either side. *The British Bandsman* agreed it was a most unfair practice and wrote: 'There is no possible way of these bands being called amateur bands'. Mr. Iles knew, in any case, that councils liked to book police and military bands because he was advised 'there is no hooliganism, blasphemy foul behaviour or petty assault at these engagements'.

There was another reason for Mr. Iles distancing himself from the argument, and it was political. He had many friends in the military bands and was on intimate terms with the officer heirarchy of the regiments. The dilemma was that on the one hand he himself had always trumpeted that the brass bands were composed of hard-working class men and he himself was responsible for the growth of the brass band. He knew that the overwhelming majority of these men were opposed to the Conservative party and were actively engaged in promoting the new Labour party by offering their services free at the rallies especially in the North. On the other hard, his lifestyle was centred around the free-marketeers, the officer class and the gentry.

However, he had his mind made up for him. He never was a supporter of the Trade Union movement but realised musicians should have some kind of controlling body to protect their interests. He took no active part in this but made it known that he was always available for advice. When he realised the great ground swell of opposition to military bands, organised by the Amateur Musicians Union, he could not afford to ignore it. He and the editor quickly allowed space in *The British Bandsman* for support on its behalf. Questions were subsequently asked in Parliament and Mr Haldane of the War Office told Mr Steadman MP who was the chairman of the Parliamentary Committee of the Trades Union Council, that he did not see any reason why the public should be denied the opportunity of listening to these 'fine military bands'.

No one got very far and the issue smouldered on until World War One. Every now and then someone would write about the 'gross and glaring injustice'. Sometimes the brass bands took to pitching themselves within earshot of military bands playing in the park and kept up a non-stop playing of *Soldiers of the Queen* until the police intervened. Finally the bands presented a petition to the War Office and then marched backwards and forwards past the startled onlookers in Whitehall, playing the *Dead March*.

Such was the behaviour of some brass bands that even the trade unions were sorely tried to continue with them. It came as a bit of a shock when the ASRS, known as the 'Railway Servants', ignored the Bristol Brass Band and booked the band of HM Royal Marines on Good Friday. A terrible blow because Good Friday was one of the few days in the calendar which provided, as one reader wrote, 'of good pickings from the public'.

A measure of support to the working class given by brass bands is best exemplified by the Government's concern for the elderly. When the Old Age Pensions Act of 1908 became operative in the January of 1909, a large crowd of pensioners

In its first 20 years many contemporary magazines published verbatim news from the B.B.

95

queued outside Braintree Post Office, Essex, waiting for the doors to open at 8.00 a.m. to draw the first money (5s.0d. per week. 1s.0d. for ladies, means-tested and must be over 70 years old). The Braintree Brass Band assembled outside at 7.30 a.m. and played a programme of music including *Hail, Smiling Morn* and, as the postmaster in his frock coat and top hat ceremoniously unlocked the door at the front, he, his staff and all the pensioners stood to attention as the band played the *National Anthem*, which everyone sung with great gusto.

This gesture by the Government was much appreciated and widely acclaimed, because the depression was biting ever deeper. Newspapers were reporting numerous court cases where action was taken against brass band debtors. The Collingwood Street Working Men's Mission Band were asked to attend the band room to sign a collective hire-purchase agreement form for new uniforms. They were informed by the salesman it was just a formality but he must have a signature. It was obvious they had no idea of the amount of shillings they were expected to pay and, in any case, some of the signatories were under the age of 21. It made no difference and in the High Court no less, the band was told to pay costs and £1 a month for 15 months. This instance was one of several reported that year.

Two other court cases were heard which, in their different ways, affected brass bands for years to come. The first evolved from the long-running vexed (and often glossed over) problem of borrowing and poaching players. It came to a head in a strange manner. Skating rinks had become popular all over the country and it was not long before skaters complained that the musical accompaniment by light combinations was drowned by the noise of the skates. One promoter heard a military band at the Olympia Skating Rink, London which not only drowned the noise of the skates but the conversation as well and he was soon employing brass bands at the provincial centres.

These bands, formed mainly on an *ad hoc* basis, provided good money for the bandsmen and soon they were playing at circuses and fun fairs. It was inevitable that players would be cajoling other players to play in their particular brass band and consequently there were more players than usual on the move.

If band committees told these errant bandsmen, 'you can no longer play with us if you continue to play with some other band', the player would resign and the band probably lose a star player. So they kept their mouths shut. There seemed nothing to stop the practice until Messrs Crosfield Limited, the soap manufacturers, stepped in when two of its players in the championship band, Perfection Soap, began to wander off to other bands to earn more money. The chairman promptly applied for an injunction in the High Court specifically to restrain the players from 'playing with or for any other band'. The firm won and the two players had to pay the costs of the hearing.

This had a sobering effect on the other crack bands which were owned by manufacturing concerns. Mr Jesse Boot, the up and coming pharmaceutical giant, pinned a summing-up of the case in the band room of the Boots Plausiance Band as a warning of what would happen should any of his bandsmen 'stoop to this ungrateful way of expressing their thanks to myself and my wife'.

The second case came as a surprise to the bands, the public and, to some extent, the financial moguls in the City of London. For some time there had been an exchange of letters between Mr. Iles and the management of Besses o' th' Barn regarding the overall responsibility for arranging future tours of this world-famous band. Besses wished to arrange their own but the bone of contention was an agreement which seemed ambiguous. Mr Iles was convinced he could arrange everything for a period of 12 months from the end of the last tour but the bands were equally convinced it could arrange what they liked and employ Mr Iles as their agent in accordance with the agreed terms.

It reached the High Court of Justice, Kings Bench Division before Mr. Justice Bray and a special jury. It excited the interest of all agents and promoters in other fields such as boxing, symphony orchestras and the acting profession. The brass band world was amazed at the rewards, the profits and the secrets of the administration which were laid bare by the skilful examination of the witnesses. The evidence was debated between brass bandsmen all over the north of the country. Figures were bandied about concerning the division of the gross receipts of tours, 45 per cent of which would go to the band, out of which all expenses were paid, such as board, lodgings, fares, printing and retainers. If the band was incapable of handling all this then Mr. Iles would do it for an extra 12½ per cent added to his percentage.

All the proceedings were reported verbatim in *The British Bandsman*. Henry Iles won, or as the *The British Bandsman* put it in heavy black print: 'Mr Iles has been victorious and judgement in his favour, with heavy costs given against Besses Band'. Before we leave this case which has been fully dealt with elsewhere, there were some facts which were illuminating to say the least.

Mr. Iles was able to establish that he was the *force majeure* in the brass band world. Was he not the proprietor of *The British Bandsman* and was he not the owner of the oldest established band-music publishing concern in the whole of the country? It seemed no band in this country could tour and give a concert and

SHAW PRIZE BRASS BAND.

WINNERS OF THE CRYSTAL PALACE 1000 GUINEA TROPHY

CLIFFE SHAW COPYRIGHT

The Shaw Prize Band taken in 1909 following success as championship band at The Crystal Palace 'National'. The magnificent trophy takes pride of place.

expect it to be a success unless it took place under the umbrella services provided by Mr. Iles.

Dotted about the country were gentlemen who made a fair living as concert agents taking their commission in most instances from the Concert Agent-in-Chief, Henry Iles. They either booked a band through him or he approached them to book a band. The going rate was 60 per cent of the 'take' to the band and the rest to the agents. If however, it took place in a town whose population was 2,000 or less then the band received only 45 per cent.

Various agents gave evidence on behalf of Mr. Iles and it was not long before readers realised the healthy profit Mr. Iles was making from his activities. From the complete reading of the transcript of evidence it emerges the whole affair both within and out of court was conducted with great courtesy and there was no rancour on either side but it was a sad affair.

To end this touchy year on a less serious note, Mr. J. Brook was introduced to a Lady Mayoress as 'and this is the soprano who will be performing with the Fodens band.' She was heard to mutter as she walked away: 'But I thought the Pope banished this horrible operation years ago'. This prompted the editor to write an article on *i castrati*.

15 *The Salvation Army, socialism and sour grapes*

The very wet summer of 1909 had meant fewer people attending contests and concerts and many a kitty was in a parlous state. The editor said 'the poor get poorer' and they did. Brass bands now, it seems, totally identified with what Lloyd George then called 'the unfortunate lower orders of our society,' rallied to the plight of the underprivileged.

Processions in support of the Labour Party took place in most industrial areas, as the party sought radical changes. The Prime Minister, Mr. Asquith introduced in 1910 some measure of social reform, the most important of which was the National Insurance Act. It was not enough and the workers became vociferous in their stated demands. Brass bands offered their services freely. One such procession took two hours to pass to the Market Place, Nottingham where the Post Office band, Netherfield Railwaymen, Old Robin Hood and Bullwell Excelsior bands all played well-known tunes to which unpatriotic words were sung by the huge crowd.

Oldham brass band organised a series of concerts in aid of the Poor Children's Free Meal Fund and Stony Stratford Town Silver Band went on parade to collect money for a widow and her six children. It made about £6 to enable her to clothe her family. These incidents were not at all unique and had their roots in the economy of the previous ten years. Up to 1900, wages had risen generally but until 1910 had remained stationary. Workers outside unions were often badly paid and a large proportion of the working class suffered from very poor housing, inadequate social services and fluctuating employment.

The new-found freedom given to unions by the Trade Disputes Act bred the most acute industrial strife Britain had ever known. In 1911 a railway strike paralysed a large part of the country and in 1912, some 850,000 miners were idle for several weeks, resulting in unemployment in other industries. These strikes and a number of lesser ones led to violent incidents. All this must be remembered when talking about brass bands up to the outbreak of the First World War in 1914.

The struggle to win cash prizes intensified and bitterness and recrimination broke out even among the crack bands, whilst 1910 saw the end of many brass bands whose members either could not afford to play or moved to find work. The editor said it was apparent that no band could win a prize 'without a paid player or two.'

Bands began to appreciate that unity was strength and supported various brass band associations to enable some order to be kept. The South Wales and Monmouthshire Association had 29 member bands yet in the south of Scotland where the brass band scene was very healthy the Association's Southern and Western divisions had a dismal response. Bands were dropped wholesale by the various music festivals which could not make a profit. Brighton Festival lost £360.

New ideas of concert presentations were put forward to make concerts more popular and it was found that 'own choice' contests made more money than test piece ones. Most 'own choices' were of the cake walk, waltz and quick step variety although the latter was frowned upon by the church as morally suspect. The editor thought this a little narrow minded to say the least and these people should go to the opera and see 'what' what'.

Jealousy between bands nearly changed the contest scene. Subscription bands began to protest about the success of works bands and a considerable body of opinion thought the contesting scene should be split into two involving, to the horror of Henry Iles, only subscription bands to contest at the Crystal Palace and sponsored bands elsewhere. One militant comment was: 'When all the players work at one mill and the master takes an interest in the band, it is an easy matter for every man to attend practices regularly for he will see work so regulated that none of the bandsmen are detained at work during the time which is generally devoted to practice and some do not have any deduction from their wages'.

'Not at Fodens they don't', wrote Mr. Twemlow, a Director. He said his band was an amateur band and the players received absolutely no special privileges or payments. A hollow laugh greeted this by bands in the North because they were aware John Foster, the owner of Black Dyke Mills, had just died leaving a

THE NATIONAL BAND FESTIVAL

Saturday 1st. October, 1910.

.......CHAMPIONSHIP..... Section.

J U D G E ' S   A W A R D.

First   in order of Merit No.
Second   in order of Merit No.   2   Band
Third   in order of Merit No.   7   Band
Fourth   in order of Merit No. 14   Band
Fifth   in order of Merit No.   9   Band
Sixth   in order of Merit No. 10   Band
Seventh   in order of Merit No.   4   Band
Eighth   in order of Merit No. 12   Band
Ninth   in order of Merit No. 15   Band
Tenth   in order of Merit No.   3   Band
Eleventh in order of Merit No.   6   Band
Twelfth   in order of Merit No. 13   Band
Thirteenth in order of Merit No. 5   Band
Fourteenth in order of Merit No. 11   Band
Fifteenth in order of Merit No.   1   Band
                                   8   Band

Adjudicators.

NOTE :- Please fill in the positions of the bands as far as possible
giving, at least, four more than the Prize winners, in case
there are any protests.
Please sign this after filling in, and seal up in the envelope
provided.
Kindly hand same to the Constable as you leave the Tent.

J. HENRY ILES. Director.

The pro forma used by judges, Crystal Palace 1910.

million pounds and they had no doubt most of the other big manufacturing concerns were awash with money, some of which was bound to find its way into the bandsmen's pockets. Surprisingly, perhaps, this was simply not true but it was a popular belief sustained by the well-cut, well-made uniforms and the very best of instruments these bands had.

If the 'two contest' agitators could have got the colliery bands on their side, the present picture would have been quite different. These miners' bands had certain advantages but not to the same extent. A colliery worked night and day and the miner's recent Eight Hour Act meant cross shifts with bandsmen working all hours, so that rehearsals were the first to suffer. Another stumbling block was that northern, southern, eastern, western, Scottish, Welsh and Irish bands and associations all trod different paths, but it was a 'close run thing'.

Hardly had this issue been settled when the editor without any warning suddenly attacked The Salvation Army, and his editorial thunder still echoes today. Why he chose to do so, no research can tell, although it was thought at the time that Iles was tremendously frustrated because no Salvation Army bandmasters could advertise for players in *The British Bandsman*.

The editor began by saying he disliked referring to religious bodies in his magazine but he had to speak out, loudly and clearly, for those in The Salvation Army bands who were frightened to speak for themselves. It was straight from the shoulder stuff. He objected most strongly to those Salvation Army bands 'seeking orders from outside bands' but which were compelled to buy from within their own organisation. This, he said, closed the door to healthy competition.

'Why on earth', he asked, 'is it forbidden for Salvation Army bands to use any other music than their own?' And he went on to say that any hint by a Salvation Army bandmaster that he would love to play 'outside' music would mean the unfortunate man would be 'carpeted' and compelled to 'endure discomfort'. He recorded where one man was so fed up that he left the band. He was very well known but The Salvation Army gave other reasons for the defection.

He was also privy to information, supplied by a 'mole' it appears, that whole Salvation Army bands were now seceding from it. He thought the whole affair quite scandalous. His inflammatory article brought sackfuls of letters. If he thought he had upset a hornets' nest, then he was disappointed. When one considers the thousands of Salvation Army musicians, then conservatively put at 16,000, and this ignores the juniors who played in another hundred bands, then those who replied were a handful. These he published because of the agreement with his views. Letters from 'outside bands' were lumped together in just one sentence: 'The majority agree with me.'

He had to go to ground for a while as gossip raged. Many brass bandsmen, administrators and promoters had a high regard for the aims of The Salvation Army and yet here was the editor alleging The Salvation Army establishment figures were at best mistaken and at worse untruthful. He was told that brass bandsmen had every sympathy with The Salvation Army. One said, 'Do not the Salvationists go with hope in their hearts into the most squalid areas where the bands play, often surrounded by drunks and harlots, to distribute food and clothing to young mothers at the end of their wits?'. The message reaching Henry Iles, the proprietor, was 'Leave The Salvation Army alone.'

Despite these disapproving nods from his friends, Henry Iles allowed the editor to return to the attack, castigating the officers for total inflexibility and writing: 'The Salvation Army seems to have curiously mixed religion with trade. It is within our knowledge that many of the players in The Salvation Army bands owe their position entirely to their music ability and not on account of either religious fervour or their loyalty to The Salvation Army cause'.

A curious episode which was about to be expanded by those who wondered if the issue had been brought about by the inability of the music publishing firm owned by Mr. Iles to penetrate the huge Salvation Army market, when the campaign came to an abrupt halt with the death of King Edward VII.

This royal death came at an inopportune time as the Whitsuntide contest bonanza for brass bands was about to get under way. There were anxious enquiries at the offices of *The British Bandsman*. Hundreds of postcards were despatched to the editor asking him if he had clarification of the 'scale of mourning for our late beloved King'. The editor, along with Fleet Street, could obtain no help from Buckingham Palace and the whole brass band movement held its breath as discussions took place. Worried treasurers used the telephone to ask the editor if any news had come through because much money was already spent on these contests and they would suffer financial ruin if they were cancelled.

Not only did it affect brass bands but the Royal Opera as well and friends of the new King were soon asking if a decision could be made urgently. At the eleventh hour the new King, George V, let it be known that his late father would not want his people not to enjoy themselves and the Royal Opera House should open and Mr Beecham's season should continue.

It so happened that the date of the royal funeral coincided with the well-attended Sunday School processions which took place in all parts of the country. Mr Iles ever anxious to increase music sales, quickly published a list of suitable music that should be played by brass bands heading these processions to show 'profound respect' and with the commercial tag, 'we can supply by return'. Brass bands were also much in evidence outside parish churches where they played the *Dead March* as the civic dignitaries and the public crowded in to offer prayers.

The *Dead March* needed no rehearsal; every player knew every note because the practice of playing it by disappointed bands at contests still prevailed. At the Shropshire Brass Band Championship the Donnington Wood Institute Prize band won first prize but, because of protests, the money was withheld, whereupon the band formed up and marched around and around the field playing the march over and over again.

As a result of these protests the columns of *The British Bandsman* were opened to the question of closed adjudication which, like borrowed, poached and paid players, was never out of the news. It asked the same questions which are asked today but it degenerated into unworthy remarks which, rather surprisingly, the editor published. Judges were called charlatans, quacks or corrupt and 'Devotees of Machiavelli'. Some judges agreed with open adjudication. One wrote that when a committee man shouted through the canvas of the tent that 'a pot of tea is outside' he did not hear him and he went without, 'which proves some tents are almost a barrier to the music'. Other judges thought it would constitute a 'bit of a rumpus' in open adjudication if they were seen not to be writing much after a band had played.

Before the year was out, Parliament intervened twice in band matters. The first concerned the new Territorial Army bands. To make a little money on the side some of these bands had headed the suffragette protest marches. Objections were raised by some people and the War Office issued an instruction forbidding the practice. The suffragettes then turned to the brass band who, knowing the risk, charged exhorbitant fees. To protect themselves many bands placed advertisements in local papers saying it was just another engagement and did not, in any way, imply 'an agreement with the cause'.

The band of the 8th Middlesex Regiment played at an Empire Day celebration in the gardens of a VIP in Brentford, Middlesex. This was quickly noticed by the local brass bands who had been engaged in previous years and they asked their Member of Parliament if this was not a 'political gathering to which a military band ought not to be prudently invited'. The War Office replied that the Minister would like to think of this event as a garden party but promised 'instructions would be given'.

The year ended on a very sad note. The Pretoria Pit Disaster at Atherton claimed 300 lives and several members of Wingates Temperance band were killed including Albert Lonsdale, the secretary and a Mr. Cowburn. They had 18 children between them. *The British Bandsman* described it as a great tragedy as all the fatherless children are 'left unprovided for and will have to rely upon a charitable public for their very existence'.

All bands rallied round to 'help these helpless women and children in an agony of despair'. The result proved, without any doubt, that the movement, although ridden with petty jealousy, chicanery and self doubt was, in the final analysis, a great brotherhood of men.

16 *The Coronation and church*

The year 1911 revealed the odd world in which the people of this country found themselves. Many were so unhappy with their lot that they listened eagerly to the seditious speeches of orators, yet showed blind loyalty to the monarchical system under which they lived.

The Wingates fund was a good example of this division. Clergy of all denominations held a prayer meeting outside the council chambers at Stockport 'to ask the Lord to rid the town of the sinful practice of brass bands playing on Sunday' and this at a time when brass bands in the area were organising Sunday concerts to raise money for the dependants of the tragedy.

Hampstead Brass Band decided to hold a concert in Trafalgar Square hoping to raise maybe £200 for the fund. It was so sure it would succeed that the approach to the magistrates for permission was considered just a formality. The bandsmen were shocked when it was dismissed out of hand with no reason given. Other bands were telling of some authorities refusing to reduce hiring rates for halls for the same purpose.

Henry Iles and his editor were not without influence and they were surprised the authorities in London considered the tragedy too remote from London and, in any case, 'like can look after its own'. Of course it did. The Oldham Temperance Band held several concerts in aid of the Oldham Mission Poor Children's Clog Fund. It was a dire necessity to raise money at Sunday concerts. If not for the various poor relief funds, then the money was divided amongst the players to supplement their meagre wages.

No stone was left unturned to make these concerts a success. Some had a lay preacher, well versed in the aims of socialism, imported to help swell the crowds. In Scotland, at Dysart, the hire of the council hall for one such concert given by the Dysart Town Band was queried by the councillors as the band had 'Socialists and Trade Union speakers taking part. It does not seem right that after singing *Holy, Holy, Holy* someone should get up and preach socialism. This is not observing the Lord's Day'.

These Scottish bands were in great demand for Labour demonstrations and did not think it was a good procession unless they marched eight miles. Some bands were kept going by workers worse off than themselves. The New Tredegar Brass Band in Wales could not have existed had not the workers in the district contributed voluntarily the sum of a penny a month. This was quite a magnificent gesture when one considers the Welsh miners and their families were suffering great distress because of the lock-out by the owners.

The plight of the miners evoked sympathy in other areas. Some bands were allowed to go collecting and others were not. In Glasgow brass bands were always out collecting 'for the Valleys of Wales where life has lost its meaning' and the City councillors helped to collect the money. In Richmond, Surrey, the Council frowned upon the bands as an evil and withdrew the halfpenny rate support grant saying, 'People who live in Richmond just do not want them.'

Scottish bands always gave their services freely. In the village of Tranent, the local colliery closed after coal had been mined there for 700 years. Not knowing where the money was coming from to sustain village life, able-bodied men travelled miles to find work and the brass band collapsed. Other bands rallied quickly to give concerts to raise money and the editor called the closure 'a sore calamity'.

Bands, apart from the crack ones, could not afford to go contesting, because railway fares were much too high and beyond the bandsmen's pockets. It became so bad that the editor predicted that by 1920 a brass band contest would be as rare 'as a horse bus or a four wheel cab'. Mission bands, which could not be sustained formed choirs instead, even the celebrated Crosfield Perfection Soap Band had empty spaces in its engagements diary. To obtain the edge on other tendering bands it promptly added four saxophones. It seemed more like a show band but it certainly increased the bookings. Brighouse and Rastrick band also suffered, but hit on the idea of sending their supporters into a town on the Friday to deliver advertising pamphlets prior to the Saturday concert. The cry, 'Briggus are coming', became quite popular.

These circumstances made committees wary of spending the little money they had in hand on music, uniforms and instruments for the Coronation festivities. Councils, too, were feeling the pinch and were not willing to pay overmuch for the celebrations, just a bit of bunting here and there and a luncheon for the dignitaries. As late as mid-May, seven weeks away from the Coronation, nothing stirred. Band secretaries asked the editor if he had heard from any source whether or not other bands were marking time.

Henry Iles was worried he would have stacks of the Coronation left unsold but just as he began to be resigned to this the flood gates suddenly opened. The catalyst was the front page publicity given by the national press for the visit of the Yorkshire Kings Cross Band to Buckingham Palace to play, at the request of the King, outside the luncheon room where His Majesty would be playing host to visiting royalty.

Sir Charles Frederick, Master of the Royal Household, informed the conductor Mr. O. Pearce, that he would give a signal from inside the window with his handkerchief when the band should thereupon immediately play the National Anthem. Mr. Pearce kept his eyes glued to the window with the band at the ready. He saw nothing and the minutes crept away. Suddenly the window was flung open and Sir Charles shouted 'Get on with it, man!'.

After the concert, King George V received the Deputy Mayor 'resplendent with his high chain of office' reported *The British Bandsman*. He was asked by His Majesty if all these men were truly working men. On the assurance that they were, the King

Perfection Soapworks Prize Band. The 1911 winners of the 1,000 Guinea Cup.

asked his thanks to be conveyed to the conductor for a very pleasant musical interlude. Such was the tremendous honour thrust upon the band that when the band returned by train to Halifax at the unearthly hour of 5.30 in the morning, a huge crowd awaited them 'with many a huzzah and the band played the complete programme again on the railway platform'.

Now councils were falling over themselves to book a brass band for the coronation festivities. In some instances they were too late. Kirkcaldy Brass Band had wearied at the delay and had gone elsewhere. A stream of abuse greeted this. The band was 'unpatriotic, disloyal and guilty of the most disgraceful conduct'. Henry Iles indulged in a quick and sharp advertising campaign to move the Coronation music from the shelves: 'Wake up you bands! Buy your Coronation music now. Easy, easy, easy terms'.

Because of the shortage of bands for the local celebrations, scratch bands with 'high falutin' names sprang up to fill the need. One called the 'Paramount Parade Popular' advertised its services thus: 'Be part of the jollities, forget your woes, book us, for the King is to be Crowned.' The editor thought little of these greedy bands and advised bands to advertise in the local newspapers in such words as: 'Support your local band, we are all bona fide'.

Strangely all this had an intriguing spin off. Henry Iles and *The British Bandsman* became aware there were bona fide bands in the country which never advertised themselves, never entered contests, had no band-room and practised where they could, be it a public house or farmer's barn. Furthermore they were not in debt, wore paid-for uniforms and had reasonable instruments. They made enough money by being quite parochial, playing in their own village for dances, fetes, weddings, high days and holidays and far removed from all the jealousy and grumbling of the known bands. Mr. Iles was quite taken aback and *The British Bandsman* enquired of its local editors and correspondents why he had never been informed of this. The consensus of their opinion seemed to be that these were family bands and therefore not part of the real brass band world. Back came Mr. Iles: 'You must introduce them to the *Champion Journal*' (The music he published).

Before we leave the Coronation it is evident the music chosen to be played at the ceremony in Westminster Abbey did not impress the editor. He wrote: 'It is not satisfactory. More room should be made for the compositions of England's greatest composer, Henry Purcell'. All the excitement died down very quickly and soon the bands were quarrelling at contests and at the Featherstone Contest, some ugly incidents occurred.

As always, somewhat like a soap opera, another devastating issue was never far away. Bandsmen, who played in sacred concerts on a Sunday, were faced with the threat of imprisonment. The Lord's Day Observance Society announced that an unrepealed Act passed in the reign of George III allowed performing bands and the promoters to be charged with 'keeping a disorderly house' and leaflets to this effect were distributed in millions: 'If we continue with Sunday Concerts beware the fearful wrath of God.'

Some bands ceased such concerts, others carried on and paid an ordained priest 'to give grace and benediction to the assembled before they parted to their homes'. The editor thought the whole episode a bit of a farce and said so, saying this dividing line between secular and sacred music on a Sunday was very thin indeed. 'Take heart', he wrote 'the band of the Royal Scots Greys march to church every Sunday playing marches to which the hangers-on sing not very nice words'. Most of his readers would appreciate this comment because it was the custom in many parts for people to return to the barracks with the band to hear a short selection played. However, in Windsor, Lieut. Colonel Ferguson put a stop to the practice 'on account of disrespect shown by civilians when the National Anthem was played'. It seems the men would not 'uncover' and kept their caps firmly in place to show their independence. So ended Coronation year.

17   A legend is born

For some bands 1912 proved to be an adventurous year with high hopes of brass music and brass instrumentation being accepted in France. Henry Iles had ideas of France being represented at the Crystal Palace and gave good publicity for the Paris Music Festival although he stood aloof financially. Brass bands began working out the cost and eventually Batley Old, Luton Red Cross, Spencers Steel Works, Houghton Main, Dannemora Steel Works, Woodlands Village, Bolton Victoria Hall, Camden Unity, Castleford, Horden Colliery, Wandsworth Boro, Great Central and Metropolitan, North London Excelsior and Shoreditch Boro, went over and captured the hearts of the Parisians.

It was only partially successful. A lot of interest was displayed but, alas, quickly died as an enormous loss of a quarter of a

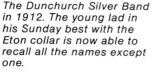

The Dunchurch Silver Band in 1912. The young lad in his Sunday best with the Eton collar is now able to recall all the names except one.

million pounds was revealed. From then on the gleam in the eye of Mr. Iles flickered occasionally but he realised a French Brass Band Movement was a dead duck.

Before the Minimum Wage Bill ended the miners' strike and the railway strike intensified, brass bands found themselves in extremely low financial water. There was no money to enter for the lucrative Easter contests and in Wales various Eisteddfods were cancelled. A fair proportion of bands were fully active but giving their services freely for the political demonstrations organised by the workers but it did not fill the kitty.

The efforts by bands in depressed areas did not go unnoticed by the press. Local newspapers praised the unstinting help bands gave in areas of appalling privation and degradation and this said one 'has done much to cement their music with the unemployed workers.'

When the strike finished the editor welcomed this 'overdue return' to normality and took the opportunity of telling bands to start rehearsing for the concert season. He was a little rude to the Scottish bands which, he said, should not go concert playing again unless they changed 'the programmes after programmes which are composed of absolute rubbish misnamed music. You'll see, no one will turn up!'

The question of how many would turn up at concerts never provided a satisfactory answer. No less a personage than Sir Hubert Parry said the wealthy did not want this type of music, yet in the prosperous town of Bournemouth, seven hundred people of all walks of life crowded into the concert hall to hear the Bournemouth Post Office Band. Yet, just up the road at Southampton, only fifty-three went to a concert by the Town Band.

Both of these bands were equal in performance and gave a similar programme, so why the difference? The answer could be that Southampton had more of the new cinemas. Entertainment habits were undergoing a profound change. Steam organs were replacing some bands on the promenade, David Griffith was abandoning his short fifteen-minute films in favour of long running stories (which culminated in *Birth of a Nation* in 1915, three hours long). People were flocking to music halls as the stages became technically better and now included illusionists, aerialists and animal acts. More music was made in the home and sheet music sold by the thousand. Brass bands had a fight on their hands.

The philanthropic ideals of the bands, however, never slackened. They came rushing to the fore when it was announced by the newspapers that a brass band had played *Nearer my God to Thee* as

the *Titanic* sank slowly beneath the waves, the sea engulfing th
bandsmen as they played. However much people wanted t
believe this heroic story, and some still do, it was not true. Th
band was basically a string orchestra of eight players whic
included one Frenchman and a Belgian and the tune they playe
was probably ragtime. True, Wallace Hartley the conducto
came from Dewsbury and true it was three members of the St Ive
Town Brass Band lost their lives but they were not members c
the ship's orchestra.

The myth persisted and brass bands everywhere played t
raise money for the *Titanic* Fund, 'to help the dependants of ou
comrades'. Now that the sinking had been elevated to a nationa
disaster, councils gave the fullest co-operation to collections wit
halls, stewards, printing, advertising and programmes bein
freely provided. A point taken by Wingates Band.

The glorious summer helped to replenish the kitty and band
were out and about in great demand, especially the soloists
know as 'swankpots' by the run of the mill player. Some of thes
soloists were followed everywhere by their own fans somewhat a
pop stars are today. It took all the time of the bandmaster to kee
them, as they were being poached by the London orchestras no
very much part of the hotel scene. One bandmaster, a M
Dallimore, claimed damages from the Amateur Musician
Union as it had conspired to lure two of his members away. H
was awarded the them large sum of £450 and this kept the li
tightly shut until after the war. 'Quite right too' said *The Britis
Bandsman:* 'Will they never learn?'.

There was a disturbing element in brass bands just prior to th
outbreak of the war in 1914. Music teachers were now appointe
in over five thousand schools to give lessons on all types o
instruments. Some scallywags pounced on the brass players a
soon as they left school and to the pride of parents, the boys wer
apprenticed to a trade. Within a few weeks the parents would b
approached and asked if they would like their sons to belong to
well-known touring band. Once in, the boys were manipulate
to make money.

One band provides a good example. The Boys of Kent Bras
Band toured Yorkshire, often walking thirty miles a day. Whe
they performed in York (just two numbers and then into th
crowd with the collecting boxes) there happened to be in th
audience an inspector from the National Society for the Preventio
of Cruelty to Children. He was aghast at what he saw. The boy
were badly shod, wore ill-fitting khaki uniform and at least on
boy could hardly blow his instrument 'for he looked fair wan'

He informed the Chief Constable and a doctor was sent to the lodgings of the boys. Vermin droppings were found on the clothing but when the doctor remonstrated with the promoter he was told 'no one dies of the itch'. Eventually the police took the man to court as the boys had sores on their feet and 'ulcerated outbreaks on their legs'. One had signs of tuberculosis and there was some evidence of malnutrition. Surprisingly the Lord Mayor of York did not think it a serious case and imposed a nominal fine.

Brass bands in the area were furious but could do nothing except to invite the editor to make some forthright comments. He agreed to give the case national coverage and printed the transcript of evidence fairly fully, which other papers soon copied. It did dampen down these enterprises but did not entirely stamp them out. At the other end of the scale very smart Boy Scout brass bands were parading the streets and attracted many recruits to the movement.

Whether or not it was because of the hot dry summer but police were called several times to intervene at contests and remove drunken players. Sometimes the bandsmen ended up in court but, more often than not, were dumped in a nearby field to sleep it off. At Willesden magistrates court a man charged with being drunk blamed the local brass band. He had tagged along with them to the ale tent at a contest and 'partook of the gallons of free beer placed at their disposal.'

This liking for ale and stout caused many a works bandmaster to choose teetotalers. One told the editor that most of his players were a load of drunks and only wanted the 'gifts, tips and subs from the band fund which they never repay'.

All this is a rather selective view of the year as it seemed the policy of *The British Bandsmen* to publish only the news items provided by correspondents. There were thousands of dedicated bandsmen who had great pride in themselves and were so disciplined they took everything in their stride. At Cardiff, a brass band was pelted with stones by hooligans from the vantage point of a railway embankment. The missiles hurtled down onto the bandstand at Splott yet they never retaliated.

Some rather odd measures were taken by councils to censor the music played on a Sunday by bands on the bandstands. One council appointed an engineer to do the job and another the inspector of Abbatoirs. The editor asked innocently if he could be appointed to examine the local plumbing.

Such was the desire to be, as the editor put it 'in the money' that rehearsals in the weeks prior to the Crystal Palace were often five times a week. All very commendable, thought the editor but he predicted that by the year 2000 bandsmen would play only for the love of music and would not be at all concerned with money or prizes. He went on: 'No one will be fined for missing rehearsals and bands will be playing compositions by orchestral composers'.

Nevertheless, dedication by these early bandsmen paid off and Herculean efforts were made to do well at the Nationals. That year the Crystal Palace attracted a record crowd of 75,000 and 182 bands competed. When the champions, St. Hilda's Colliery, went home by train, fog repeater explosive signals were placed on the line to indicate how far away the conquering heroes were. 20,000 packed into the station and another 20,000 lined the route 'of triumph'. *The British Bandsmen* said: 'The band is made for ever'.

With crowds equal to those which went to the FA cup final there were many criticisms levelled at the organisers of the Crystal Palace contest and these were not always the fault of Henry Iles. He saw the Crystal Palace authorities could never assess, within reason, how many people would go through the turnstiles. Some of the complaints concerned inadequate catering arrangements and the scramble for transport, but the most frequent over the years were the lavatory facilities.

Thousands upon thousands would detrain in London and make their way to the Crystal Palace, some arriving in the approach roads in Sydenham before dawn. Old residents can still remember the excitement. No one went to bed and stayed up to look out of their windows at the flood of humanity, the street vendors and the groups of Welshmen singing their patriotic songs. But they also remember the disgusting scenes of men and women urinating in the streets and gardens. These complaints reached the local clergy who suggested to Henry Iles that he hire the Crystal Palace from an earlier hour. 'Open the gates', one said 'and let them in a couple of hours before time' and this was done.

Touts were also a cause for complaint but Iles and the police could do nothing about them. Not surprisingly, with so many men from all parts, milling around, most were extolling the erotic delights of Soho, Piccadilly, Pimlico and, somewhat startlingly 'the joys of Putney Tow Path'. More sophisticated tricksters mingled with the crowd and jostling pickpockets had a field day. Bandsmen took all this in good heart and, as usual hundreds of letters of appreciation came from all over Britain. J Henry Iles and his contest were on the way to becoming legends

18 'Yes, they are working men!'

The year before war broke out, Castleford Brass Band raised money from its subscribers and undertook a tour of Germany. It played before immense crowds culminating in an audience of 18,000 in Frankfurt. The working class of Germany took the band to their hearts and as one of the workers leaders said at the farewell ceremony 'Your band of working miners has given us faith in our struggle to better ourselves'. Goodwill and fraternal love overflowed. These scenes were reciprocated when St. Hilda's and the Berlin Philharmonic played before thousands of people in the Edinburgh Marine Gardens.

When Castleford returned to this country, the bunting was strung across all the streets in the town. Everyone turned out *en fete* and the councillors and the clergy made speeches all of which praised fulsomely the success of the tour and 'knew now, if not before that the mission had found a tremendous brotherly love with our kin across the water'. One newspaper said it had cemented the friendship between the two working classes of Germany and our country for ever.

The news of this tour soon reached other subscription bands and the editor was asked for his advice on travel arrangements. Henry Iles was quick to exploit this and within weeks let it be known he could manage all tours to Germany. He asked a contributor, 'Veritas', to sound out bands on his behalf. In the course of this exercise the correspondent was able to tell Iles that there were 9,975 brass bands in Great Britain. 'Well,' he said, 'They are not all buying the *Champion Journal*.'

Not all these bands had a full complement of players because better players went to better bands. Teetotallers went to temperance bands because, as the editor said, 'the booze element was destroying comradeship'. As bands settled down for the summer engagements so the 'full' bands extended their repertoire and were soon exciting the onlookers with *Everybody's Doing it* and the toe-tapping *Red Pepper*. It did not please everyone, Grays Urban District Council at a full meeting called a halt to this as the music was frightening the horses.

These bands were not too sure of the new Copyright Act, for modern music attracted a fee often beyond their purse. 'It was £200 to play an operatic selection by a living composer' said *The British Bandsmen* but this was a gross exaggeration. Bands fell foul of the recent Betting and Lotteries Act because they sold draw tickets in shops and public houses. They appealed to the editor as this source of revenue was vital to the band funds. Henry Iles made enquiries of his friends in the law courts and it was thought a way round all this was to have lucky number programmes. In some areas the police stopped the practice, but whatever the outcome, band draw money dropped dramatically and they did not want to know about 'this new fangled copyright business'.

The British Bandsmen certainly wanted to know and pointed out the pitfalls. Henry Iles was wily enough to escape some of its effects by using a test piece from a living composer. *The Daily Telegraph* agreed because, it said, the whole of the best music written in the last 50 years 'is now denied the workers bands'. *Music Opinion* thought it a great step forward but was concerned it would be too much for brass bands and they would be unable to cope.

When the specially-published test piece for the Crystal Palace Contest *Labour and Love* reached the bands there was a mixed reaction. Conductors were none to sure how to approach a tone poem and frowned upon its colouring problems. One professional conductor, Mr. Halliwell, said it opened a new frontier and added that bass trombonists 'will be removed from providing just a noise to partaking in a beauty of sound'. Nonsense, said others, all instruments will just be playing a noise for it is simply a very inferior piece of music. The debate raged for months and, with less intensity, still does.

There was, of course, music being specially written for and arranged for brass bands and the number of good bands increased as they settled down to dedicated rehearsal. As contests approached, some bandsmen went into strict training and abandoned alcohol for the time being. A story had got around that if one went to the doctor and bought a bottle of 'tonic', and drank it for three days before a contest, it would sharpen the senses and increase confidence.

Inevitably some wag suggested Irwell Springs Brass Band must have drunk a gallon or two to win the National Contest.

Others said tonic should be forcibly fed to judges, who unfortunately brought a lot of the wrath from bands upon their own heads. Now very mindful of the laws of libel, following some spectacular fraud cases heard recently in the High Court, the editor could only hint at a sense of fraud being practised at some contests. It appears everyone knew, via the grape vine, which judges were 'approachable'. Some committees had a list which they used whenever it was decided to invite a good band to enter a contest to give it lustre or to have an edge on another contest held on the same day a mile or two away.

Naturally, the good band would not come unless it was assured of first prize and the only way to ensure this was by bribing the judge. These judges were known as 'drop judges'. One was booked at a well known provincial contest but, the day before the contest, went sick. The committee searched frantically for another 'on the list' but in the end booked a judge which it found was a man of honour (and there were many such judges)

Satirical maybe but close to the truth (1913).

who read between the innuendoes and turned a deaf ear to the questionable approaches. In the event the good band was not in the prizes, passions had to be controlled and a brave face put on it, for no one could do anything about it. The editor was asked to name names but he refused, mainly because of gaps in the evidence.

This was seized upon by a contemporary magazine which thought it ought not to have been discussed and then went on to say that surely there was a dubious practice going on between Henry Iles and William Rimmer, the prolific composer of marches for brass bands. It thought Mr. Rimmer was churning out a new march every day so that Mr. Iles would publish the music and shout out loudly to all bands to buy, buy, buy. It was a fact that Iles did tell bands to save their collection money to buy the Rimmer masterpieces.

Bands were also asked by *The British Bandsmen* to donate some of their collections to the fund for buying the Crystal Palace for the nation. 'After all', it said, 'the King and Queen head the list of subscribers.' The bands ignored the appeal and said perhaps Rimmer and Iles should donate some of the profits 'these marches are making'. The Crystal Palace was eventually purchased for half a million pounds. Some bandsmen considered this a dreadful waste of money and if that sum of money was available then it should have been paid into the funds for poor relief because 'people are more important than glass'.

As if to echo this sentiment, arrangements were made for the King to visit the distressed areas of Lancashire and make a 'personal acquaintance with the working conditions of His people'. Councils engaged brass bands to play the *National Anthem* and selections at Accrington, Blackburn, Manchester, Preston, St. Helens and Oldham. Some of the entourage had never heard a brass band before and thought it quite odd that 'these military bands had chaps playing in them with civilian clothes'. When they were told the men were factory workers, it is to their credit that they shook hands with the players and were dumbfounded at the expertise displayed.

By command of the King, Fodens played before their Majesties at Crewe Hall and, as was now usual, *The British Bandsmen* reported the King 'was amazed when he was told they were all working men'. A few months later, St. Hilda's Colliery band played before the King and Queen at Lambton Castle. The Queen was so delighted with the performance it was extended another 45 minutes, and yet again *The British Bandsmen* wrote: 'Her Majesty was amazed when told the bandsmen were all working men'. When the Queen spoke to some members, she was informed that

they played in contests against other bands and the finals were played in London every year. One player, in answer to a 'royal question' said that thousands went to the massed bands concert in the evening. The Queen apparently answered 'How lovely' and an aide was asked if Her Majesty would be interested. This was, of course, polite conversation but when Henry Iles heard about it, he beavered away among his friends, who had the necessary contacts, for a royal coup.

How close he came to succeeding one will never know but it must have been considered, as the editor said an objection had been raised saying that 'among 100,000 people there must be some rum ones'. In fact, over 100,000 actually paid to get into the Crystal Palace complex in the last contest before the war, more than went to the F.A. cup final. Irwell Springs Brass Band won and the *Manchester Guardian* wrote: 'Heroes all and all working mill hands.' The majority of the press included the words 'working men', 'miners and mill workers' or 'factory hands' in their news items about the 1913 contest. It seemed as if it was not quite right that ordinary workers should be able to play such beautiful compositions and read music. A good band had only to play before the gentry and the same question was always asked 'Are these really working men?'

'Royal' Foden, all dressed up in new uniform before meeting King George V in 1913.

19 *World War I*
1914-18

The brass band movement, like almost every other movement under the sun, be it industry, art or pastime, had its ebb and flood tide. It had its periods of depression and briskness, apathy and enthusiasm. These periods may or may not run concurrently in separate parts of the country and they may vary in duration. This was the position in the first few months of 1914.

The British Bandsman was reporting lack of interest here and enthusiasm there. Some bands were folding and others springing up, some had few engagements and some full diaries. Some bands could not retain players and other bands had a waiting list of those wanting to join.

The year had a glorious, happy-go-lucky summer. Brass bands in their hundreds contested, played at fêtes and on seaside promenades now thronged with people who had taken advantage of the cheap railway excursions. They played for various disaster funds, workers' demonstrations and for high days and holidays. Colliery bands played at welfare outings and village festivals and the territorial bands marched and counter-marched at carnivals and fairgrounds.

The music to the new two-step was played and the youngsters danced to *Pumpkin Pie*. The editor was hard pushed in this warm summer of contentment to find anything to write about that would be controversial and excite his readers. In the end he settled for a campaign against brown boots with blue serge.

The Salvation Army bands gathered in London for the Band Festival. The spectacle attracted thousands of people who lined the Embankment to watch them go by. The Aldershot Tattoo was a big success with every seat taken, 1,500 musicians performed and, to the country at large, the Army seemed to be the essence of pomp and circumstance. The music trade was buoyant and crack bands were at their peak because of a new found loyalty among the players.

'Truly', said the editor, 'the sun shines benignly on brass bands'. As the weather held, more seaside excursions were laid on and the railway companies hired brass bands to play at the arrival termini. There is no doubt brass bands were an accepted part of the worker's summer. The editor thought bands should take advantage of this goodwill and play throughout the winter instead of the usual hibernation. He advocated winter contests as 'travelling in this twentieth century cannot be bettered'. Brass band associations began to hire halls and all augured well.

The declaration of war on Germany was five days away but no rumour entered the pages. People were aware of the assassination of the Archduke Francis Ferdinand but the Balkans were remote to ordinary people and in any case disagreement between Germany and Serbia was none of their business. So far away was any hint of hostilities that the recent success of the Dieppe Music Festival, in which over 100 bands entered, the editor was telling brass bands to visit Europe before the winter came. He said 'Brass bands are all *à la mode* now.'

His edition on 1 August was full of rather bland news and comment, although by a cruel coincidence the music supplement which was published with this number was Percy Fletcher's *In Solemn Strains*. The next edition was printed before the outbreak of war but published afterwards. It was optimistic and looked forward to the great Crystal Palace contest.

To the editor and most people, the mobilisation came as a complete shock. The declaration of war was so unexpected that people asked themselves if it were true. The next issue contained lists of cancelled contests. Secretaries were reporting the bands had been seriously depleted as many members were on the reserve list and had already left for their regiments. The declaration even crept up unannounced upon the military bands, some of which were actively preparing overseas tours. The band of HM Grenadier Guards were due to sail to Canada and only at the very last minute was it cancelled. Some choirs and bands from overseas were touring Britain. There was a mad scramble for berths on liners leaving on hastily rearranged schedules.

As the German advance came within an ace of success, line regiments were rushed to France. Brass bands, which got to know by word of mouth of this, were quick to supplement the territorial and regimental bands and played at the railway stations amid the poignant, patriotic scenes. There were hardly enough bands to go round. In Llanelly, the 4th Welsh and the

Royal Engineers marched through cheering, hat-waving crowds headed by the Salvation Army band with its Corps flag flying. It played hymns to accompany the sad farewells.

The editor, caught up in the martial fervour, swore it would all be over by Christmas and assured bands to keep practising because contesting would soon be with them again. The Olympia contest was the first to go but even this was not a worry to the editor because, as he said, 300 German spies had to be housed somewhere. His optimism was dented somewhat when he heard the whole of the well-known Manchester Postal Band had been called up as the players were all reservists. Twenty-one members of Batley ambulance Corps enlisted at once and left for Chatham Naval Hospital. Thousands marched with them behind Batley Old Band which played *Auld Lang Syne* as the train drew slowly away.

These scenes were enacted all over Britain during that August. A fair number of Frickley Old Band were reservists and, with supporters carrying their cases, they formed up behind the remaining members of the band who played them in great style to the railway station. The police had to clear a way through the cheering crowds.

Salvation Army bands were everywhere, raising funds and holding street services to pray for 'our gallant heroes'. The bandmaster of Coventry Salvation Army band reckoned the *National Anthem* was more popular than *Abide with Me*. Troops passing over the Monmouthshire canal came across an open-air prayer meeting. The band of the Salvation Army immediately

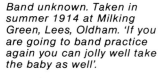

Band unknown. Taken in summer 1914 at Milking Green, Lees, Oldham. 'If you are going to band practice again you can jolly well take the baby as well'.

played the *National Anthem.* The Commanding Officer called the soldiers to a halt, they removed their caps and stood, at attention, to sing it. This was followed by a hymn and then everyone cheered and cheered again as the Salvation Army Band formed up in front of the column and played them to the station with a rousing march and colours flying.

From Messrs Brunner, Mond and Co., Winnington, 333 workmen immediately volunteered 'to put the Kaiser in his place.' The firm marshalled them at the factory gates and two brass bands took them to Norwich railway station to the sound of detonations from stolen fog signals. At the station the band played as the farewells were made and a correspondent wrote: 'The trombones were the best I ever heard.'

By September the editor was still optimistic it would all be over by Christmas and urged bands not to stop rehearsals and to start making plans to contest in 1915. Nothing seemed different. *The British Bandsman* was still an issue of 24 pages and was crowded with advertisements; urban contests did not seem to be affected, then it all changed. The London County Council cancelled the park engagements and bands were reporting they were losing their best players as they had received mobilisation papers. Suddenly the paper was reduced to 16 pages and it contained a further list of cancelled contests. Engagements at horticultural, agricultural and flower shows were postponed until the next year. Smaller contests did continue and were to do so throughout the war and the Belle Vue contest managed to carry on. Sadly the bands did not go to the Crystal Palace Festival until the war finished.

The crack bands lost many members to the colours and, finally, the various brass band associations declared all contests promoted by them had had ceased until 'the final shot is fired. Let us hope we will celebrate Christmas in peace.' The country was yet to experience any hatred for the Germans.

The German liner *Kronprincessin* was trapped by the war in Falmouth harbour. The passengers were accommodated in St. Columb workhouse and the ship's band and the Falmouth Band gave joint concerts. This feeling of both peoples all being temporarily in the same boat did not last long. Governments had stumbled and staggered into a war that was to cost 10 million lives.

The small British expeditionary force under Sir John French which had rapidly been deployed in France had no sooner pushed forward to Mons in Belgium than it was forced to retreat. As this news came in the editor became convinced this set-back was because information regarding the strength of the British had been conveyed to Berlin by spies. He blamed the German, or so-called, German bands still roaming the country. He said, 'They are not true musicians but spies and they get a small salary from the German Secret Service.'

He still thought it would be a nine days' wonder and our gallant army would overrun the Germans. 'Everywhere', he wrote, 'is full of patriotism' and went on to tell his readers that Sir Edward Elgar had been sworn in as a special constable in Hampstead and had been issued with a gun. He reported that the great Russian bass, Chaliapin, and the entire male section of the Russian ballet were now on the Eastern Front and that Seigfried Wagner and Rachmaninov were in the German front line together with Franz Lehar. Henry Iles hoped the countries involved would soon come to their senses. His opinion was that the German High Command just did not realise the terrible might of the Royal Navy and he wrote, 'Brass bandsmen have answered the call to arms to defend our Motherland. You are heroes all. Do not worry lads you'll soon be back in the good old band-room with some tales to tell I fancy'.

Still there existed a holiday mood. The casualty lists which were published were light. Bands still played regiments to stations and brass bands on the South Coast seemed to be always at the embarkation ports to play the troops on board ship. Bandmasters were having difficulty in restraining their younger members from volunteering 'before the show is over' but volunteer they did. Some bands played at the recruiting centres and immediately lost members caught up in the patriotic fervour. In Wolverhampton a brass band finished with the *National Anthem* and ten members promptly stepped forward to sign on the dotted line.

Rumour became rife that the stubborn resistance of the vanguard of our troops was taking its toll. Then came the first news that sent a chill through the brass band world. Mr. J. Ord Hume the composer reported he had not had his usual postcard from his friend Ernest Vass, the last one had been posted in Mons. The casualty lists grew longer and so did the hatred for anything German.

This reached such lengths that no piano of German make was allowed inside the Queen's Hall, London and foreign gentlemen playing in the various symphony orchestras pinned badges to the lapels of their jackets to show their nationality. Edward German, the composer, let it be known that his real name was Edward German Jones and for a different reason, Arthur Sullivan dropped his middle name, Seymour.

The editor soon published a list of bandsmen killed at Mons and his readers were horrified at the slaughter. *The British Bandsman* printed a poem:

The men who have left the Homestead,
the men who have left the band,
to march in Ranks of Glory,
to fight for the Mother land.

Bandsmen, who often treated the Salvation Army bandsmen with ridicule, swallowed hard as these men figured prominently among the dead and wounded. Some called at the local citadels to offer their respect and sympathy. Salvation Army bands worked hard turning out all day on Sundays with their comrades, collecting, giving succour where needed and provided spiritual support to the growing number of people who attended the outdoor gatherings.

The orderly retreat from Mons produced several stories from bandsmen, one of whom told the editor he was one of the lucky ones. He said he and his shattered battalion were in retreat for some miles, all the time harassed by long range guns. When they reached the hastily prepared transit base they collapsed with fatigue only to be joined by thousands more staggering in carrying what weapons and ammunition they had been able to salvage. The officers were as exhausted as the men and they too lay on the ground for the first real sleep in many days.

Then suddenly, over the still air of twilight he heard the unmistakable sound of a cornet playing the Welsh air *All Through the Night*. The tune was unchanged as it got louder and louder and men moved their tired limbs to look down the approach road where a dozen men of a Welsh regiment marched with heads high and rifles shouldered behind the cornet player still playing the tune. He was 'from a Cornish band and had taken his cornet to war'.

Other letters reached the offices of *The British Bandsman*. One said, 'I have come through the last battle without a scratch but men fell around me. It is a wonder any survived. Remember me to Mr. Brunt and all the football engagements.'

Now the reservists had gone some young boys volunteered from the band leaving only half a band to carry on. Some bands never played again and some decided to withdraw for the duration. *The Cornish Post* wrote, 'When are we to expect a programme from the town band? St. Agnes people will appreciate, as before, such efforts as a relief for an hour from the overwhelming topic of the war'. Gradually the bands came back to life and *The*

British Bandsman, and the national press, welcomed the return 'to normality'.

To help counter the grossly exaggerated stories of a defeat by the Germans in Flanders the editor published another poem:

Our lads are no stranger to noises,
they've been to a contest before,
we can rest quite content that the Germans,
will get all he is seeking and more.

The flood of volunteers increased. By November 2,000 bandsmen had enlisted including the entire family of six from the Richards family in Llanelly. Men went from the instrument makers (23 from Bessons alone), uniform fitters and the music publishing houses. Stock lay on the shelves and to shift it discounts of 50 per cent for cash were offered; W. Brown & Son finally gave 60 per cent. The bands managed to remain viable by using semi-trained boys and often, without being asked, turned up at the funeral of soldiers who had died of wounds in the hospitals in this country and played suitable music.

The military campaign had, by the end of 1914, solidified into a vast seige operation with the opposing forces facing each other in lines of trenches from the Swiss frontier to the North Sea. From the end of the year until 1918, these lines never varied by more than some 20 miles to east or west. It was in the small strip of Flanders where many an attack and counter attack resulted in hundreds of thousands of deaths and it was there so many brass bandsmen lay down their lives and won their medals.

The year ended sombrely and with the grim realisation that it could be a long war. Trite as the poems of the editor might now seem to our sophisticated eyes they were written from the heart and accepted as such from the readers. His last poem this year read:

The British Bandsman we can see,
has done his little bit,
And while he's there, you will agree,
He's sure to make a hit.

In 1915 the editor began contributing to the propaganda successfully sustained by the daily newspapers. He told his readers the entire German Fleet had turned tail and fled at the first sight of Sir David Beatty and his glorious ships of the line. It was to be the year of just one more push and the editor heaped lavish praise upon the unending stream of volunteers. 'Hurrah!' he wrote, 'Mr Watkins and the Llanhilleth Town Brass Band have enlisted en bloc in the Gwent battalion. Again Hurrah!'

Pontyberem Brass Band joined the 4th Welsh and Penicuik enlisted in the 3/8th battlion, Scots Guards. The Hillingdon Church Temperance band and the Oldham Postal Band, which included Robert Maders, just 16, were amongst dozens who went in strength to the recruiting sergeant.

By the middle of the year, 5,000 more bandsmen had gone to fight, the latest batch included 20 from Irwell Old, 23 Musselburgh, 14 Melingriffith and 14 Towyn Silver Band. The entire band of the 24th Battalion, Manchester Regiment was composed of brass bandsmen, 14 from Chadderton, two Oldham Postal, and one each from Gladwick, Irwell Old, Nile Street Mission, Oldham Temperance, Kingston Mills, Royton and Besses' Junior bands.

Alex Stevenson, famous bass player with Hucknall Temperance Band, transformed within weeks from a sensitive musician to a trained killer (1915).

One player from the Goodwick Brass Band said: 'Well, we had a meeting and thought we ought to go. We played in the room all together for the last time. The bandmaster said we ought to play the *National Anthem* to end with and when we all come back we can start with it. We all shook hands and some of us cried. We went home and told our loved ones our minds were made up. In the morning every member turned up and joined the 4th Welsh'. Sometimes, after discussion and a prayer, entire Salvation Army bands went. Halifax and Long Eaton Salvation Army bands were in Flanders within five weeks of leaving their homes.

A number of men in the Boots Plaisaunce band joined the Army and within six weeks of reporting to the barracks were gassed in Flanders and home again, their lungs not to last the rest of the year. In June Mr. W. Heywood of the Ynyshir Colliery Band joined up. In less than six weeks his family were informed of his death, such was the need to feed the trenches (happily, he turned up safe and well). 'To all you brave men who are enlisting we say well done. You are answering the call to fill the ranks for your King, your Country and your God', wrote the editor.

The battle of Ypres took a terrible toll of brass bandsmen. Mr T. Murray of Brownley Silver had hardly written to the editor thanking him for the weekly arrival of *The British Bandsman* when he was killed in action. Some letters were quite dramatic 'Fighting at an unknown village we were hard pressed in fierce hand to hand fighting from house to house. Suddenly the *Marseillaise* rang out and the French arrived in the nick of time. The grey legs trembled because they do not like the bayonet. No shots were fired, just the cold steel. I feel sorry for Fodens and hope they soon get together again.'

He was referring to the strike called by the workers at Foden because of the refusal of the owner to increase the paid wage by 5s.0d. per week. Mr. Foden gave the band an ultimatum: 'Leave the union or get out of the band'. Those who withdrew their labour were told to surrender their uniforms and instruments at once or face legal action. By April the only members left in the band were the bandmaster, principal solo cornet, third cornet second trombone and two bass players. The editor asked, 'Is this the end of Fodens?'

It was a nervous year. The people of Britain realised what endurance and effort would be required of them with the transformation of a civilian people into a nation at arms. This was carried out with difficulty and strain. General conscription of adult males, including married men, was only imposed in 1916 after a long delay. Until then, if any eligible looking man in a brass band took the stage he would be subjected to boos and hissing until he withdrew. Girls cried out, 'Cowardy cowardy custard' and, 'who is hiding behind mummy's skirt?'. Several young bandsmen were assaulted with walking sticks and handbags. The feeling of anger towards the 16-30 year age group was so venemous that passion overrode reason.

This led bands to chalk on blackboards or print in programmes 'All the members of this band are either medically unfit or cannot be spared from work of great importance.' The War Office caused comment because of its insensitivity. The editor wrote 'Who ever allowed a German Prisoner of War band to parade through the Lancashire villages playing German marches, when one entire village was mourning the flower of its youth killed in the recent great battles'.

Galston Brass Band protested vehemently because it had lost its band room. It was commandeered for a home for Belgian

efugees. Other bandrooms met the same fate, which did not
lease the editor especially as collections for these people sprang
p in the localities. He wrote, 'The way in which these relief funds
re administered is open to strong criticism. Brass bands should
op collecting.'

The published lists of casualties made terrible reading. They
ontained names of members of the same brass band who had
nlisted together, trained and fought together and died together.
riends who played for Rhyl and Abergavenny brass bands were
illed on the same day together with Lieutenant Boosey, the son
f Charles Boosey the music publisher. The editor, although
lways emphasising the need for an honourable peace and the
utile waste of war, was not beyond glorifying the role of the
oldier. He wrote, 'Private McStay, a bandsman, has died with his
ayonet in the breast of a Prussian guardsman. No soldier could
ave passed away more gloriously'.

In the dangerous area of no-mans-land many soldiers were
eported missing presumed killed and the editor was beseiged
ith letters asking if any of their sons had been seen by others
fter the attack. Partly as a result of this, parcels of *The British
andsman* were dispatched to the front.

In Britain bands were experiencing a change of mood from the
ublic at concerts. The Wicken Street Band reported the public
id not want dance music any more. 'It wants music to suit the
ightening times. Whatever we play there is a dull reaction. They
el the war cannot be won this year.'

Churches were crowded with people at prayer for peace and
rotection for their loved ones. Sacred concerts were still given
y brass bands and in Coventry 11,000 people attended a concert
iven by the Coventry Brass Band to listen to appropriate music
reading the return home in case a telegram had been delivered.
hese Sunday concerts prompted the Rev'd. G. F. Upton to say
e place to pray was in church — 'It is a shame and a disgrace
hat the public should be attracted away from the church in this
ay'. The editor would have none of this and countered: 'Some
re saying people want more music and less of the sermon'.
)ther clergy corresponded on behalf of the Rev'd Upton – 'It is
n God's House that God listens' and other views which were
ertainly open to debate. Finally, the editor wrote, 'By what right
o the minority of busybodies seek to deprive concert goers on a
unday of such innocent recreation'.

Not all religious reaction was so dogmatic. It took the clergy to
oint out how 'doomed already a battalion looked when
narching to the station without a band'. And right they were!
Jothing could sustain the soldiers pride more than a band. With

no band they felt unwanted and were very often moved at dusk. The Salvation Army bands were the first to react. One soldier wrote: 'The order came at 9.00 a.m. for our Regiment to entrain at 1.00 p.m. The officer said sorry lads I cannot get a band. A Salvation Army man who had been making tea for us thought he might be able to help. He sloped off and within three hours we heard a band and over the hill came a wonderful sight. First two flags with the brass tops glinting in the sunshine and then a big band all in the uniform of The Salvation Army. As word got round the women left the factories, shops and houses. People got off the waggons and buses and they all lined the street shouting good luck Tommy and come back soon. We marched in grand style I can tell you and the regiment never forgot this, never'.

What about *The British Bandsman* itself? Its pages were fewer and advertisements dwindled. No longer were the firms of Boosey & Co. and Hawkes & Co. at each others throats. It seemed to be a clearing house for war news as it affected the movement. One item read, 'We have received intelligence from the Army Service Corps to say many brass bandsmen have passed safely through the Neue Chapelle fight.' Bandsmen wrote in from 'Somewhere in France' or wherever, asking for music to be sent out. Brighouse and Rastrick Band dispatched a cornet to their soprano, Ellis Dyson, who had written to say a tune or two would keep them happy in the trenches. The offices of *The British Bandsman* were very nearly moved to outside London because Henry Iles was worried about the Zeppelin raids.

The paper withdrew the trophies and prizes awarded in its name for contest winners. It reported in full adjudicators remarks on those contests still running or especially cobbled together. It did not take kindly to the remarks of one judge, Mr Charles Hassall of the Irish Guards, when he said the instruments were dirty, players had two days' growth on their chins and a little soap would ensure better engagements. A contributor said it was not only soldiers who were fighting the war but the grimy miner, the weary factory workers and the munition girls all working 'day and night, they haven't the time to be at their Sunday best'.

For some reason the most popular request was *Finlandia*, but most concerts ended with *Oh God our help in ages past*. No longer was it necessary only to play the first few bars of the *National Anthem* at the end. Mr. Rimmer said, 'The public want it played in full and, by golly, the people stand to attention, with heads bared and believe it or not, sing it!'

The editor had the last word as this dismal year drew to a close 'German soldiers are given three books. A pay-book, a prayer book and a song book. His official prayer reads 'Let me b strengthened in heart and hand to live for and die for my German Fatherland. Therefore, still, therefore till go I forth to do God's will"'. The editor wondered, as so many people wondered, friend or foe, on whose side God was. It was an issue constantly referred to in churches here and in those of our allies and in churches in Germany and her allies. Mass was said and communion given on both sides and it was a talking point of the thinkers.

The editor thought 1916 would be the year of decision. The German High Command were of the same opinion but the attempt to force an early decision floundered. Profiting from a respite, the British Army went into action in greatly increased numbers with good, reliable and plentiful equipment. The area chosen was astride the River Somme. On the first day of the big offensive, 60,000 were killed but it failed to push the Germans back any appreciable distance.

Returning soldiers told stories in band rooms of utter chaos as their comrades were mown down by the machine guns. It seemed a question of 'touch and go' despite the flattering accounts put out by the Government agencies. The 16 page *The British Bandsman* carried list after list of fallen bandsmen of which 640 were killed.

The editor wrote an open letter to all bandsmen engaged in this titanic struggle. 'You are not forgotten. The more Germans you kill the sooner the war will end'. He seemed to have made up his mind which side God was on. He went on, 'More losses and more appeals from the pulpit for volunteers. You cannot do better, you lads in bands than accept the reverend gentleman's invitation. God is on our side'.

The advance on Loos was a disaster and the wounded could now be seen in the streets of villages, towns and cities of this country. Hospitals were full and brass bands and those of The Salvation Army, went from place to place, day after day, to give concerts and boost morale. The editor was not sure what to make of the War Office and the conduct of military bands in this respect . . . 'How come the Coldstream Guards Band can play at the circus? How can an agent offer £200 for another military band to play at a private function? How can one of the Guards bands play daily at a London Tea Room? The troops march to Waterloo Station without a band. What do you make of that? Why do they not play at hospitals where the wounded are? Are we at war?'

The Government withdrew all annual grants to orchestras. the editor, Henry Iles, the civic authorities and such giants as Beecham, Stanford, Parry and Elgar protested but did not get very far. Indeed, some people thought certain famous musicians conductors and composers had 'waxed fat' on music in the war and should replace the grants with some of their own money. *London Opinion* was quick to draw attention to the house owned by Sir Edward Elgar in Hampstead: 'It has a studio the size of a concert hall. It is like a Venetian Palace rather than a London house with a billiard room and a comfortable library'.

This backlash was understandable, for the appalling losses on the Somme continued and in five months the British Army had casualties equal to half those on all fronts in the 1939-1945 war. This set-piece battle produced some stories worth repeating. As the battle of attrition ground on with both sides only a few yards from each other fighting desperately for supremacy, there came amidst the din and anguish of battle, the plaintive notes of a cornet. As if by mutual consent, a small sector ceased to fight and no shot was fired. Men on both sides lit pipes and cigarettes and listened in wonder at the beautiful sound. For fully 15 minutes the strains of folk songs filled the air when suddenly, the player broke off and gave a spirited version of *Rule Britannia*. The fighting 'renewed with great ferocity'.

Cavalry charges were still common. Trooper Harry Hamilton of the Dungannon Brass Band suffered severe injuries when 'at the gallop and charge he fell into a disused trench and was crushed by other riders and horses'. Tunnellers were at a premium and many brave ex-miners died. Robert Dunshire of the Dunniker Colliery Band won the Victoria Cross.

He came back to this country to appear before HM King George V, who pinned it to the chest of this unassuming man. Mr. Dunshire deposited the medal with his loved ones, returned to the front and was killed a week later. Another bandsman, Corporal Edward Quinn of Ballyrashane Protestant Band, was awarded the Distinguished Conduct Medal. These were the first of many bandsmen to receive medals for gallantry.

Men were now enlisting not so much to be in the victory parade but to prevent defeat. As the battle raged the call went out for more and more volunteers. Twenty men of the Bridgetown Thistle Temperance, and 11 from Southend Mission, joined the Army. Only shortage of pages prevented the editor naming at least another 500 bands which were losing players who 'had downed their instruments and picked up the gun'.

More and more men were pushed into the Somme battle and people read the published lists of casualties with disbelief. The editor could hardly bear to open his paper and answer the telephone. He said, 'The flower of our youth will soon wither and we shall be left with old men and babies'. Those who fell at the

Somme included too, the flower of The Salvation Army. The editor wrote, 'Before the war we would say "Oh! He is a bandsman but only in the Salvation Army". We apologise. They have shown real British pluck and we have discovered something none of us realised. The casualty lists in *The British Bandsman* are eloquent of this.' This was very true. A study of the awesome lists shows many a junior Salvation Army bandsman killed, some hardly of age, S. Orton of Cambridge Heath, E. Williams of Kings Lynn and scores of others.

As the battle of the Somme died so the troops on both sides were once again in a seige situation. Requests arrived at *The British Bandsman* for more music to be sent over. The Press Association correspondent wrote a dispatch which included the words, 'I am just behind our front line. It is quiet now except for the big guns and patrols. Those who are alive cannot fight any more. They have been to hell. I would like to see a good brass band come over and play to the troops. It would be a big morale booster and take their minds back to Blighty. It is surprising how many of our trench weary soldiers like a brass band'. And it was surprising too how much the Germans liked a brass band. At Gillsen Prisoner of War Camp in Germany, an enlightened commandant asked the prisoners what hobbies they had. There were so many brass bandsmen that a German regiment gave some instruments and the Gillsen Brass Band was born. In the British rest camps the call went out for brass band players to identify themselves. They were ordered to form the Welsh Divisional Band which had suffered severe losses. Sergeant C. George (cornet, Abedare Brass Band) became bandmaster and his band became known on the front as the Cardiff Band, much to the annoyance of the officers who were paying for it.

Mr. James Farley, late of the Walsall Brass Band said: 'we managed to save our instruments but lost our music'. Henry Iles had no hesitation in sending a 'weighty parcel' to him and Mr. Farley wrote back, 'Now the Base Horse Transport can hear some music. Already other bands have heard of your generous action and will be writing to you'. The more this music was played the more the soldiers would find bawdy words to put to it.

Sam Cope went to a public concert in London arranged by the 'Regimental Ladies Committee' to raise funds for the 'children of the men'. It began and ended with a march. In the audience were young officers fresh from the trenches, all living on borrowed time and they sang, according to Mr. Cope, songs which 'were obscene, indecent, ribald and with unseemly words to the marches'. He was surprised no one took offence and was puzzled at the co-operation of the girls who expressed their appreciation by asking for encores.

The lull in the carnage did not last for long and soon attacks and counter attacks were mounted to straighten out a line, extend a salient or salvage some pride. In one advance, soldiers experienced stubborn resistance and frantically began to dig in. They unearthed a huge crate in a shell torn Belgian country house. Curiosity prevailed over self preservation and, despite the pleas from the officers, the soldiers dismantled it and found a grand piano. A pianist and a cornet player, 'whose cornet came next to his Bible', held the men spellbound. The bombardment went on unabated and as the men fortified the position the unusual duet continued. Unfortunately, there is no record of the names but the cornetist came from Stenalees Silver.

The operation of the Home Rule Act for Ireland was suspended for the duration of the war and Englishmen forgot about the Irish until the Sinn Fein rebellion on Easter 1916 jogged their memories. *The British Bandsman* took to task the Irish brass bands which 'headed the processions of these notorious rebels'. The editor condemned the whole business and told his readers 'this is a help to the wily Hun!' The week after the Easter uprising there was no Irish column in *The British Bandsman* or any item of news from Ireland. It had all been removed by the censor. Martial law prevented any more parades and brass bands were forbidden in the streets of Dublin. The players stood outside the shell-pocked post office and tore up copies of the *National Anthem* and joined the crowds in shouting 'Long Live Sir Roger Casement'. When the editor heard that all the Post Office Band instruments had been destroyed in the fighting he told his readers to have nothing to do with any fund which collected for their replacement.

Sam Cope, Henry Iles and a host of well-known stalwarts were working behind the scenes to make sure the brass band withstood this grief-stricken year. They travelled far and wide to association dinners, annual general meetings, and fund raising activities. They asked band clubs and band institutes to open their doors to soldiers on leave, harried the overworked Post Office along to improve the delivery of parcels and letters to the troops and became unofficial welfare officers to those who wrote hundreds of letters seeking news of the missing. The Christmas issue was very sad. On the front page it carried two lists. One for those enlisting, which contained 15 members of Burnhope Colliery Band eager to get into the fight. The other was of those killed in action and this contained the names of 17 Salvation Army bandsmen and three from the list of those enlisting from the

Burnhope Colliery; S. Morrison, E. Smith and F. Ward. All killed within a few weeks of joining their regiment.

The British Bandsman was not, of course, all war news. The readers enjoyed articles on music, on playing and comments of judges. One of the best debates was the plagiarism evident (or so everyone reckoned) in *God Save the Prince of Wales*. Most correspondents thought it a little bit of *From Greenlands Icy Mountains, Oh Never Look So Shy, The Flag That Waved a Thousand Years* and *Goodbye My Love, Goodbye*.

The British Bandsman did not think it could wish its readers a happy Christmas, as 'it would savour something of a mockery when so many families are plunged in anxiety, grief and mourning' but it did print a letter from Private Joseph Taylor (Mansfield Colliery Band) from somewhere in France wishing all his friends in the bands a Happy Christmas. This sombre year was closed with a poem:

> *Little Mary will be watching,*
> *Disappointed she will be,*
> *if there ain't no Santa coming,*
> *and there ain't no Christmas Tree.*

On 1 January 1917, *The British Bandsman* was reduced to eight pages with very limited advertising but it sold well and hundreds of free copies were dispatched overseas. It did not make a profit and Henry Iles kept it going out of his own pocket. The food situation was becoming grave. In one month – April – 423 Allied ships were sunk. Henry Iles personally contributed food hampers as prizes in contests, quite anonymously. No one could deny his philanthropic activities and these were never referred to in *The British Bandsman* at his special request. No appeal involving brass bands went unheeded. He gave generously to the efforts of the South Elmsall Brass Bands in playing and collecting money to provide every child in the district, whose father was fighting abroad, with a new pair of boots. This is only one of many examples.

Although they were by now in a state of shock, the people of the country began to seek an antidote to all the misery and this reflected itself in the growth of brass bands which could call upon players from exempted work. There were now scores of bands writing to R. Smith & Co. for music, new army and navy bands, cyclist bands, German Prisoner-of-War bands (yes, the commandant wrote on their behalf) bands of special constables, munition factories, collieries, transport and public utility services. The editor thought it would not be long before he saw a band attached to these 'new tank things'.

The conscription of youths of 18 scythed through the bands. Llandudno Town Band lost half of its members and committee secretaries were informing the editor they were suspending activities as they had no 'exempt' members and the 'papers to enlist were being posted to our best young players'. The Salvation Army had the answer: girls and more girls. Oldham Salvation Army Band boasted it had now 13 lasses playing instruments 'including the big 'uns'. (Instruments, not lasses!).

Several Salvationists protested to the editor about the growing practice of brass bands giving concerts to collect money for the various cigarette funds. The London Salvation Army were particularly disgusted at this practice and wrote asking the editor for his support. The editor did play it down a little, but not so Henry Iles. He praised the efforts of the London Band Association which had sent thousands of 'fags' to the front. He wrote: 'You are doing good work for the lads fighting for your country'. He thought it a truly wonderful gesture when the Association delivered 3,000 cigarettes to the Edmonton Military Hospital. The Salvationists wrung their hands in despair and when Mr. Iles prevailed upon his friends in the brewery at Pimlico to donate crates of milk stout, pale ale and brown ale to the wounded in the hospitals on the outskirts of the City, he was personally 'asked to desist by my friend in The Salvation Army.'

Mr. Iles was by now a very well-known figure, both in the business world and the brass band world where he was recognised as a man with drive and purpose who never said 'No.' He appealed to the London Association to provide a band which would enrol *en bloc* in the London Volunteers, because 'these brave lads march to the strains of a gramophone either strapped to a soldier or wheeled in a perambulator'. Needless to say, two bands volunteered but the records of the Volunteers do not reveal which ones.

The Irish rebellion rumbled on and some Irish brass bandsmen were sent to prison 'with hard labour' for playing at seditious meetings. This news reached the editor but he thought it wise not to make it too 'newsy' as he was now aware the censor read the magazine. He was not too sure when the censor saw it because he never submitted anything he wanted to publish to anyone. When it was censored the year before it was only because it had reached the Censor Office by word of mouth. It speaks well of the freedom of our press in those life and death days that the editor was able to print critical and scathing remarks on the conduct of the war without an eyebrow being raised.

In the first three months of the year 701 brass bandsmen were killed of whom 256 were Salvation Army bandsmen, including on one day alone seven members of the Keighley Salvation Army Band. Penge Salvation Army Band reported 42 of its members had joined the army and other Salvation Army bands were suffering 'because those returning on leave are so shell-shocked they cannot pick up their instruments'.

Those who returned blind were referred to the famous St. Dunstan Hospital and there was never any lack of brass and Salvation Army bands to play in the grounds and, indeed, many of these musicians were responsible for forming a brass band entirely composed of blind players. 'There you are,' as bandsman Knighton said, 'now we need not come any more'.

The young, the middle aged and the not so young anymore, and their wives, watched each other like hawks in case they were exempt on flimsy grounds. The editor contributed to this when he wrote a piece of news nothing to do with brass bands, 'Lord Derby has obtained a four month exemption for one of his gardeners, a Class A man.' Brass bandsmen and orchestral players had to make sure audiences knew the band was composed of the 'too ill, too young, too precious and too old,' not that age mattered; some bandsmen of 60 and over volunteered for the army. To ignore this was to invite pointed remarks during the interval between pieces. 'Hey there! You with the dark hair and trombone. Get your bum off to war'. It looked very much as though the correspondent substituted 'bum' for the other word which was considered very indelicate in those days.

Other bandsmen wore the medical certificate, which pronounced them C2, prominently on their uniforms, even when marching with 26 other bands in the Lord Mayor's Show in London, or else they would have been physically assaulted. It is here that one sees from the issues of *The British Bandsman* that tradition carried on, Mayoral processions still happened, so did contesting, so did the consequent bickering and players were still borrowed and poached.

Those who were the most vociferous at concerts against any eligible looking man on leave, were the returning wounded and those on leave. This was not the only thing which upset them. Systematic rationing of meat, bacon, fats and sugar, unbelievably did not take place until 1918 and before their eyes they could see friends they had left behind now rich people because of the manipulation of the market. They could also see friends who could not get enough to eat. At a Camberwell Contest the first prize was a sack of potatoes which, when shared out, came to 17 per player.

The returning brass players in London often visited *The British Bandsman* premises at 210 The Strand, London. The number of stairs to reach the editor were many and steep. It was not an unusual sight to see Sam Cope and Henry Iles sitting on the pavement outside to greet the wounded bandsmen using sticks and crutches and talk to them downstairs. The most serious complaint was the failure of food parcels, sent by wives, mums and sweethearts, to reach the Army post offices. Arthur Hoyle of the Bethel Mission Band said his mum had knitted two scarves and sent three tins of toffees but he had not seen 'head nor tail' of them. He said he blamed the cowards in the Post Office. This was not strictly true because as many postmen in proportion to bandsmen were also killed in the war.

Those in the Post Offices were either too old, exempt or were ladies. Or, as Sapper Hoyle put in, 'light fingered women!' When Henry Iles took this up with the Postmaster General he quickly established it was 'not a large scale thieving operation' but was due to the overworked and harrassed Post Office which led to delayed delivery often in the wrong place. He was able to assure the Postmaster General that readers were always writing to him from places as far away as Singapore to say *The British Bandsman* was arriving albeit a month late. This was patently an exaggeration but it sounded good. Bandsman Harry Rice of Rushden Temperance Band had his *British Bandsman* delivered at irregular intervals whilst serving with General Allenby in the deserts of the Middle East! Shortly after this, postal codes were introduced in London (e.g., SW14, EC2 and, for 210 The Strand, WC2). Henry Iles was not adverse to letting it be known that he was more than responsible for this.

What tickled Henry Iles and the editor pink was the astonishing gaffe by General Sir William Campbell who took the salute at a big military parade of over a thousand soldiers at Stockport. After column after column had marched past the saluting platform, crowded with military and civic dignitaries, he asked his aide to call the conductor of the band before him. He congratulated the band on its performance and complimented the men on their immaculate turn out and impeccable drill. He hoped to have the pleasure of hearing them again and asked that his regards be sent to their Commanding Officer who must be very proud of them when they led the regiment. No one had the heart to tell him it was the London and North West Railway Brass Band which had been asked to play as there were few military bands left in the area.

The revolution in Russia filled the pages of the National newspapers and speculation was rife if it would end or prolong the war and whether it would end in victory for the allies or end in a draw. One would be hard pushed to see the word 'defeat' in hese news reports. The editor only made passing reference to it and wondered what would happen to the Royal Russian National Anthem. 'Torn up, I suppose' he said. He also made passing reference to various acts of bravery by civilians. One such report concerned a young boy scout. It was the practice in London for these young lads to blow the 'all clear' on a bugle after a Zeppelin raid. One youngster was standing in the open to give the signal when he was killed by shrapnel. Another boy scout immediately took his place.

This year saw a more ghastly blood bath than the Battle of the Somme. It was the third battle of Ypres which ground to a halt eventually in the mud of the battered village of Passchendale. The long casualty lists re-appeared in *The British Bandsman* and the call for volunteers intensified. Many bands were reporting their inability to fulfil engagements. What started off as a year full of promise for brass bands ended in total sadness. A news item from the bandmaster of the North Bank Silver read, 'A dull, melancholy cloud has descended upon us, we have no grit to rehearse or perform. All our best players, the mainstay of the band have gone to fight for their King and Country. We saw them off with a jar or two but we all know it would be a miracle if we shook their hands again. We were all frightened but made the most of it. Our ladies made some cakes at the farewell and then the lads went, full of their own special thoughts. As the year closes we remember them in our prayers'. Others said, 'There is no one left in the village to come into the band, our average age is 63 and the men do not like the travel' and finally, 'even if we join up with other villages in this part of Suffolk we cannot raise a decent band. All we have round here are schoolboys and pensioners.'

The last year of the war began with no end in sight. The editor asked 'Are we to witness another Thirty Years War?' He imagined the war would not be over until there were no chess pieces for the generals to play with. He was pessimistic and his words summed up the growing feeling of disillusion among people when he wrote: 'We are becoming grey and we ask whenever will the boys be coming home. Are we sharing our sacrifices equally? We are all giving our services by playing for relief funds, for boots for poor children and for cigarettes for the front. A true pathos, but look around, there are plenty of examples of facile sentiment'.

When he wrote these gloomy words he could not know that the early months of 1918 held out the last hope of a German victory. The long sustained effort was draining their resources. Their allies were faring badly and the great Austria-Hungary empire was crumbling. The all-or-nothing attack was launched by the

Germans on a 43 mile front on 21 March and it swept away the entire British Fifth Army.

A dark hour indeed, which inflamed public opinion against those not in uniform. Reports reached the editor of violent reaction against eligible men who had yet to join up or be conscripted. Several bandsmen were assaulted when leaving engagements because they looked fit enough to fight.

One charity, anxious to book the popular Horden Colliery Ragtime Brass Band, wrote to the secretary seeking assurance that no man under 40 years was in the band. The committee then decided to include in its advertisements for engagements, these words, 'We are a band of 40 players, all miners. Some have seen action at the front and others are above military age. Most carry exemption cards'. The Chess Valley Band changed its title to the CV Military Band in the hope it would escape the demonstrations when its younger men walked on stage. Herbert Ashleford, the soprano player was badly beaten as he left the hall and was forced to seek hospital treatment. The poor fellow was medically unfit for he had one arm shorter than the other.

The wives of serving soldiers were the spearhead of such outburst. As the casualty list grew so the rage against the 'lillies' increased. A meeting was held in Hereford and called upon 'all fit men and to stop getting fat on the corpses of their kin'. In Stockport, 700 soldiers marched to the music of two brass bands. Placards announced it was 'to weed out all fit men and take them to the recruiting sergeant' or 'Miners are fit yet cowards.' Castleford Old lost many middle aged men because of this excessive, yet understandable zeal. No one would listen to excuses.

Wives were particularly proud of their husbands and often asked the editor to publish letters from the regimental chaplains, which sometimes arrived before the telegram announcing a death. One letter received from Mrs Auter was about her husband, John, late of Cudworth Old. It read, 'As your husband's chaplain I must write a few lines. He was detailed at a post to help me to make a hot tea for the wounded. Later in the morning a shell burst beyond the shelter which served as our kitchen. The shell killed your husband instantly and so were three German prisoners of war. It will be comforting to you to think that his last acts were those of mercy and administering to the suffering of others.' Mr. Auter left a widow and seven children.

On 8 August, General Haig launched his counter-attack and by a supreme feat of arms breached the formidable Hindenburg line and the writing was on the wall. The discipline and heroism of the British troops pushed the enemy back along the entire

British sector. Philip Parker of the Dewsbury Brass Band wrote to say he had not had his clothes off for a fortnight and his gun had run hot. Ben Parker (no relation) Chadwick band wrote about the poison gas that smelt like flowers. It had been a sad sight in band rooms throughout the war as 'gassed' bandsmen on discharge haunted rehearsals knowing they would never blow again.

Contests were still held and at one a minute's silence was observed as a mark of respect for one of England's foremost cornet players, Edwin Firth of Fodens, who had been killed in action. In the last few weeks of fighting the last member of a Welsh male choir was killed. The entire choir had now been killed since it enlisted *en bloc* three years ago.

As September ended the editor felt that the German war machine, although very much intact, was at last faltering. Letters arriving at his office spoke of retreat. Newspapers, however, never gave a hint the war might soon be over and Henry Iles said at a function that he expected to hear of the inevitable counter-attack. But the optimistic feeling persisted as the editor showed the following sort of letter to the staff. 'Tiny' Dobbs of the Pershing Band (so called because it had one American trombone player) wrote, 'Our band has to be driven in vehicles to keep up with the troops because they like a good sing-song at night.'

At last the editor felt he could turn to the more controversial subjects such as he had encouraged before the war. He reported a speech by Sir Thomas Beecham in Manchester, 'Brass bands are tosh! They have made more money from Park engagements than the Halle makes in a week. Go out on to the street and break windows and when you get before the magistrate tell him the Halle is going to the devil. It will look good in print'. The editor deplored the lowering of moral standards in mixed bands and warned bandsmen to beware the Jezebels, not, you will notice, the other way round.

He, Henry Iles and famous judges and conductors began to consider the post-war instrumentation of brass bands. The editor wrote: 'Most of our brass band greats are saying the addition of six clarinets, an oboe and a bassoon will make a tremendous and acceptable difference to the present sound.' This feeling was widespread because many a war-depleted brass band had encouraged other instrumentalists to make the number up. Henry Iles said at a dinner organised by the Central Charities for Fatherless Children, 'I love brass bands but after the war I think I shall have to learn to love half a brass and half an orchestra.'

During the last week of September there was a crisis meeting between Henry Iles, the editor and the three printers. *The British*

Bandsman was selling well but government restrictions precluded any worthwhile profit and Mr. Iles felt he could no longer sustain the magazine from his own financial resources. The paper was not alone in the struggle to survive, *The Salvation Army and Songster* had ceased publication and the weekly *Musical Standard* was now published fortnightly and was a shadow of its former self.

After an agonising debate, including how on earth the Crystal Palace Festival would survive with no publicity, it was decided to cease publication within a month and the small gathering broke up with heavy heart. On his way home Mr. Iles had second thoughts and on 5 October it appeared as if nothing had happened. It was reduced to four pages and the price was 1½d.

Four weeks later news was received that the call up had ceased. Reserve camps in England were bursting at the seams as no men were being transferred to the battlefields. The day after the armistice, Henry Iles called the staff together and shook hands over a celebration drink. He referred to the two great crises *The British Bandsman* had suffered. The first, whether or not it was transferred to the Midlands following 'the great daylight zeppelin raid on 13 June, 1917, and the trauma of a few weeks ago.'

In the next issue the editor wrote, 'I am so profoundly touched by the fact that the fighting has stopped that I find it quite difficult at this stage to go into the question of its effects on brass and brass bandsmen. I do not think they will pick up the threads of 1914.'

The period of the Great War was not all a litany of woe. To those left behind it was a sobering experience but the bands, committees, administrators and judges did their best to keep going. The pages of *The British Bandsman* provide astonishing reading as concerts, contests, gossip and comment were published weekly, everyone ever mindful of the sacrifice of others.

The following has been culled from *The British Bandsman* and is a proud note on which to end the Great War of 1914-1918:

AWARDS FOR GALLANTRY

The Victoria Cross
R. Dunshire (Dunniker Colliery Band)   W. Clamp (Motherwell S.A. Band)
J. Raynes (Leeds Police Band)   W. Kennell (Wellingborough S.A. Band)
Lt. Colvin (Belfast Citadel S.A. Band)

Distinguished Conduct Medals	45
Military Cross	6
Military Medals	71

Those who were bandsmen before 1914 and enlisted: 12,888.
Total of all brass bandsmen who enlisted: approximately 25,500.
Total of Salvation Army Bandsmen who enlisted: 8,000

Killed or died of wounds	1,234
Wounded	1,461
Missing and prisoners	356

20 *Would the crowds come back?*

When the war was over, disillusioned survivors joined the ranks of the wearied civilians who wanted nothing more than to forget. It took *The British Bandsman* some time to settle down as a good part of the working day was spent replying to hundreds of letters and telephone calls regarding news of returning bandsmen. It was constantly sold out during 1919 although it contained only four pages of news and gossip.

As if the suffering had not been enough, a great influenza epidemic swept the country, taking with it the lives of many bandsmen and their families. Touring bands left hurriedly for home but for some it was too late. The Italian Carabinieri band left behind several members too ill to travel and some of these were detained in hospital.

When the epidemic died down, almost spontaneously the victory celebrations began. The band of the Ambulance Corps, toured the country and was mobbed wherever it played. Special services were held in all citadels as The Salvation Army welcomed its heroes home. Brass bands waited patiently for the return of their players and then staged mammoth welcoming-home concerts where, more often than not, these ex-servicemen would be played on to the platform with Handel's *Here The Conquering Hero Comes* and Union Jacks waved everywhere. The volunteers who had left the Paulton Silver Band all returned from the fighting and were welcomed home by the eight players left behind and hundreds of well-wishers. Some bandsmen found their bands were no more but this did not matter as other bands invited them to the concerts, the spirit of the trenches was still ever-present. Some bands collapsed due to the circumstances of the sudden end of the war. Military, special constabulary and various munition works bands were never heard of again. The

1919 following peace celebration concert. The Lees Christian Brethren Temperance Band. A typical palindrome style photograph.

peace celebrations were a good stimuli for everyone; bands, advertisers and promoters; and everybody echoed the cry of Lloyd George: 'A land fit for heroes to live in'. *The British Bandsman* increased to eight and then to 16 pages but had enough news to print 32.

The euphoria did not last long. The vision of Utopia was soon to fade as the country struggled in a morass of economic difficulty and stumbled into industrial strife. The Housing Act of 1919 was passed to help the local authorities provide more houses but it brought little result because of economy cuts. This see-saw effect stopped bands from being too ambitious although Chalk Farm Salvation Army Band made plans to tour the USA by airship.

Many firms which had famous brass bands found themselves suffering from the burgeoning trade unions which were by now, experiencing the strength of unity. Strikes for better pay and conditions shut the Belfast and Clyde shipyards and the railway network was soon paralysed. Transport became a very hit-and-miss affair and bands cancelled contests. The editor advised bands to keep contesting even if it involved only the bands in the immediate vicinity as 'surely not only you but brass bands in parks will die.'

The question on everyone's lips and in the daily papers was, 'Will the crowds come back to the contests?' All eyes turned to the Bugle Contest in Cornwall, as over 20,000 bandsmen had now eturned and were raring to go. The organisers knew money was tight and in some areas trains were unreliable. In any case, railway fares had been increased. Even the night before the contest, Mr. F. Richards, the Bugle contest secretary and the editor, had their doubts; certainly Mr. Iles was apprehensive and was prepared to see a 'sparse contest crowd'.

The day dawned dry and bright and the Bugle committee were completely taken aback at what they saw. Shortly after dawn the first Cornishmen arrived and by 9.00 a.m. all roads leading to the village were thronged with thousands of people all eager to be in at the start of the big parade. It was a happy, delirious day and still spoken of by the older residents. It was a good day too for contest promoters, especially Henry Iles, who began at once to dust off their files and start planning.

Belle Vue shook itself back to normality and long queues formed to enter the hall. At Huddersfield, 40,000 people entered the park to listen and other areas and associations reported huge crowds but, alas, only for the better-known contests. Many of the minnows never survived. Henry Iles was reborn and dug deep into his personal finances to once again promote the Crystal Palace Contest.

One reader said: 'What good news the Crystal Palace is coming back next year, a good day out and a good night out.'

This helped the movement too, for news was coming in from area correspondents showing over 2,000 brass bands had restarted and, in one month alone, 500 were newly created. These bands had to struggle in some places for recognition by the councils. Some councils hankered after the 'gipsy'-type orchestra and some after the sedate string ensemble. Cheltenham Town Council, with several military types among its ranks, promptly opted for a big brass band and spent £1,500 to get the best but, at Tynemouth, the council refused to spend £10 saying: 'It is far too much to spend on music.' In Lancashire, the cotton boom generated better wages and this soon filtered through to the bands in the area and new instruments and uniforms could be purchased.

One would have thought the bands in London and the South East would have the benefit of a boom but they did not. Their uniforms were shabby or non-existent. The economic recovery over the country as a whole was very patchy. Where it was good, the councils were able to afford to build bandstands and advertise park concerts to which thousands flocked. This in turn was good for the deck-chair business, the catering industry and fun-fair operators, not to mention the three card tricksters and other fly-by-nights.

As the contesting season began to blossom so did th
acrimony. The Lindley Band at one contest protested vehementl
about being drawn No. 1 because the audience consisted of 'on
woman, three men and a child' and demanded they play again a
the end. The judges at first agreed but one of them looked at hi
watch and said he had a train to catch and he had no time to liste
again. The *Dead March* was again resurrected.

It was felt among the cognoscenti of the movement that 191
was the right time to stop players being bought like footballers
Cornet players especially were well sought after. Harton Collier
poached one from St. Hilda's for a retaining fee of £100 and 12s
6d. for each engagement, 6s. for each rehearsal and all expense
paid. *The British Bandsman* wondered if there would be an
amateurs left. To be fair, Harton Colliery had lost a playe
following its Belle Vue triumph. In any case, Jack Mackintosh,
famous cornetist and trumpeter, the man involved, still had t
work for a living, not like some virtuosi in the music world.

'How come', said the secretary to the Steamshed Band, 'tha
the other bands get the park jobs and not us. I know we tende
low'. The reason, according to the editor, was simple – 'Get in si
saxophones'. Bands which decided on this instrument did mak
money. They learned the new dance rhythms and were hired b
charities, works and social clubs to play in dance halls and schoo
rooms. The Walmer Bridge and Lees Temperance bands wer
becoming very well known as good dance bands and thei
engagement diary left little time for anything else.

The industrial unrest continued with the miners on strike and
as the slight recovery ceased, the slump increased. Advertisment
by the score were received every week at the offices of *The Britis
Bandsman* from bandsmen seeking work. Brass bands an
Salvation Army bands played almost around the clock at th
soup kitchens which sprang up. More men joined the ranks o
the unemployed as conscription was abolished and yet they wer
welcomed back with open arms by the struggling bands an
often a whip round would be made to buy them some clothes
'and we gave the lads a little bit of baccy as well' said one repor
A new band was formed called the Llanelly Demobbed Brass Ban
and this was followed by other returning soldiers forming band
to make 'a bit of brass'.

Some were *bona fide* outfits with correct administration an
joined associations; others took to the streets with, according t
The British Bandsman 'a big drum, a kettle drum, lots of clinkin
medals, notices to say the children were starving, a crutch or tw
and the blast of trombones but very little music' but the crowd
loved it and gave over their pennies in appreciation. It is said tha

at a Llanelly rugby match, the Demobbed Band made more than the entrance fees. 'The collectors boxes were heavy and their hearts were light'.

Just as the paper was gearing itself for the intense publicity campaign to promote the 'return of the world famous Crystal Palace Festival' a disastrous fire broke out at the printers and the premises were gutted. Henry Iles quickly set up shop elsewhere but the fire could not have happened at a worse time. Hundreds of copies were lost for several weeks and, unfortunately, so were some precious files.

By March over 100 bands had already confirmed they would take part at the Crystal Palace the owners of which were already in close contact with Henry Iles and the police. It was thought the occasion in the aftermath of the war might well allow emotion to run riot. All that summer, contests were watched keenly and Mr. Iles asked the various promoters to let him know how the contests were received and how many 'turned up to pay'. Stalybridge and Hull Whitsuntide contests gave great hope but others reported meagre attendances 'owing to the lack of trade in the district!'

The British Bandsman was then unashamedly used as the masthead for the propaganda. No week passed without some reference to the Crystal Palace and in some cases the rhetoric of the editor would make a political orator blanch. Bands were reporting to the paper that the giant prize draws (so necessary before the war to provide funds to induce a band to go to London) were being abandoned owing to police pressure and, even worse, whist drives and club games were under suspicion by the police, as mere gambling methods to raise money.

Another trouble arose. Bands were always hired for concerts, parties, dances, fêtes and festivals but these were being cancelled because of lack of support. On the other hand huge labour demonstrations were held. On 8th May, 1920 hundreds of brass bands were engaged by the local trade unions to head processions but, of course, the band committees never asked for a fee. It just did not enter their heads.

A pattern was set this year which continued for the rest of the decade in the editorial department of *The British Bandsman*. The reports from the district correspondents were printed as received which, naturally from time to time, had serious omissions and false information. Nothing was checked and the editor often had to hide behind such phrases as 'We print what we receive.' Totally different to the present day when contests results are checked and doubled checked. The reason for this was expense. In 1920 there were two monthly magazines and one weekly catering solely for brass bands. All three faced very serious problems because of the high cost of paper and *The British Bandsman* was purchasing paper five times the pre-war price, but it still maintained its price for 2d. per week, whereas other weekly magazines had been increased to 3d.

Henry Iles thought that an increase in price would lose readers because of the financial straits in which they now found themselves. He floated the idea that *The British Bandsman* would, possibly in the future, withdraw adjudicators' remarks from the columns. According to the editor these were 'a relic from the past and no one reads them nowadays'. Until now every contest judge had his lengthy remarks on every band published and these filled half the paper. When they were withdrawn it meant more space to write about the Crystal Palace; what it was, where it was, what its attractions were, and so on. No stone was left unturned to interest the readers.

Then calamity! As if the reports from failed contests in Scotland, Wales and Cornwall (some abandoned and others curtailed) were not enough, the Crystal Palace would not be and, perhaps never would be, available for all the classes of bands which had hitherto taken part. The government had assumed control over part of it for a museum and exhibition. This meant the demise of the contests for military bands, the consolation and preliminary shield sections. The prizes and cash for these sections were passed on to the brass bands. This was the beginning of the format which we have at the National today.

It was all very well for the editor to write again and again of 'the enormous interest shown this year in the Crystal Palace' and 'thousands might well be locked out' but he and Mr. Iles were analysing, with some disappointment, the returns from bands which simply could not afford to come without the massive support of the pre-war enthusiasts. Railway companies were reporting lack of support for special excursions and he awaited the great Handel Festival at the Crystal Palace with some apprehension, as he imagined this would provide him with a useful pointer to the popularity of the Crystal Palace. It did not help at all. The attendance was officially described as 'thin'. However, Herbert Whiteley, the editor of *The British Bandsman* was optimistic. He thought 50,000 would go but Henry Iles put the figures at no more than 20,000. 'It is,' he said, 'the year we go on or the year we shut the door. If the door is shut in our faces then the brass bands will knock in vain to be readmitted as disaster befalls them'.

The contest was held on 25 September and up to 21 August 1920 the message was not too hopeful. As the remaining weeks went by so did some good news roll in. Such-and-such a band was coming by 'motor charabanc' and others had been hired to bring the supporters. The Great Western Railway traffic manager rang Mr. Iles to say there had been a last minute rush for excursion tickets. The caterers hastily revised their logistics and the Sydenham police division made plans for reinforcements to be at hand. Professional photographers of bands advertised their wares and rates and finally all those at the Crystal Palace, with a finger in the pie, braced themselves to face a crowd of 100,000. On the grapevine the message reached the 'get-rich-quick' brigade and they too were out in force, picking pockets, fleecing gullible gamblers, exhorting them into tents to watch 'The Great Rope Trick' and the spectacle of the fattest woman, the smallest man, half man half beast and, of course, the ladies of the night.

There was indeed a crowd of 100,000 and of these 60,000 passed through the turnstiles. Henry Iles took advantage of this surge of interest and doubled the size of the paper and increased the price by one penny.

From *The British Bandsman* and its contemporaries, it can be seen quite easily that the 1920 contest released seven years of pent-up emotion. North mixed with south, east and west. Old acquaintances were met and friendships renewed in very emotional circumstances, sad tales were told as some faces did not appear. The *National Anthem* was the occasion for an eruption of patriotic passion, played majestically and slowly by the massed bands followed by three cheers for His Majesty the King.

Of course the ale flowed and men got drunk but the police entered into the spirit of the great occasion and few arrests were made. Thousands lost the homeward-bound trains and hundreds milled around the railway stations and the streets of London. Extra presents had to be bought for wives and sweethearts to offset the enforced absence. The editor reported some bandsmen buying expensive items 'to offset the cackle when they got back'. The day was succinctly summed up in *The British Bandsman*. 'What a day! What a crowd! What a concert! What test pieces!' It was a musical feast and the great national newspapers agreed. The Prime Minister, Mr. Lloyd George, sent a telegram of congratulation to the winners, St. Hilda Colliery conducted by W. Halliwell and South Shields, its home town, went mad.

Yes, the crowds had come back and, in no small measure, helped by the efforts of *The British Bandsman* which kept the Crystal Palace contest before the ears and eyes of the movement and did so for many years to come. Congratulatory messages were received by the sackful and Henry Iles was fêted wherever he went.

21 *Life Divine*

In 1921, the government chose to lower the proportion of paper currency to the gold reserve thus increasing the real value of money. This, in turn, caused a decline in prices, profits and a shrinkage of trade. The spectre of mass unemployment loomed and by the end of the year two million were out of work. The high promise of the politicians in 1918 could not be kept.

This slump, as the crisis was called, made if difficult for the lesser bands to hold together and sorrowful letters were received to say the band had tried but without money to spare to keep going we played our last piece and our instruments are up for sale. The editor, for ever optimistic, wrote, 'The slump will soon be over. It will not be long before an equitable system of exchange will be agreed and trade and bands will boom again'. He was partially right as 1922 did enjoy a small recovery but the slump, the depression, despite encouraging words from successive prime ministers that 'we are turning the corner,' lasted for another 20 years.

The carrot for the bands was the magnificent cash prizes to be won and bands stooped to any kind of chicanery to win. The editor viewed such underhand antics with horror and wrote 'They flagrantly break every rule that the wit of contest promoter can devise and they have the effrontery to protest against another band doing what they are doing themselves'. Only the threat of a writ prevented him from naming names. It was not unusual in the space of the contesting season for at least six bandsmen to play for six different bands in six different contests. One correspondent said that the trouble lay with the cornet players 'They are self-seeking and selfish in the extreme, they do not know when to stop bowing'.

There was dissatisfaction for another reason. At contests bandsmen mixed with each other all day and found that a common grievance was the elitism which was creeping into the bands, separating the rank and file from the committee, the latter being admitted free to contests, concerts and various dinners. *The Courier* said, 'Some bandsmen have had enough and have downed tools'. Others reformed into street bands and went busking. The players were incensed when they heard on several reported occasions that beer and sandwiches were provided free for the committee by the publican of the place in which the committee meeting was held.

At the annual general meeting of one band it was discovered that two committee members had received interest-free loans. To the editor the solution was simple – make every player a committee member and call the band 'The Committee With Voting Power (inset name) Brass Band'. This year did see, however, the start of a truly democratically-run brass band, band leagues and band associations.

These committees had to look over their shoulders all the time as competition mounted against bands playing in the parks. Councils had learned quickly that choirs were notoriously exhibitionist and would gladly perform for nothing. The bands responded by providing entertainment. The Liverpool bands decided to compete with the dance bands and the conductor would announce: 'We have now decided to introduce the quick step into the programme, so please take your partners'.

At Mexborough in Scotland, comic band contests and concerts were run and in the West Country it became the habit of the soprano player to play among the dancers. The Darvel Brass Band played *A Sailor's Life* in the park on board a specially erected ship effect, with dummy guns, fireworks and searchlights. This created a new dimension.

It was necessary to obtain a park engagement to remain in business but councils refused to book bands unless they were in uniform. It cost £155 to kit out a band of 30 and it was impossible for bands to invest in this amount as the park engagement might only pay £10 to a lesser band in one year. *The British Bandsman* said, 'Yes truly the rich get richer and the poor get poorer'. Crack bands could hold draws in accordance with the law, that is among *bona fide* members and families and friends, but the lesser bands often desperate for funds sold tickets to all and sundry and broke the law.

The paper said this was a very risky business and the penalty for being found out could be prison. This did not deter the Darlington North East Railway Brass Band which made a sizeable amount for the band funds, but horror struck when it was found that a member of the police force had been sold a winning ticket and, what is more, he had nothing to do with the band in any way. Everybody kept quiet and awaited the inevitable question but it never came. The recipient played in the Darlington Military Band and like, apparently, looked after like.

Bands had to raise money or finish. The main concern was to 'dress up like Dyke'. When the Denton Original Brass Band suddenly appeared in a uniform of rich colour, the other Manchester bands took a gamble with the illegal giant lotteries to help the uniform fund.

It had been the practice in over 50 years for brass bands in their Sunday suits to go to church each year on a day set apart as 'Band Sunday'. This was changed in 1921 to 'Labour Sunday' and *The Post* reported: 'The bands now proudly and with determined step march in their majestic uniforms to the service in church followed by hundreds of the Labour supporters'. Yes, uniforms had come to stay and were a necessity for survival. After all, as *The British Bandsman* said: 'It identifies the band with its power something like that enjoyed by 'The Salvation Army'.

Not that Salvation Army bands escaped criticism this year but it was more blistering than usual. It began with the Hanwell Band petitioning the Middlesex County Council to prohibit the playing by The Salvation Army band on the streets because of its discordant music. Whilst the committee were sitting, The Salvation Army Band marched past. The councillors opened the windows and listened and then promptly agreed with Hanwell.

The 'power' to which the editor referred was the power of The Salvation Army authority. He asked why it was that every piece of music submitted to the music adviser had to include at least one melody to which sacred works had been set. 'Why have special music at all? The bands only play hymn tunes from the special book'. He was also somewhat objectionable in his approach and wrote, 'Do you know Salvation Army bandsmen cannot go to a football match or any other game where an admission fee is charged?' He was soon the butt of criticism for this onslaught both secular and religious. He realised he had gone too far and within weeks was exhorting brass bandsmen to follow the 'discipline and dedication' of the Salvation Army bands and turn up regularly for rehearsal.

Bandsmen could never understand why they were often precluded from playing in the streets on a Sunday and yet Salvation Army bands could 'bang and blast away at full tilt'. In the City of Bath, one councillor proclaimed that 'Brass bands should not play on the sacred Sabbath because the inordinate love of pleasure had been the principal reason for the break up of the empires of the past. Our great British Empire must not be allowed to suffer the same fate'. To which the editor remarked such balderdash could be effectively answered by the slide trombone. The harsh economic conditions apart, it was a great year of cut and thrust.

Refreshed from a two month tour of Egypt, Henry Iles pursued 'the Derby Day of the working class', the Crystal Palace Festival, with much vigour. He immediately attacked the other big contests. 'There is one thing,' he wrote, 'you are certain of receiving the money and trophies in your hands on the same day at my contest'. He was referring to the Glasgow promoters who did not present the shield to Fodens in 1919. Wingates band had to wait for their trophy in 1920 and the St. Hilda band only got their trophy with great difficulty.

Mr. Iles then began to think of royal patronage for the Crystal Palace. He badgered his contacts in parliament, as he thought the patronage of a lesser member of the royal family would lend some prestige to the occasion. He was absolutely dumbfounded when Buckingham Palace wrote to him to say the King himself would be graciously pleased to grant his patronage to the festival. A tremendous achievement and reported in most of the national papers, one referring to it as a 'spectacular honour for brass bands and for Mr. Iles'.

It was the talk of the whole movement for weeks. The mystique of the monarchy had touched the workers and the bands loved it. Bands played and sang the *National Anthem* at the beginning and the end of their concerts. The stature of Henry Iles grew. Bands made collections and eventually in 1921 he was painted in oils by Archibald Barnes. The cost of this was borne by over 100 brass bands and dozens of conductors, adjudicators and association officials. Henry Iles was often far too busy to sit for the hours demanded by the artist and when it was presented to him at the Crystal Palace Contest on Saturday, 24 September 1921 it was unfinished.

The painting, called by the press 'The National Testimonial', was organised by the London and Home Counties Amateur Bands Association to mark the twenty-first National Band Festival and also to commemorate the 21st anniversary of his presidency of the association.

At the presentation Mr. Iles was cheered to the echo by the huge audience yet, behind his back, many who were privy to the fact the painting was not finished were none too pleased with him. The murmurings accused him of not caring, of pursuing money to the exclusion of everything else, of relegating brass bands to just a nuisance value and much worse, putting his thumb to his nose at the marvellous and sincere efforts of bands to acknowledge his true worth to the movement.

And all this because the painting required a touch here and there. Of course the criticism rankled but he was too much of a gentleman to reply. He had been 'under the weather' for much of 1921 yet had steadfastly done everything brass bands demanded of him. His business pursuits had grown and he had given as much of his time as he possibly could to the artist. But this was the penalty of being 'larger than life' and already a legend.

Finally it was finished and displayed at the galleries of the Fine Art Society in London. Many bandsmen took the opportunity to go and see it.

The year was already assured of its place in the story of brass bands but it was not over yet. Cyril Jenkins, a composer of note wrote the test piece for the Crystal Palace but could not decide on its title. Herbert Whitely, the editor, read the music but looked in vain for its name. He telephoned Mr Jenkins who told him to choose it himself. One would have thought the editor would have agonised over this but almost immediately whilst on the top of a Number 14 London bus hit on *Life Divine* and for years he told friends it must have been divine intervention which brought it to him.

It was a bold title, very well received by the critics and brilliantly played by the winners, St. Hilda's, whose record of this is now a priceless collectors' item (Zonophone 2168). Not to be outdone, Fodens Band also recorded *Life Divine* (Winners series 3588) and at 2/6d each the records were sold out. To win this championship really did call for severe discipline. St. Hilda's rehearsed seven days a week for six weeks, the men emerging from the coal mine, begrimed and hungry, and going straight to the band room for at least three hours.

The Daily Herald reported, 'The extraordinary interest aroused by the Crystal Palace Festival, and the keen rivalry of the skill in the arts, are a good answer to the gentry who think that the three R's are quite good enough for the poor and the arts are quite beyond them'. It was the greatest Festival in 21 years and attracted saturation publicity mainly because of the astonishing test piece. Even the ever-critical editor dismissed the drunks and hooligans as 'a few restless souls' and *Life Divine* became immortal, a classic.

22 'Those who sit are cissies'

The editor, prompted no doubt as others were from the optimistic noises emanating from No. 10 Downing Street, thought 1922 would see a return to pre-war prosperity. He wrote, 'The Old Year is dead and to its turmoil, unrest, unemployment and bad trade, we all say good riddance'. It turned out to be a thoroughly miserable year and he was soon writing about the Glasgow and London hunger marches by the war veterans.

To offset the bad trade figures, Bonar Law, the Prime Minister, decided upon a complete protection scheme, subsequently improved by Stanley Baldwin, by imposing hefty duties on goods from overseas. It became a protectionist year with brass bands seeking some sort of defence against the blatant under-pricing for engagements, the poaching of excellent players and borrowed players. The latter was so bad that it affected contests. At the Swindon contest, Cirencester Silver Band won with a borrowed cornet player who lived 60 miles away and had not heard of the band until approached.

Worse was the flagrant breaking of contest rules and the underhand payment of money slipped into a player's hand as he took the stage. Bribery too was always hinted at until the matter exploded with the celebrated furore at Swansea when Mr. Parker wrote a somewhat innocuous and ambiguous letter to the adjudicator, Mr. Hawkins, informing him who he was, what he was and the name of his band. A chatty letter but it ended with the words, 'I conduct the Treharris Band and that is the band I want to win'. This sentence resulted in a 12 months suspension from the South Wales Association.

It was Yorkshire who led the way for the formation of a national governing body with national rules.

A meeting was held in Sheffield which was reported, by the organisers, as a huge success but a correspondent wrote it was a fiasco. The idea caught on for a while locally but the majority of brass bands gave it the cold shoulder. Their main task was to survive and they did – just. The slums expanded, the money went nowhere and brass bandsmen turned to street concerts and touring.

In the big cities, street bands paraded the shopping centres and made up to £8 per week per man, more than three times a weekly wage. Collectors often had one leg and a crutch and placards were displayed: 'Ex-Servicemen with starving families'. The War Office frowned at this and a general was reported in *The British Bandsman* as saying, 'Street bands are not compatible with the dignity of man who has stood between the enemy and his country and now blows a trombone to feed his family'. All very well, thought the editor, but the general does not have to keep the wolf from the door. 'Let him see what I see: The tall gaunt figure of a man poorly clothed, wearing a muffler and carrying his only means of support, his instrument'.

Half-a-dozen bands in the West End of London soon multiplied to 50 or so playing on the same day. There were often six bands playing in and around Trafalgar Square, London, and *The Daily Telegraph* said: 'The matter is now quite out of hand,' yet in the same article praised the high quality of performance. A Mr Henry Allan surfaced as the agent of the street bands in London. He soon had them properly organised and made sure the 'pitches' were not overworked. He advertised in *The British Bandsman* for players of all instruments and spread his activities to other towns and cities.

Wye Prize Band 1922. No uniform and boots give way to shoes.

He tried to keep within the pertinent sections of the Vagrancy Act and if fines were imposed he paid them. Many Salvation Army bandsmen joined his bands, the members of which were paid £3 per week plus maintenance. He boasted he had a waiting list of thousands. He was probably right because his so called 'street empire' soon broke up as those on the waiting list took it upon themselves to go busking on their own.

The police were soon breaking up fights between Allan's bands and the 'freebooters' as they were called. Bass drums were kicked in, bottles of Stephen's ink were emptied over clothes and makeshift uniforms, and instruments used as weapons. The press said the public enjoyed this more than the playing. *The Burnley Express* welcomed the free enterprise and wrote: 'A brass band is better than no music at all.'

The law said it was all right for them to play as it was entertainment and not begging. Mr. Fry, a London magistrate, discharged six players and three collectors much to the dismay of the police. *Bona fide* brass bands kicked up a fuss. 'We know', said one bandsman, 'that as soon as they have collected enough then they go to a well-known loose hostelry and spend it all in an hour'. The editor was unimpressed and replied, 'There is only one question. Do you want the German bands back again?'

Touring bands had mixed receptions. Apart from the crack bands who were fêted wherever they went, other much poorer bands, with sometimes all the players unemployed, tried to tour the better-off parts of the country to make some money to buy coal during the winter. Sometimes they met opposition from discharged orchestral players doing the same thing. There were many of these wind bands busking as the slump had hit the municipal orchestras. Bournemouth had lost £5,000 and Hastings £10,000 since 1920.

The Grassmarket Mission Prize Silver Band from Scotland fancied a long trip to the South because 'that is where the money is' and wrote to the editor seeking advice. He referred them to the Mansfield Band which was experiencing trouble in London from other mendicant bands and reminded the band of 'a particularly nasty incident in the West Country'. Apparently a touring band from the Midlands was set upon by the local bands and a free fight broke out resulting in broken noses and hospital treatment.

As always the brass bands supported the poor and Labour politicians. Three bands accompanied Communist and Labour leaders to political meetings giving their services free and there was hardly a Labour gathering that did not have a brass band to play *The Red Flag*. Bands were responsible for outings for the children and Hoxton, in the East End of London, is where it all began. There had been other such outings but the great national daily papers reported this outing in full. Hoxton Hall Brass Band organised an outing for the poor children of the district. It raised a large amount of money, quite adequate for the project, or so the committee thought. After a census it was found 'there are hundreds and hundreds, and hundreds more are discovered every day'. Finally it had to be limited to the children whose fathers had been killed in the war. This fired the imagination of leader writers and so the Epping Forest Outing made the headlines and thousands of bands, organisations and churches followed suit.

There were 11 brass bands within a square mile of Knightsbridge and Kensington, London, and these would mass to give three concerts on the street corners for the unemployed, knocking on the doors of the wealthy for collection money and to their credit the wealthy gave handsomely.

The real support for brass bands from the general public was hard to win for it had become synonymous with the poor, the unemployed, and the working class. It attracted a grotesquely spiteful press which could be quite hostile. *The Liverpool Echo* said 'The Music is a triumph for blatant brass' and went on to sarcastically describe its playing. *The Huddersfield Daily Examiner* said: 'It has been a long time noticeable that the enthusiasm which characterized many of our local brass bands has for many reasons been on the wane'. Another said: 'We agree with the Southport Town Council who do not wish to employ brass bands. People get more enjoyment singing and dancing around a barrel organ. Even Salvation Army bands can drown the noise of the railway engines'. *The Daily Press,* a lone voice, said: 'No one should sneer at the Brass Band, it deserves encouragement and recognition. It is the music of the masses'.

The good pickings for brass bands were always found on a Sunday in the parks and on the promenades. Some council welcomed them, others certainly did not. Here are two examples. At Southend, Essex, it was decided to have no brass bands on the pier. One councillor and a Justice of the Peace said they would rather support the Ten Commandments than a brass band. At Richmond, Surrey, the council provided tea and biscuits for the band playing in the park.

The balance sheets for 1922 reveal the majority of the bands were showing a deficit. Expenses had to be judged very carefully and it meant accepting adjudicators from the advertisements in local papers. Well known judges were in great demand for the big contests. J. Ord Hume had travelled over 10,000 miles in this year alone, but the lesser contests were run 'on a shoe string'. The

British Bandsman reported the arrival of one judge who was shabbily dressed, drank all day and gave some odd results. At the end of the day he was put up in the house of a committee man. The judge left early in the morning before the family were up, and he had used the fireplace as the lavatory. Only the law of libel prevented the naming of the man.

Some bands never received the prize money. At Airdrie and Scotstown, prize winners were not paid, Black Dyke losing £90 and Wingates £71. After the Glasgow Cattle Market contest no prize money was paid because it was a financial disaster. What did emerge from these failed contests was that many were promoted by people far removed from the brass band world. One was called Archie Pincher, but *The British Bandsman* refrained from any punning.

1922 saw the end of the 'square formation' of bands when performing at the Crystal Palace and the adoption of the 'concert formation'. Most bands sat in the chairs provided but some still stood 'as we have always done and always will. Those who sit are cissies and wallflowers'. *The British Bandsman* and Henry Iles were proud of the 1922 Festival and said, 'Most of us have been to the contest where bad language offended our ears on every hand and drunken men could be bought for ten a penny. Now it is the cleanest contest conducted in the Kingdom'. Maybe so, but it certainly was not the best organised. It was over an hour late in starting, food ran out before the afternoon and huge queues formed for the beer tent. One wag said, 'This is why there was so little drunkenness because you couldn't get near it'. If Henry Iles had strayed into Sydenham he would have seen the usual Crystal Palace scene enacted in the streets, which were crowded with drunks being sick in the gutters.

Musically it was a great success and the press devoted column after column to it, sometimes going right over the brink. 'Every manufacturing concern should have a brass band as it promotes harmony, beauty and joy for the workforce who would be too happy to strike'.

The economic blizzard meant indescribable conditions for families of the working class and the brass bands. Bandsmen began to emigrate in their hundreds. Dalton Town Band lost five players but all this, *The British Bandsman* said, helped fashion the healthy brass band scene 'in our empire overseas'.

And so ended the year; the year in which *The Liverpool Post* said that brass bands 'Should not be made to pay the entertainment tax because they do not entertain.' On the other hand in February, prior to the Arsenal *v* Newcastle football match the conductor of the Arsenal band, Mr. J. Kitchenside, after spontaneous

The Arsenal Football Club Brass Band taken in 1935. The Sousaphone always a great hit with the spectators.

applause by the huge crowd, was presented to HRH The Duke of York who said he was entranced by the performance of the band, and, yet again, a member of the Royal Family expressed his astonishment that the players 'were all working men.'

Footnote: *I am indebted to Mr E. J. Dodman who told me Mr. Kitchenside was connected with the Prudential Insurance Company which, in turn, was connected to the Arsenal FC. The band was a breakaway from the Highgate Silver Band and then changed its name to the Arsenal Band which helped to organise championship contests on the football pitch throughout the summer.*

23 *Towards the General Strike of 1926*

Always alive to the prospect of bigger contests, bigger prizes and bigger profits, Henry Iles asked his friends and correspondents if there was any practical method for determining the number of brass bands then existing in the country and how many of these actually contested. He received various suggestions including the formation of a National Register and one, from R. Smith & Co. — his music publishing concern, that he approach his friends in Parliament to consider licensing brass bands for a peppercorn fee.

Eventually the concensus of opinion decided there were 9,000 bands of which 900 contested. What a great movement it is, everybody said, until wiser heads took a long, hard look at these truly healthy figures. Spot checks revealed that some district correspondents were counting the same band with different names, bands which had recently finished and those which were twice counted on the borders between districts. Someone then decided to try and reconcile the sale of R. Smith & Co's music with the purchaser.

No one wanted to believe the revised figure of 5,000 bands of which 1,000 contested and it caused some anguish at *The British Bandsman*. The distortion of the figures is demonstrated by the method employed by one correspondent. He asked the Essex County Council how many different bands performed in the parks and was told that in all the parks in Essex the total came to 77. When he asked for a list of these bands, the reply was that no record was kept as a lot of the parks played gramophone records of bands over 'the new loud speaker machinery'. When the editor was told of this, Henry Iles took it up with the Council Chairman and was told it was much better to broadcast the records because they could not spit, throw rubbish about or play wrong notes.

The only thing people might miss were the conductors who took more care of their flash appearance than the musicianship of their players.

The popularity of the brass band was still quite unpredictable, especially in these troubled years. Sir Thomas Beecham never stopped criticising them and told anyone who would listen that 'brass bands are a blot on the pure, beautiful music landscape'. Hannen Swaffer of *The Daily Herald* disagreed but added 'their forte is definitely in a club for the deaf'. All good hilarious stuff but unconsciously directed against the working class. The bands retaliated in like manner: 'We do not play at Rugby matches because the crowd sing indecent songs to the music which even their ladies enjoy. We would rather play at football matches among our friends who appreciate our playing'. In this small way, the franchise battle lines for the next few years were being drawn.

The bands tried to enhance their status in the community by dressing in more garish uniforms and invented more and more medals to pin on the jackets. *The Daily Telegraph* wrote: 'Fodens took off their jackets, rolled up their sleeves and showed they meant business', but, in fact, they were removed because of the tap, tap of the medals against the instruments.

A letter from China in 1923. The 'B.B.' still goes all over the world.

AGENCY EXPRESS
Bookseller-publishers
HARBIN CHINA

PRINTED MATTERS

Redaction

„ British Bandsman "

London

via Siberia

If any item of news belittling the brass band could be unearthed then the so-called 'quality press' used it to the full. One such story made the rounds which was grossly exaggerated, yet it had a grain of truth. When it reached the London press it read: 'False teeth for brass bandsmen are a nuisance. It is the practice in the north of our country for these brass players to insert a cork inside their mouths for the outer edges of the two sets to rest upon. We are informed that at a recent concert the cornet player rested his instrument after his solo part, sighed and blew out his breath in satisfaction. Unfortunately a cork flew out and fell upon the lap of the Lady Mayoress sitting in the front row with other worthies. Despite the horrified looks of the band, she said with great aplomb, 'and from whose mouth, pray, does the bottle come?'

No band owned up although the editor thought it should disprove what he thought was pure journalistic licence. It was true corks were used for the purpose described but the story seemed fictional as no band, no place and no date were given. Another news item reflected on the fact that the big orchestras, in the 'posh' hotels of London, were now performing on revolving stages. 'Our brass bandsmen have been performing on revolving stands in fields and halls for years'.

Sometimes the press were favourable to the bands. In Darwen, Lancashire churches of all denominations held services on a Sunday to ask for God's guidance to be given to brass bands not to desecrate the Sabbath by using the Lord's Day to play music. Apparently *Horsey Keep Your Tail Up* was considered indelicate and *Felix Kept On Walking* was set to sinful rhythm. The northern papers thought this very shortsighted and suggested these songs kept the people happy because 'Goodness knows, they have little to be happy about'.

Working people thought they would have something to be happy about when a Labour government was returned, only to be shortlived, but they did see the age requirement for the old age pension reduced from 70 to 65 years. Later a Royal Commission sat to report on the miners' conditions of pay and hours and the Unemployment Insurance Act was passed. Brass bands tried manfully to live through this grey period, even learning to play the Charleston to bring a little excitement to their concerts. Rochdale Council shuddered at this innovation and accused brass bands of robbing the workers of their Sabbath rest. The editor reacted immediately and accused the council of being a relic from the prehistoric age. It should wake up because people would 'rather see Charlie Chaplin than read Shakespeare'. For a while it looked as though the tirade against Salvation Army bands would recommence. Abingdon Town Band was giving a street corner concert in aid of the uniform fund, when the local Salvation Army band 'pitched camp just ten yards away and then began to bellow and blow'. Just as the editor began to get into his stride to make capital from this, letters began to arrive in great numbers reporting bands in bankruptcy. It affected the good bands and some really struggled. Batley Old had a debt of £400, but it might just as well have been a million. Strangely, this was also the time *The British Bandsman* urged bands to buy a special reproduction photograph from 'real life' of Henry Iles, to be hung in the bandrooms. It was on sale 1/-. Sales met hard going and some of the letters of enquiry to bands were returned 'Not known as addressed'.

Again the alarm bells rang. Surely this was just a scare and new bands would be formed. 'You must entertain', boomed *The British Bandsman*, 'You will be lost if you don't'. Bedford Town Band took the editor at his word and played from a floating bandstand on the river — and it sank. As the players waded ashore, there were cries of 'Remember *The Titanic*'. Other bands dressed up, sang, danced and played by torchlight. Some used saxophone quartets and Oldham Brass Band found itself allied with 'The Cheer Up Entertainment Society' visiting hospitals and workhouses.

If a crack band, with the expertise to entertain, and able to attact a crowd of, say, 10,000, then in came the three card tricksters, the fattest lady, the smallest man, dice rollers, budding Houdinis and the take away eels and pease pudding vendors. Very often the band became a secondary attraction. The publicans did well, applying for extension of hours to cope with what one called 'the swilling money'.

These years saw a great step forward in broadcasting. The BBC, founded in 1922, was quick to realise the potential market among the working class and found that the brass band, if properly balanced for radio — which then it was not — provided cheap and stirring music. Furthermore it might well encourage sales of wireless sets amongst that section.

These same years also saw a bit of a step backward for bands. The practice was now prevalent for 'top-call' players to be imported, at a fee, to assist the bands contesting in the lower sections. No one seemed able to control what had become a thorn in the side of contesting bands. This would remain so until the problem was dealt with in a sane and businesslike manner. It was not, and contesting went somewhat flat.

From the beginning of its publication *The British Bandsman* had witnessed brass banding muddling along without any serious thought or direction. Contesting was originally intended to stimulate enthusiasm amongst bandsmen to make them more efficient. Now it was the case, more often than not, of learning a test piece parrot fashion. It was accepted that professional bandsmen could be borrowed to gain a snap win over better all-round bands at contests.

There was a host of complaining letters after most contests and the editor blamed the early pioneers of contesting who did not take into consideration the sporting and fighting element in the contestants. In other words: 'All's fair in love and contesting'. Far ahead of his time, the unassuming editor proposed a grading system, as in the football leagues, with five sections, the competition allowing for three up and three down. This was only one of the many of his ideas. The editor, Herbert Whiteley, was responsible, more than any other, for moulding the movement into what it is today.

'The Jazz Age' was a futher complication. To counter the threat of these 'jazzers', as they were called, dressed in white shirts, white flannels and boaters, taking over the park engagements, brass bands tried to play jazz. Too much super-syncopation made them realise what a long way it was from ragtime. The brass band player found there was too much accentuation — on every quaver and several semi-quavers of a bar of common time. After a few disasters, brass bands left this passing fad alone. Incredibly the crack bands seemed to be able to take this in their stride and the editor was thrilled when he heard top bands 'negotiating the twisting and turning' of the music.'

The bands missed the saxophone and clarinet so necessary for this type of music but the drummers had a wonderful time as some of those still living have said. It is interesting to note what the press said. *The Times* in January 1925: 'The saxophone anyway is a drab instrument and jazz is devastating to anyone with a normal musical ear'. The *Daily Mail*, in the same year: 'The Queen's Hall Symphony concert attracted a small audience but down the road, Debroy Somers and his Savoy Orpheans were playing to packed houses with the saxophonists and trombonists being lionised by the crowd'.

After this flirtation with jazz, the brass bands marked time and so did *The British Bandsman*. The paper printed long articles on other subjects such as opera, composers and technical data. All this seemed to while away the months until the Crystal Palace festival.

The big story of 1925 concerned the Open Championship at Belle Vue, Manchester, which had a mixed reception from the press. *The Manchester Guardian* wrote: 'A zoo is just the place for a brass band,' and *The Manchester Evening News* added: 'Brass bands should, in future, stick to military marches and snatches of familiar songs'. However, the music correspondent of *The Daily Telegraph* gave some praise. He wrote: 'These men from the North amaze me. They speak correct Italian. It made me turn my head quite sharply when hearing, in flat Yorkshire, such phrases as *allegro marziale* and *un poco agitato* as if it were normal on the Pennine Way'.

This was the year that the editor of *The British Bandsman* wrote: 'We are becoming a money-making mob; even Belle Vue is a second class affair'. Without warning it was announced that the celebrated Jennison family were to sell Belle Vue and the editor made great play with this news. It must be realised that for very many years the owner of *The British Bandsman* and his editors had deliberately underplayed the importance of Belle Vue and the Open and for one very good reason . . . it was the main rival to the National at Crystal Palace which, of course, they organised.

Equally sudden was the volte-face. The editor was now using such phrases as 'The Great Belle Vue', 'The Mecca of the North' and 'the place where thousands queue to get in'. As the sale deadline approached, anxiety grew. 'Who Will Save Belle Vue?' 'Who will the new owners be?' Some thought it would remain as it was, others that it would be redeveloped. One strong rumour was that it had been sold to a property company and would be pulled down. The more erudite music press was asking what manner of man was there who would maintain its great tradition.

Of course, *The British Bandsman* knew all along who it would be for there, standing in the wings, was John Henry Iles himself. It had been purchased by a London syndicate for almost a quarter-of-a-million pounds and both he and Sam Cope were among its more important members. Quite a few readers were horrified and asked if it was the end of the Crystal Palace. 'No', thundered the editor, 'we will march forward together'. And so they did, the Open and the National or, as the late Frank Wright used to say, Tweedledee and Tweedledum.

Henry Iles conducted most of his business over this transaction in hospital, where he had been taken in January for a serious operation. It was entirely successful but he did not leave hospital for two months and did not return to *The British Bandsman* until May. It is a measure of his popularity that hundreds of 'get well' messages were received from the bands.

Although *The British Bandsman* was now responsible for promoting Belle Vue as well as the Crystal Palace, no extra staff were employed. Mr. W. D. Cooper, business secretary to Henry Iles, found himself working many more unpaid hours and Herbert Whiteley, the editor, was placed under ever-increasing pressure as every directive from the owner had to be evaluated, commented upon and then implemented. This extra burden settled heavily upon his shoulders and four years later he resigned, utterly exhausted.

The weeks leading to the Crystal Palace contest were hard going for *The British Bandsman* staff and the bands. The economic conditions worsened and more players were unemployed, on strike or locked out. Soup kitchens and self help groups were everywhere. Headed by a brass band, 10,000 striking colliers in the anthracite area of the Amman Valley made a 20-mile night march over the mountain to Gynant, near Neath. Elsewhere, this manifestation of the great dissatisfaction of the working class, resulted in demonstration marches in the towns and cities all over the country with brass bands in their uniforms bringing a colourful splash into the monotony of the shabbily dressed marchers. On the other hand brass bands were at carnivals and fetes where the workers laughed at themselves in distorting mirrors, or tried to ring the bell and win a coconut as if they had not a care in the world, yet already their fingers were edging towards the trigger of the revolutionary gun. Truro Town Band flatly refused to head the Mayoral procession to the cathedral. *The Glasgow Evening News* reported 'breaches of decorum by the crowd as the brass band played the *National Anthem*'. *The Newcastle Weekly Chronicle* said: 'Men would be vastly better employed playing in a brass band than standing idly at street corners listening to the frothy ebullitions of the Communist orators'.

For the record, the 1925 Crystal Palace contest obtained another 'first'. Bands in all sections used more borrowed players than ever before. Everyone broke the rules but no one objected at the time, although a fortnight later the slap on the back became a stab in the back as letters full of recrimination were printed with accusation and counter accusation bandied about in the most libellous fashion.

24 *No light or brightness anywhere*

The irony of the origins of the General Strike of 1926 was not lost on the thousands of bandsmen from the colleries who had answered the call to fight for their country in the Great War. They had helped to vanquish the German Army and yet, within a few years, the Ruhr valley was producing enough coal to export to traditional British markets.

The British mine owners asked for further reductions in the pay of miners to compensate for these lost orders but the men would not stand for it and used the slogan 'Not a minute on the day, not a penny off the pay.' The government began to support the owners and the embittered miners turned to the Trade Union Congress for aid. A general strike was called and lasted from 3 May to 12 May.

The strike carried with it the germs of civil war and the Prime Minister, Stanley Baldwin, proclaimed: 'Anarchy and ruin stare us in the face'. Had it been successful, it would have meant the surrender of power of the lawful government of the country. Throughout the strike, His Majesty's Stationery Office published *The British Gazette*. It was full of strike news, of riots and other disturbances but, as if loath to ignore normality, reported a news item from Australia: 'Mr. Albert Baile, who recently won at Belle Vue and Halifax contests, now conducts the Newcastle Steel Works Brass Band. He will be visiting this country shortly to conduct the Australian Brass Band'.

This was sandwiched between news that the cinemas were open, but operating theatres in hospitals were closed, that huge food dumps had been set up in Hyde Park, London, and that armoured cars were escorting food convoys and soldiers were accompanying bus drivers. *The Daily Express* (a foolscap sheet printed on one side) found room to print the cricket scores and one headline read, 'Bands hold up coaches' but it referred to pickets not players. When it was over *The Daily Mail* (one small sheet) carried the headline 'Revolution routed'.

The British Bandsman said: 'The General Strike and the miners' strike, not yet adjusted, has put the clock back in the brass band movement. Brass bands, being working class organisations, are among the first to suffer. Shortage of money means less new music and, consequently, less interesting music. Instruments and uniforms suffer and so does the contest movement, the life blood of progressive bands. Let us hope we can all get into our stride again very quickly'.

Bands tried to keep the standards of contesting high but the lack of money meant the lowering of these. Some of the most well-known, skilful and dedicated judges, whose fees reflected this expertise, had no engagements at all this year. *The British Bandsman* urged bands to support 'these fine gentlemen' and not to engage 'fly-by-nights' as 'fighting will certainly break out again because of these cackling old hens'.

As a direct result of corporate decisions, some bands decided not to contest again and, quite a few bands broke up. This worried *The British Bandsman*: 'If we do not watch it, we shall have less bands than The Salvation Army which now has the huge total of 1,050 bands in the British Isles'.

This was not the only reason for the editor calling 1926 'a black year indeed'. The breakdown of worker discipline had led to disgraceful scenes at brass band concerts. At the De Montfort Hall, Leicester, brass band concerts resulted in rowdyism, obscene singing, indecent behaviour and, worse, 'total disrespect for the Crown'. Some idea of the latter is shown in the fact that over 3,000 prosecutions took place in the country for sedition and its menacing violence.

During the last weeks of May, the editor received pessimistic letters and telephone calls (for over 100 band secretaries were now on the telephone) about the slow recovery of banding. Some viewed the scene with foreboding and thought the brass bands would have to sell instruments to survive. The editor would have none of this, 'The Crystal Palace will shine as a sunbeam to illuminate the suffering hearts of the worker bandsman'.

Some bands found the term 'worker' an obstacle in obtaining engagements. One, known as the Gravesend Workers Band, lost money because of the prejudices of political opinion and disbanded. Some odd titles then emerged including 'The Holy Family Brass Band'.

Politically, the editor sat on the fence but this did not stop him from fighting injustice. He was incensed that the band of the Kneller Hall Royal School of Music had played at the London Coliseum. He kicked up a fuss and eventually questions were asked in Parliament because of 'the prevailing distress among civilian players'. The War Office was told 'it was a disgrace that students who receive training from public funds should be so employed.'

The editor could not understand why in the North, brass band players were pawning instruments whilst in the South a trombone player in the 'Kit Kat' night club in London was earning £80 per week. When *The British Bandsman* printed the news that the famous dance band leader Jack Hylton had been quoted as saying 'the best players come from brass bands', many wrote to Mr. Hylton asking for auditions. John Pursglove of the North London Excelsior Brass band became internationally known and was a star turn at the Savoy Hotel where Jack Hylton held court over the 'bright young things.'

'Why is there this discrepancy between North and South?' the editor asked (the nearest he ever got to being politically minded) 'Certainly there is no money in the North. It is all in London'.

The General Strike and the miners' strike seriously affected the circulation figures of *The British Bandsman*. It could not publish for two weeks during the strike fortnight in May and became the first casualty as bandsmen searched for economies. The revenue forecast for the year was revised and it made chilling reading for Henry Iles.

The editor wrote: 'The darkest clouds have settled at their lowest in the sky. There is no light or brightness anywhere'. It had to be said that if it were not for the generosity of Mr. Iles, not only *The British Bandsman* would have ceased publication, but the brass band movement would have disintegrated. His philanthropy had largely gone unnoticed. He could afford to help out for he was well on his way to a fortune.

He had returned from a month's holiday in Monte Carlo and was soon to go cruising in the Mediterranean for five weeks. In between, he devoted his energy to making the beloved Crystal Palace a success and often gave a substantial sum to the many 'thousand shilling funds' begun by bands to ensure their attendance and this year he saw a dream come true at the Crystal Palace.

He had always been full of admiration for the bravery of brass bandsmen under fire in the Great War and donated a bronze plaque erected in the Crystal Palace which was unveiled on 2 September, 1926 by the Hon. Esmond Harmsworth, MP

Opposite: An appeal to the people of Somerset for funds in the catastrophic year of 1926.

WELLINGTON (Som.) TOWN SILVER BAND

President—Lt.-Col. A. Hamilton Gault, D.S.O., M.P.

Vice-Presidents—

J. Howard Fox, Esq., J.P., C.C.; W. H. Ham, Esq., Portreeve; Sir Gilbert Garnsey; John Pope, Esq., J.P.; Councillor W. F. Stone; George Corner, Esq., M.A., T.D.; Gerald Fox, Esq.; Councillor W. H. Garnsey; H. J. H. Bryant, Esq.; Mrs. J. N. Campbell; J. H. Carrick, Esq.; Councillor J. E. Shapland; Miss A. P. Fox, J.P.; P. E. Clarke, Esq., F.R.C.O.; J. H. Jackson, Esq.; Col. The Hon. R. T. St. John.

Bandmaster—Mr. J. C. Baker. Conductor—Mr. F. Noble. Hon. Treasurer—Mr. E. M. Warren. Hon. Secretary—Mr W. J. Tucker, 5, Foxdown Terrace.

Dear Sir or Madam,

We, the Members of the above Band, do hereby tender our sincere thanks to our patrons for past support, and, as working men amateur musicians, respectfully appeal to the gentry, traders and general public of our locality to kindly devote a portion of their subscriptions to the help of our Silver Band and the noble cause of music.

The Band at present is greatly handicapped and frustrated in their efforts to excel by the poor, worn-out instruments now in use. A complete new set of "Excelsior Sonorous" Contesting Instruments, silver-plated and engraved, complete in solid leather cases, valued at £350, has therefore, been ordered from the well-known makers, Messrs. Hawkes & Son, of London. It would be quite hopeless for the Band to attempt to raise so large a sum from their own private resources, but they hope to receive the generous aid of the public to help them in this matter.

It is the intention of the Band, at a later date, to go in for contesting, and they hope, with the aid of the new instruments (which will place them, as far as instruments are concerned, on a level with the best bands in the country), to shortly bring back a prize, thus doing honor to their patrons and themselves.

The Band has, on many occasions, given its services free in aid of local charities, and will be quite willing to do so in future.

Duly authorised representatives will be appointed to visit every house in the district, and whatever amount is paid or promised, it will be thankfully received.

The Band will be only too pleased to repay in good music, and trusting that a hearty response may be made to this appeal, as the members are desirous of bringing the Band to the front rank.

On behalf of the Committee,

W. J. TUCKER, Hon. Secretary,
5, Foxdown Terrace,
Wellington.

P.S.—Instruments on view this week end at Mr. E. H. Ayliffe's.

171

MEMORIAL TO BANDSMEN.

The above is a photograph of the Memorial to Bandsmen (together with the donor, Mr. J. Henry Iles), which was unveiled at the Crystal Palace by the Hon. Esmond Harmsworth, M.P. The Memorial is in bronze and bears the following inscription: —

To the glorious memory of the thousands of bandsmen who fell for their King and Country in the Great War, 1914-18. Erected under the auspices of the London and Home Counties Amateur Bands Association and the National Brass Band Club, by their president J. Henry Iles, Esq., director and founder of the National Band Festival, September 25th, 1926.

After the unveiling ceremony, wreaths were placed at the foot of the Memorial from Mr. J. Henry Iles, The National Sunday League, the National Brass Band Club, the London and Home Counties Association, the Scottish Association, Messrs. Besson and Co., Ltd., and the Crystal Palace Band. On the following day (Sunday) the wreaths were deposited at the Cenotaph, in Whitehall. Forming up at the 'Horse Guards Parade, the champions of the previous day—St. Hilda Colliery Band, marched slowly at the head of the wreath bearers playing "Lead, Kindly Light." They halted at the Cenotaph and after the wreaths were deposited played "Nearer, my God, to Thee."

This year Henry Iles purchased the leisure complex at Margate for £120,000 and built a swimming pool there for £60,000 for the use of the general public. He owned a coal mine and looked forward to 1927 as a year of expansion for his enterprises. He hoped, with Royal approval, to place money in trust for a College of Music for Brass Bandsmen and the right for it to confer degrees. It was not to be.

1926 would not be complete if no mention was made of the solidarity of colliery bands with their colleagues on strike. *The British Bandsman* made for sorrowful reading, because the miners' strike continued into November before it collapsed. It is to the ternal credit of these bands that they did their utmost to alleviate the stark tragedy so evident in the mining towns and villages. These efforts have gone down in mining folklore. Not all bands can be mentioned but the following selfless examples are typical.

Oakdale Colliery Band walked all over Devon making collections on behalf of 'the hungry wives and families'. Nine Mile Point Colliery Band left its home, Cromfelinfach, Wales, and walked over the mountain to Caerphilly, a distance of six miles, playing from village to village into Dorset and Hampshire. After many privations and inevitable disagreements, the band arrived on the streets of London, tired, wan and below par but proud and triumphant in their efforts to raise money. Finally it gave a concert in the East End where the Bermondsey people raised £4,250 for the miners of Blaina.

Ryhill, Yorkshire, Band marched south to Kettering, Northamptonshire, giving concerts along the route, sleeping rough when unco-operative councils gave no shelter. Carluke Band travelled over 800 miles and collected £200. None of these efforts were unusual. If some miner's bands did not walk then they were out in the near vicinity of their homes, day after day, wet or fine, to give street corner concerts. These bands were the backbone of fund raising activities and helped to sustain the moral of the strikers beset on all sides to end the dispute.

In all cases collecting boxes were full of money. Not like the concerts given by some bands for the benefit of the public. Brighouse and Rastrick played before a vast crowd in Greenhead Park, Huddersfield, but the boxes were full of nails and buttons and only £2 in cash was found. In the end, the government survived, the General Strike was a fiasco and *The British Bandsman* hung on by its teeth.

25 Three years of little progress

1927 was an unusual year in that it ushered in a slight recovery i
trade, produced the first talking film and provided the first sign
of over reaching which was awaiting this remarkable man, J
Henry Iles. It was also the year when all factions of the wobblin
brass band movement came together with one voice. The catalys
was the appearance of the rules laid down by the Performin
Rights Society. These caused great dismay and caustic commen
from all quarters. All agreed it was a tax on the pleasure of th
working man and *The British Bandsman* led the protests to
crescendo of complaint.

'Why,' it asked, 'should brass bands provide this goodl
income to the publishers? It is only an addition. Absolut
rubbish', snorted the editor. His argument was that the compose
received a fair cut of the profit made by the publisher and it wa
sheer greed for him to line his pockets with the very hard-earne
pennies brass bands were making in these hard times. He likene
it to the profit made by the tobacco barons who could say: 'W
will gladly supply you with cigarettes at so much per thousand
but if you sell them you must pay us for our kindness in allowin
you to do what you like with your own property'.

The music publishers, alarmed at the amount of highly critica
letters being received, pleaded poverty caused by the effect o
wireless on the sales of sheet music. Back came *The Britis.
Bandsman*, its readers and associations with much stronge
language which, in essence, read: 'Why choose us for you
compensation?' This not only affected music but also the pundit
in the City of London who were asking why free marketin
principles did not apply, for, if no fee was payable under th
rules, would it matter? Composers would still compose an
firms would still publish!

The Performing Rights Society countered with: 'There is no justification whatsoever for this kind of language'. *The British Bandsman* was quite incensed at the attitude of the Society and published the old Calvinistic hymn to push home its anger:

> *We are the elect and chosen few*
> *Let all the rest be damned*
> *There's room enough in hell for you*
> *We don't want heaven crammed.*

The campaign lasted for months. Every few weeks someone would write in comments like: 'Nonsense, the next thing will be a tax on instruments to play the music'. With hindsight it all seemed to be a bit of a farce. The rank-and-file of village bands were told if they played selections from *Carmen*, published by R. Smith & Co., then no fee was payable, but if the music was published by Chappels then a fee was not only asked for, but demanded. It was ignored by bands for months: 'Nowt to do with us until the bill comes'. Henry Iles was quick to launch a big advertising campaign: 'Every piece published by R. Smith & Co. is entirely free of performing rights. Play it anywhere, any time'.

With a decrease in strikes, this year saw Fodens go back to a six-day week with overtime when necessary. The coalfields were in full production but the miners were still full of anger. Nevertheless, almost without exception the anger was controlled and the miners began to support their bands by contributing 1d per week to the band funds. There was enough money around for an unofficial tariff to operate: Retaining fee for the bandmaster £2.00, solo cornet £2.00, soprano 75p, solo trombone 85p, solo euphonium 85p, solo horn 75p, secretary 75p, treasurer 75p.

One band had a 'fact fund'. If payments to soloists became privy to other members, then an amount of money was paid to these players 'to keep their mouths quiet'. The payments to the officers of the band were always contentious and why not! Seldom was a balance sheet published and, as annual general meetings were always excuses for raiding the band funds for cheap ale, many questions were not asked. If they were, they were simply not answered.

Of course some bands were wholly democratic. Camborne Town Band shared out all fees received from summer engagements equally between all playing members. *The British Bandsman* encouraged this because it thought otherwise there was great scope for fraud and deceit. The editor said: 'If some of these brass bandsmen were in an orchestra they would shine as fiddlers'.

Not that orchestras had much money as the upturn in the economy expected after the last disastrous years never materialised.

Sir Henry Wood said that all the leading symphony orchestras and brass bands would have to perform superhuman efforts to get out of the rut. Councils were losing thousands of pounds in the summer of 1927, more than the previous year when Southend lost £2,825 on military band concerts alone.

Henry Iles was on one of his jaunts abroad but when he returned he revitalised the brass band propaganda in *The British Bandsman*. He was saddened by the death of his loyal secretary, Mr. W. D. Cooper, who had done most of the entrepreneurial work dropped on his desk by Mr. Iles, who knew there was really no way he could ask the editor to take over. Although only nibbling here and there at the various discussion papers given him by Mr. Iles, Herbert Whiteley found his cup dangerously close to overflowing.

Henry Iles stayed long in the office reading every news item which came in hoping the tide would turn and the depressing news of bands began to decline. He seized on the news that the famous Carlisle St. Stephens Band had never borrowed a player, paid no fees, salaries or wages, paid no retainers and allowed no drink in the band canteen. He held this up as an example to other bands. He was always conscious of his wealth in these grim times and his takeovers in the business world were always for the good of the workers. All around him he saw the evidence of the deprived and needy brass bandsmen and, whatever his high flying business wheeling-and-dealing required of him, his first love was the brass bands. Some cynics said it was because he had milked them dry, put up fees and fed them overpriced music. This talk became more and more familiar and lasted on and off for another seven years.

There is no doubt that Britain before the end of the 1930s was a land of the rich and the poor. The rich and not-so-rich had their own cultural pursuits; opera, classical concerts, art galleries, poetry readings, ballet and recitals. But the poor, even if they did enjoy themselves by listening to a brass band, were sometimes reduced to tears by the press. *The Daily Chronicle* wrote: 'Is there a law which compels local authorities to organise brass bands to disturb the peace in the parks? Stop them and save 10 per cent'.

Those who organised Conservative Party garden fêtes and the like did not re-engage brass bands because of the attitude of the players in the General Strike. Players began to weed out the trouble-makers to enable the band to ingratiate itself once more into the welcome and well-paid engagements provided by the gentry. One letter to the editor said: 'We have a red hot bolshie in our band. He is always busy with his pernicious behaviour'.

People looked back on the General Strike with a shudder and by 1928 the playing of *The Red Flag*, by some bands had given way to *Yes, We Have No Bananas*. A groundswell of a feeling of 'live for today' began in the north as a little more money was available for pleasure and the editor wrote that this was a good sign. He said the General Strike had done more harm to brass bands than the whole of the Great War and it was a terrible thing to contemplate that now only one in ten bands bothered to enter brass band contests.

A significant contribution to the dwindling number of contesting bands was the high railway fares which were disproportionate to the national wage. *The Leicester Mercury* wrote: 'It is too expensive to travel by train. Because of this bands did not come to the Leicester Brass Band Festival and there were many empty seats. One band usually came with 90 supporters but not this year.'

If a band decided to hire a char-a-banc then it was often not plain sailing. News items abounded with bands arriving too late to participate because of mechanical troubles. The secretary to the Winnett Street Brass Band said: 'The water in the radiator became too hot and boiled over like a kettle and we had to stop by the roadside. Still we had us a blow. It was a lovely hot day and we had to wait a couple of hours for it to be mended and some of us had a sleep. Mr. Banks said it was too late to go to the contest so we went home. We stopped at a pub in Stoke and gave the customers a couple of numbers and raised £1.7.5½d.'

Henry Iles spent some time in New York this year on business but before he went he organised opposition to the growing practice by the BBC of playing records as he said 'through the air'. The bone of contention was the fact that a brass band cut a record and this was used time and time again on such programmes as *Records at Tea Time*. Live broadcast by brass bands suffered as a consequence.

He lobbied Parliament with little success but rallied support from bands and even from the church for a reduction of hours devoted solely to records. It snowballed. Before long he was agreeing with church leaders in North Wales who said, 'It is not a miracle broadcasting records. God would not allow it to be'. The clergy of Peebles demanded the practice ceased forthwith as it was keeping people away from divine service. The Mayor of Grimsby cursed the playing of records in one place to be heard in another and said it was a backward step. Publishers and instrument makers were sure it would kill the trade.

The national press joined in the argument and it was a debating point for a couple of months. However public opinion won the day and bands began to make more and more records

they could ill afford for programmes to be brought back.

Yet the programmes prominently featured advertisements for foreign holidays and Mediterranean cruises. Certainly there was no media agency ad work. Just Henry Iles casting around his friends to defray expense.

The advertisements meant nothing to bandsmen and some queried bluntly the frustrating glimpses of the rich. Even in 1937 money was scarce and two competitors, who could not afford the fare to the Alexandra Palace, London, walked over 100 miles to compete.

1912 was a year of grave industrial unrest and 1927 was still in the abyss of the general strike from the previous year. The workers in these years had no money, lived day by day often dependant upon foreman patronage and, with few exceptions, well in debt.

But the Crystal Palace Festival programmes were bought in their thousands (31,000) in 1913 alone). They were souvenirs to be cherished and mulled over. Those left behind handed over coppers

and found themselves household names. It was the beginning of the formation of an elitist group of record makers in the brass band movement which has, more or less, kept itself intact.

It also bred enthusiasts who, until now, had never heard a brass band play anywhere let alone under studio conditions. Sales of records leapt and the phenomenon did not go unnoticed abroad. A Leipzig paper said: 'Bands known as brass bands in England can earn high money with the new record business because it can be heard in the homes of those who can afford a wireless set and some, like us, can make their own'. This referred to the 'cat's-whisker' set so popular with do-it-yourself enthusiasts.

The older bandsman seems to look back on 1928 as a good year for bands. He remembers the Crystal Palace contest filled with the fog of cigarette smoke, of more money to be spent on beer and also in the fun fair. One said it was a year in which he enjoyed a good standard of living and his wife, a district nurse, agreed as there were now more healthy babies.

These same bandsmen remember 1929 as a disaster. The economy took one step backwards and the first to feel its effects were the colliery bands. The mining industry suffered chronic unemployment. In Wales, Lancashire and Durham, one in three of the workforce was out of work. This had a damaging effect on colliery bands as many players left to find work in the more affluent South.

Scores of these bands, especially in Lancashire, found it difficult to carry on. In Yorkshire, contests dwindled and in Wales bands barely existed. In the Wigan district bands died and those which survived could pay no travelling expenses or honorariums to officers. In Cowdenbeath the bands met just to keep their hands in but there was no money for the places to be lit or heated.

Besson's, the instrument makers, were rumoured to be in trouble and looking for amalgamation with another firm. This was strenuously denied by Besson's but the writing was on the wall, as 1930 was to prove. Street bands reappeared. The poorer bands looked on helplessly as the name bands made money with touring concerts but, said the letter writers to *The British Bandsman*: 'they do not do much for charity, only themselves'. This was an unfair comment for almost without exception some money was given to worthwhile causes. The Pilling Brass Band was specifically formed to raise money for charity. One of these bands turned out in the Market Place in South Shields on Good Friday and collected from 10,000 people who came to sing the Easter hymns.

Bands collected every day and the public, happy to sing and dance with the busking bands, barrel organs, strolling players with ukeleles, concertinas and pram gramophones, were disenchanted because collecting boxes were rattled every few yards. One person wrote: 'After putting up with all this on a weekday why do we have to put with the euphoniums, drums and cornets of The Salvation Army. The Sabbath is to be enjoyed and not marred by such goings on.'

One band reported it felt the top judges were too full of their own importance dressed in frock coats and top hats and having the impertinence to ask for ten quid for an engagement. The secretary said: 'It fair made us laugh our heads off'. There was a move to give these judges 'a fiver and no more'. Some asked for an adjudicator from the ranks of The Salvation Army as it was thought such an individual would not be allowed to charge – 'and all we would have to do is put a penny in the box.'

Salvation Army bandsmen were still fair game for brass bands and they never ceased in their efforts to entice the better Salvation Army players into their ranks. *The British Bandsman* joined in and wrote that these Salvationists were not allowed to go to the cinema or football matches 'so no wonder eleven of the twenty-three players of the Newton Abbot Salvation Army Band have left'.

When paper money fortunes crashed in America in 1929 it had an immediate rippling effect on the economic condition of this country and it was surprising how quickly it affected the take-home pay of the worker. Not particularly as a result of this, but surprising in view of the general strike, Ramsay McDonald became Prime Minister of a Labour government.

There were some reforms introduced with which the editor agreed but he wrote he could not understand why the young bandsmen preferred to draw the dole rather than work. He thought this unemployment benefit was not only too much but should be withdrawn completely. Even if these bandsmen travelled, they found themselves ostracised by other workers who physically prevented these outsiders from lining up outside the docks, factories and quarries to be called by the foreman for piece work.

Many unemployed players left their home towns often for months on end to go busking in other towns and cities. Some took their uniforms with them to give a splash of theatre to their playing and these soon became travel-stained and frayed. Bands had priorities; instruments, music and rehearsal facilities, with uniforms way down the list, unless they were name bands already nationally recognised by what the players wore on stage.

At this time, and somewhat insensitive some thought, Henry Iles introduced a new rule into the conditions for entering the Crystal Palace contest. In essence it read that no band could enter the contest unless every member of the band was dressed in uniform. There was a sizeable rebellion against this arbitrary decision but Mr. Iles was adamant it was good for the public image of brass bands and he was right.

Some bands were absolutely broke and told Henry Iles that they would have to withdraw. His first reaction was to cross them off the list and secondary sources reveal he advised them to borrow the money. Herbert Whiteley, the hard-pressed editor, found he was taking sides and all this contributed to the frustration which was to boil over later on and place him in medical care.

Finally, it seems there was a show-down between the two and Iles gave special dispensation to selected bands. Others purchased second and sometimes third hand uniforms. Some raided the so-called 'welfare funds' and others obtained money from grants from the councils. It brought a much needed fillip to the uniform makers but left no money for anything else.

Comments from readers ranged from, 'Do we play better in war paint?' to 'money would be better spent on our children'. During this period King George V fell ill and when he recovered the country celebrated in fine style. Bands were in demand (and on payment) for street parties, processions, parades and church services. 'Hurrah', wrote *The Citizen*, 'His Majesty is still with us.'

It was not long before bands realised that the uniform makers were making a good profit. (Good, yes, but handsome, no.) This did not prevent some people saying that some of this profit should be returned to the movement. The editor agreed and wrote: 'The trade wax fat on contests. Why do they not give financial support?' The 'trade' did not reply in print although, being in business, the various members were well aware that Henry Iles was rich enough to buy everybody out. 'Had he not purchased a huge area of Aberdeen to build yet another Dreamland?' and 'He goes on more cruises than the Rockefellers' were some of the comments made. Privately the various trade organisations thought 'millionaire Henry' could easily pay for all contests both here and abroad. This was a time for all kinds of questions. One read, 'Why cannot brass bands do without putting ale in the judges tent? Cannot he give a good decision unless he is stimulated?' *The Courier* interpreted 'stimulated' as 'three sheets to the wind.' Yet it was sometimes the eagerly awaited high spot of a contest to see an almost legless judge being helped to a chair at the concluding ceremony. *The Royal Cornwall*

Gazette thought this tippling by judges would be stopped if all 'judging was done in the open air and in any case he would not be able to doze as he does in the tent on a warm day.'

The scandal of borrowed players was finally killing off the contests. Herbert Whiteley dedided to act and told Henry Iles to make it a condition that players physically registered and signed a registration form, the signature to be verified on the contest day. It was successful at the Belle Vue Contest. At the Crystal Palace in 1929 it was common knowledge that one star player received £15 to play for a band. 'He did not tell us which one', said *The British Bandsman*, 'but he saw eight other players borrowed at £5 a time'. The registration procedure for the Crystal Palace Contest quickly followed.

About this time the residents of South London were getting fed up with being invaded by 100,000 people every year at the National Brass Band Contest. Inevitably this huge crowd contained a hard core of trouble makers, vandals, hooligans and alcoholics all hell-bent on creating street disturbances around the Crystal Palace. Many complained to their local MP, who raised the matter with the Labour MP and First Commissioner of Wales. He thought the answer might be to bring the Crystal Palace back to its original home at Hyde Park. Fortunately, or unfortunately, although it excited the interest of the Cabinet, there was no money for such a project. In anycase the Government purse was quite empty.

After the 1929 Crystal Palace, Henry Iles went on one of his long holidays abroad. This time he went to South America to supervise the building of one of his new enterprises, a dirt track for motor cycles. When he came back, the office telephone number of *The British Bandsman* had been changed to Central 1166, as famous internationally, some said as Scotland Yard's Whitehall 1212 or perfumes 4711. The cheerful message from the editor for every one to have a 'Happy New Year' in 1930 sounded hollow even before it began. 'Why,' said the Market Military Band, 'we bothered to go carolling this Christmas no one knows. We made less in three weeks than we made in one day last year.' And so began the great depression.

26 *The hungry thirties*

The media tag of 'the hungry thirties' did not apply to the beginning of the decade and 1930 opened on an optimistic note for brass bands. During the lazy months of January and February, encouraging noises reached the editor that bands were awakening from the winter determined to go contesting. He, in turn, gave a rosy picture of 1930 to Henry Iles only to find that by April the regional correspondents were reporting a worrying reduction in contests, concerts and park engagements. This was because of a lack of funds but, oddly enough, there was a more serious reason. Some brass band associations failed to impose firm control over their member bands which still borrowed players for contests. Worse, many associations did not uphold the rules they themselves made.

It was not until the Scottish Association shocked the movement by suspending the Peebles and Knightswood bands for incorrectly registering players, that other associations grasped the nettle and severely tightened their supervision. Yet, bands still sought a way out of 'bona fide registration'. One of the most popular methods was to make borrowed players honorary members for the day of the contest!

Northern newspapers applauded the new-found supervision and, as one wrote, 'It would help to correct the naked greed for the prize money and the hoo-ha which always follows the announcement of the winners.' *The Halifax Courier* was not so sure about this hoo-ha. It did not approve of the prolonged booing and cat-calling from disappointed bands at contests but on the other hand said, 'we do not expect brass bandsmen to be a load of lilies'.

As the year progressed rehearsals became more infrequent and were often reduced to a desultory meeting on a Sunday morning when music making gave way to pessimistic talk of the financial plight in which they found themselves. The brass band movement no longer vibrated and Herbert Whiteley was under great pressure from Henry Iles to get it moving again. An impossible task for one man. It was a full time occupation to produce *The British Bandsman* week after week let alone organise and carry out the many instructions pouring from Mr. Iles regarding the Crystal Palace contest.

Herbert Whiteley did his best but it never seemed good enough for the paper's owner. Finally his work suffered and his health deteriorated. He was told by his doctor to take a long rest and there is no doubt he was in the throes of a nervous breakdown. It was a sad day for brass bands when he resigned.

Henry Iles was generous in his tribute to his former editor but one gets the impression *The British Bandsman* and the Crystal Palace contest were sacrosanct to Mr. Iles and he was determined they would succeed and, if an editor could not stand the pace, then it was as well he left. He approached his old friend Sam Cope and persuaded him to return as editor and also to take over the music publishing firm of R. Smith & Co. which he owned.

By now, Mr. Cope had many outside commitments and it was soon apparent an assistant editor was necessary. *The British Bandsman* found 'the man of the hour' and Alfred Mackler joined the staff. From 1930 to 1940 when he joined HM Forces and

The Knaresborough Silver Band. Now well over 100 years old. Despite the economic blizzard of 1930 here are the players displaying their new instruments purchased that year.

How styles have changed!

The Wellington Band, now 100 years old, showing the different uniforms in 1890, 1912, (which was thought to be somewhat avant garde with blue and gold trimmings) and 1931 (with guardsman type uniform).

served with distinction in the war, he was effectively the editor. Mr. Mackler recalls with great pleasure his association with Mr Cope and both of them soon brought an intimate style of communication between the paper and its readers. Mr. Mackler realised the present grading system to place bands in the various sections at the Crystal Palace posed ethical problems. The arbitrary judgement employed hitherto was frustrating many bands. He and Albert Sharpe, the business manager to Henry Iles, re-organised the system on a fair and proper basis which has stood the movement in good stead being refined over the years to what it is today.

Both the editor and his assistant were concerned with the lack of interest shown this year in the Crystal Palace. Their first priority was to persuade the bands that, despite the appalling economic conditions, they should 'pull out that little extra, raise funds and go'. Unfortunately Henry Iles was unable to stomp the country advertising his beloved contest. He too fell ill. He was advised to have a complete rest for three months and went to recuperate in the South of France.

Every week, news reached Mr. Mackler of bands folding including famous bands such as Wellingborough Old after 60 years of existence and other once-busy bands; for example Southend Silver. If the bands were not in trouble then their administrators and players were. Secretaries, treasurers and band-fund collectors appeared in the courts for offences from embezzlement to illegally pawning instruments.

Sam Cope and his assistant turned a deaf ear to the gossip that Henry Iles had lost his enthusiasm for the banding scene and the Crystal Palace had had its day. *The Courier* said, 'The Great Trek to London Town by brass bands is as good as over. This year, if it takes place, will only see a trickle. Second thoughts abound because of the lack of funds and the lack of interest. The pockets of supporters are certainly not as full as they used to be. We all know the terrible difficulty there is for even scraping together enough money for food and clothes. There is little, if any, to spare for the annual get-together in the capital city.'

But was this true of the country as a whole? *The British Bandsman* was constantly reporting packed crowds at concerts and reasonable support for contests. On the other hand, treasurers were reporting decreased takings and the 'trade' underwent its periodical breast-beating, wailing that instruments, music and uniforms were gathering dust. Outstanding instrumentalists were now on the busking circuit risking being knocked down by drivers of cars who scarcely knew the clutch from the brake pedal, (driving tests were not introduced until 1936) and, of course, the occasional

rrest and subsequent prosecution under the Vagrancy Act as an
dle and dissolute person'.

The grim shadow of 1931 began to loom as early as August
930. Businesses went bankrupt as unemployment increased
nd, as surely as night follows day, revenue fell. Expenditure and
nemployment benefit rose rapidly while the yield to the
xchequer from taxes was reduced just as quickly. Britain
uffered as world trade suffered and its export market shrivelled
ithin months.

For sometime the staff at *The British Bandsman* had heard
umours of the ruinous trade figures experienced by the
nstrument manufacturers. Profits had plummetted overnight.
Cash needed from the hire purchase agreements by bands
eased to arrive because everyone was in the same boat. Yet it was
 surprise when in late August the well known firms of Messrs
Booseys and Messrs Hawkes merged. Until August 23 they were
eparate firms in desperate competition and advertising as such
n *The British Bandsman*.

Over the next few years many firms engaged in music
ublishing and instrument sales ceased to trade. Old-established
ailors, who had for years made a comfortable living, were
orrified at the sudden competition for the making of uniforms
hen the new firm of Boosey and Hawkes and the energetic Civil
ervice Supplies entered the market with sufficient capital to
nder-price what had hitherto been a cosy agreement.

Eight weeks away from the 1930 Crystal Palace contest and still
orthern newspapers were pessimistic about its success. Some
ub-headings read, 'Crystal Palace funds not healthy', 'Whist
rives poorly attended' and 'Police act on lottery'. However, Sam
Cope told the staff that it would take place, it always had taken
lace and, furthermore, over the years he had heard it all before.
He was right. The 25th anniversary of the National Championship
vas oversubscribed and a complete sell-out with all records
roken. 200 bands, 4750 bandsmen, their wives, families,
upporters, hangers-on and the curious, all adding up to 65,000
eople. No wonder *The British Bandsman* and Henry Iles toasted
ne success in champagne.

More food and drink were consumed at the contest than in
ny previous year. The manager of the brewery in Pimlico,
London, had to put his bottling staff on overtime as Reid's stout
old out throughout South London. There was little trouble
nside the Crystal Palace complex but there were many arrests for
runkenness in the area outside. Quite a few bands returned
ome less a player or two.

When it was all over came the reckoning and in the homes of many bandsmen there was little money for food and a bleak Christmas beckoned. Whether or not this lack of money was acquiring political overtones, the fact remains that for the very first time there was a distinct murmuring in the movement against the words used by Henry Iles in this usual telegram on the day of the contest to HM the King, the Royal Patron to the Crystal Palace Festival. It had always included 'We, the working men musicians etc.' 'Why,' some asked, 'Does Mr Iles insist on calling us working men musicians when over 75 per cent of us are out of work, on the bread line, feeding at soup kitchens and going to jumble sales for our clothes?' (a composite question from primary sources).

Henry Iles replied through the columns of a contemporary music magazine. He wrote, 'His Gracious Majesty realises the marvellous power for good of the brass bands when he extended His Patronage to their movement. They are doing something to raise the standard of patriotism and they are doing something for the good of the people themselves and that is indispensable to our country.'

This was re-stated in *The British Bandsman* and, with variations for sometime after. It was as if it were necessary for Mr. Iles to justify himself and did not want to distance himself from the working class, the base of the brass band. Of course, jealousy of his life-style was apparent within the movement. The source of his wealth also caused comment. Rumours began to circulate amongst his enemies in the world of brass bands that he even had a finger in the Performing Rights Society. He was annoyed when they reached his ear. He could easily have opened his books to the whisperers which would have shown the extent of his financial support for *The British Bandsman* and the bands. Finally the paper published a statement that neither he, Sam Cope nor any member of his staff were in anyway associated with the Performing Rights Society.

Despite the tenor of the new tunes, *There's a Good Time Coming* and 'Live, Laugh and Love', 1931 stretched before brass bands like a desert. Henry Iles told his readers it was his sincere wish that happiness and prosperity would pervade their hearts in the coming year. But it became worse. Mr. Iles had his usual commercial success and made a lot of money. It was in this year he was elected Warden of the Musician's Company and the movement held its breath to see if his name was in the New Year' Honours List. His instinct for making money was still good and he ignored the advice of his friends to retreat behind a stockade as shares collapsed. He was his own man and went hunting in the ock market for the inevitable bargains. He survived because of is boldness but, soon after, this was to be his downfall.

The dance bands in the luxury hotels of London were playing *When You're Smiling*, *Painting the Clouds With Sunshine* and *Dancing With Tears in my Eyes*. Certainly if they were dancing in South Wales then there were tears in their eyes. The area was particularly hard hit by the deepening depression and *The British Bandsman* commented, 'The valleys are a grim shadow of the past. The depression has laid a heavy hand on banding in the South. Its cry of 'Halt' has to be obeyed. Many bands are defunct and others hold on with depleted membership'. The paper's Welsh correspondent called the whole of 1931 'a black, black night'.

Bands in the north and other areas of growing unemployment saw the trickle of players to the south become a steady stream. Mr. Mackler has since called this the time of emmigration for the British and he was the first to realise the tremendous uplift this was giving to southern bands.

The dialects of Yorkshire, Lancashire, Cheshire, Durham, Scotland and particularly Wales, could now be heard in most rehearsal rooms in Home Counties and some of these immigrants poured abroad. The Stoke Newington Branch, British Legion Brass Band, went to Paris and others went to Brussells. Not all the money collected by these reasonably well-off bands was spent on pleasure. The Arsenal Band gave regularly to the 'Fatherless Children's Fund'; St. Hilda Band performed for charities as well as itself and the 'Shoeless Children' and 'Aged Miners' funds were generously donated to by the band. Tooting Central Hall Silver Band managed to make enough money to feed 1,000 old people.

There was a feeling in brass bands of the poor getting poorer and that they must help each other to survive. Hunger, degredation and embarrassment haunted the North. One newspaper wrote in February, 'Our brass bands are setting a most unselfish example but we feel it is only the poor providing for the destitute'.

Much of the money for band funds and charities was in fact coming from concerts held on Sundays. For some unknown reason, a press campaign was mounted against the 'dilution of respect for the Day of our Lord'. One said these concerts were quite illegal and the law was being broken every time a brass band played on the Sabbath. Consequently brass bands abandoned these concerts. *The British Bandsman* said, 'This will be the death of the movement with no money, no instruments, no music, no uniform, no contest'. Despite the rhetoric it was basically true and Mr. Cope added, 'The Acts want burning. Our brave British Tommies became imbued with the Continental Sunday whilst fighting the enemy and expect to enjoy themselves on the Sabbath.'

This prophecy about the death of the movement due to various external pressures, was made frequently in the thirties but the movement, although leaner, actually flourished and good bands were in great demand.

The Edinburgh Charities Band Association was established for the purpose of helping the 'unfortunates' in the city. This was a good example of the desire of band associations 'to keep going and do good' as *The British Bandsman* put it. Bands were sometimes in name only, others sold off their assets, paid their debts and never reformed. Professional teachers and bandmasters returned to the ranks of the unemployed from whence they had been plucked during a lull in the economic storm the year before.

But again, was it all so bad? Sam Cope wrote 'There is evidence the brass band world is getting busy. We have not enough space to mention all the activity that is going on.' Small news items had arrived and these formed the basis of his optimism. For example the newly formed Perranporth Brass Band headed the parade to welcome home Donald Healey, the winner of the Monte Carlo car rally. Helston contest had a record entry and the annual quartet contest at Ettingshall, Wolverhampton had to cope with 15 quartets and 35 soloists. It lasted seven hours. Small villages refused to let their bands die. Regular fund-raising activities were organised and the contribution of the bands to community life somehow continued. Some thought Sam Cope was whistling in the dark as soon, more reports of abandoned contests poured in to the office. For the first time ever the Belle Vue May contest seemed doomed but the steady hand of Alfred Mackler settled the bands. 'Buck up', the paper said, 'for goodness sake get your entry forms in now'. And the bands did just that.

The famous Harton Colliery Band experienced very hard times as the colliery had been closed for nine months and no money was circulating in the area. Many bands brought some light relief into a drab dreary way of life in the industrial North by playing at street corners and squares during the day without a collection box in sight.

Much more money circulated in the south of the country but it did not particularly benefit brass bands. People preferred to buy records and stay at home for their entertainment. So popular did this become that one gramophone factory covered 60 acres and employed 8,000 workers. Patents for improved gramophone needles swamped the Patent Office.

At the top of the hit parade were the melodies of *Tip Toe Through the Tulips, Little White Lies* and *Valencia*. Southern brass bands soon realised the financial potential of making records, a lesson learnt by the northern bands years before.

If the public were not playing records then it was listening to the wireless. 80 per cent of all radio programmes in the London area alone were solely devoted to music, with brass bands taking a fair share. Not that these bands were everybody's 'cup of tea'. Some listeners complained to the BBC of the strident sound and compared it to 'cat music'. One reader told the editor that these brass bands were the curse of the Sabbath.

Mr. Mackler believed the 'mechanical music' as he called it, would make inroads into live performances and said, 'We will have to live with it and make the best of it'. With foresight he realised radio performances by bands would reach a far larger audience than was the case with concerts and 'might this not be a good thing and produce a surge back to the concert hall?"

The Belle Vue September Contest, to the surprise of many, was one of the most successful ever held with players and spectators very appreciative of the new rules of registration. Apparently there was not a borrowed player in sight. A topsy-turvy contest scene had developed. Records were broken at Truro but the Corwen contest was a fiasco. Some bands were down-at-heel and dressed in uniforms more fitted to a scarecrow, yet others, such as Camborne Town were able to parade in completely new uniforms of good quality cloth. Galashiels Town Band were much in demand but within a 20 mile radius other bands seldom met for practice. They could not spare the money because of the more pressing demands of feeding the family. These times were indeed 'Lean and Forlorn Days' as *The Daily Telegraph* headlined its 1932 New Year message.

Worthing Council thought the day of the brass band had now finished. It was said in full council that the bands had enjoyed a long run but now it was over. 'Members of the public have let councillors know that "hot" music is all the rage and we now agree to engage only those bands which can supply this. Brass bands certainly cannot.' All this was good fodder for the letter writers to *The British Bandsman* but the fact remains that in some seaside towns brass bands never played on the bandstand again. The 'hot' music this year gave way to 'Gypsy' ensembles, string and wind bands, concertina and regimental bands, civilian military outfits, dance and show bands, and – the most popular of all – Palm Court orchestras.

All a blow to the finances of the brass bands. Brighouse and Rastrick band tightened its belt and were compelled to dispense

C. P. CONTEST 1933
THE ADJUDICATORS IN THE SEVEN SECTIONS.

Back row, left to right: J. Eaton, T. Eastwood, D. Aspinall, H. Morris, G. Nicholls.
Centre: Dr. Keighley, J. T. Rees, W. J. Parry-Jones, I. Perrin, F. Rogan.
Front Row: H. C. Hind, J. Brier, H. Bennett, H. Geehl, C. Ward.

with the services of its resident conductor. Corporations, borough and town councils ceased recruiting and reduced staff. The unions watched carefully for any luxuries which could be dispensed with to prevent further unemployment of their members. Among the first to go were the park engagements. In some areas they were severely curtailed and in others completely abandoned.

Football clubs dispensed with brass bands entertaining the vast crowds at half time, yet the Arsenal Band flourished and played regularly throughout the slump at all home matches.

It was a worrying crisis. Sam Cope wrote once more, 'Stick together lads. Things can only improve'. Henry Iles dug deeply into his pocket to keep *The British Bandsman* going for without his generosity it would have ceased publication. The trade, too, was reeling. Messrs Boosey and Hawkes were desperate for business and advertised extensively using the headline 'Alright! You fix the terms. We supply you with the goods.'

A Kent newspaper reported an outburst by Alderman Westbrook at a meeting of the Royal Tunbridge Wells Town Council. He said, 'We do not want brass bands here. They are no longer popular.' *The Manchester Evening Chronicle* reported his comment and said the world would be a drab place without brass bands. *The Newcastle Weekly Chronicle* wrote in its editorial comment, 'The question is, will brass bands, long the pride of the colliery villages, be able to last? They are in danger of disappearing for there is no support these days.'

Half of Fodens Band and Wingates Band were unemployed and it was necessary for them to be able to draw the maximum unemployment benefit as this was essential to provide for their families if not for themselves and their wives. To their horror the unemployed bandsmen found their 'dole' money cut. On enquiry they were told they could not claim for those days set aside by the firms for rehearsal by the bands which they sponsored. A court judgement said they were 'following an occupation as such'. In other words they were at work for the benefit of the employer. It was a crushing blow to their morale and when news of this perculated through to the work force, tempers flared and ugly protests were made to the management.

Fred Mortimer, the conductor of Fodens Band, with the help of the directors, protested vehemently to the government office responsible for payment of the 'dole' and to the government itself. His reasoned argument was listened to courteously and the unpopular decision was rescinded. It was a major triumph that went largely unnoticed in the press until Mr. Mortimer successfully campaigned on behalf of other bands caught in the same circumstances. It led to many people, who thought they had been wrongly means-tested, establishing to how much they were entitled and Fred Mortimer's victory was quickly exploited.

Brass bandsmen were not backward in realising the earning potential of dance bands. Because of the wireless, Henry Hall, Jack Hylton and Debroy Somers were all household names in London and the provinces soon followed. The figures for the listening public were enormous. Towns and villages advertised 'Flannel dances', 'Blazer dances' and 'Crooner dances' and all this created a huge market for dance bands most of which had a fair sprinkling of brass bandsmen on trumpet and trombone.

A spin off of this was that the music publishers increased the brass band repertoire to satisfy the desire of brass bands to play for dances organised on the lawns of big houses, in school playgrounds and regattas. Pillings Brass Band had a go but gave it up as it found the rhythms too adventurous.

By and large people did not consider the new Chancellor of Germany, Adolf Hitler, a threat to themselves but there was an uneasy feeling when they heard of Hitler's chilling order that all Salvation Army bands in Germany were forbidden to play in public or private. What a contrast to this country. Chalk Farm Salvation Army Band not only played before the King and Queen of England but toured Denmark, Sweden and Finland.

1934 saw no easing of the poverty some people were experiencing and news items were sometimes biased. One report read, 'the poor workers of this country playing in brass bands lose their teeth early, but in America, where everyone gets regular meals, teeth last much longer.' Quite untrue. The bread lines of the unemployed this year in America are remembered now in films and novels.

The Bristol Evening News wrote, 'All is very dismal. Why does not someone organise a big brass band to march through our streets at full pressure, blowing, blaring, plenty of brass and cymbals? Goose-step preferred.' The success of the St. Hilda Band caused jealousy but little resentment among the struggling bands. Some thought they too should turn professional as some truly remarkable figures were returned by St. Hilda's management. The band had travelled 250,000 miles in three years, were playing only for 40 weeks in any one year, were self-supporting and were making a handsome profit.

If it was not unemployment which monopolised the conversation in the bandroom then it was the vexed question of borrowed players; it just would not go away. The practice of borrowing players had prevailed since the beginning of band history and was considered quite legitimate. It had also helped to foster a feeling of togetherness. It was not until this crept into contesting that the issue became contentious.

In one contest a third-section band was composed of half Fodens and half Wingates, both championship bands. In 1934 the evil was getting out of hand again but not all agreed it was a bad thing. One bandmaster is on record as saying, 'if any band of equal or higher grade applies to me for a specialist player at a contest then I am quite willing for him to go without any regard for any rule.' Another said, 'Borrowing players is a good system. Players practice harder to get on the list as they can bump up their earnings.' Yet another commented, 'Borrowed players are, in the main, decent chaps and often play for nothing. They do enhance the standard of play and cause other players to try harder.'

One would have thought the time was ripe for all bands to adopt the contest rules as laid down by the National Brass Band Club but the pressures to succeed were too great. Entertainment tax was another bone of contention. Bands coped generally with its complications but some legal decisions were made which reached the importance of 'stated cases.' The question before the judge was, 'Does a person who occupies a deck-chair to listen to a brass band place the owner, who lets out his property in the deck chair to the occupant, liable to pay the Entertainment Tax?' After much legal argument it was decided the owner *was* liable. This increased the price to hire the chairs and several bands reported people only came to listen to them if the grass was dry and they could sit down.

Another question concerned the loss of good players from lesser bands because of unemployment problems. These bands complained to Sam Cope that bands maintained by employers could offer employment to their star players and offer 'perks' such as the 'availability of the disbursement funds' as an inducement to join. This was not considered fair play, which begs the question, was there ever any fair play in the brass band contesting scene up to that time? One thing is for certain; it caused a tremendous feeling of ill-will between the affected bands.

In the opinion of Harry Mortimer, CBE, the virtuoso of the cornet and trumpet, celebrated conductor of brass bands, well-known adjudicator and now Father of the Movement, 1934 was a watershed and it was touch-and-go if the contest season survived. A disturbing element now appeared with outside entrepreneurs promoting contests for profit. If, when balancing his books just prior to the contest, the promoter found the effort was not worthwhile, he would cancel it as late as the day itself. Scores of bands reported the delivery of a telegram to say the contest was off just as they were about to board the coach. Naturally they were peeved, as money already spent could not be claimed.

Nothing, but nothing, could stop the steam-roller, the Crystal Palace Festival and Contest. The circulation of *The British Bandsman* always increased before the festival and then fell back again a few weeks afterwards but in this year it retained the new readership mainly because of Fodens Works Band creating a record by winning the championship for the third year in succession, and equalling the record held by the St. Hilda Band, by becoming winners of the championship five times.

The result fired the imagination of other bands and a new resolve was abroad to renew their chances of winning with energy and enthusiasm. They read of the concert given the evening after

The pictures on the following four pages are reproduced directly from 'The British Bandsman', 1934.

A scene at the 1933 National Band Festival. Many Bands are already preparing funds for this year's event.

The Doyle Brothers, Arthur (euphonium) and Charles (trombone), and Mrs. A. Doyle (accompanist). They have attended 18 contests and have won 17 first, 10 second and 4 third prizes.

Hayes and Harlington Silver band (conductor, A. T. Matson).

The band of the Brecknock S. B. School. Instructor, Lieut. L. Julien.

Two most genial personalities.
Above right: *W. Lowes*. Below:
Harry Mortimer.

A picture taken at the Jubilee
Dinner and Presentation to Mr.
James Alexander, secretary of
the Scottish Band Association,
in Edinburgh, including Messrs.
W. Lawson, A. Lawson, J. Beattie,
H. Bennett, J. Alexander and W.
F. Hannaford. (Glasgow Daily Record
photo).

The late James Ord Hume.   Right: *The May Belle Vue Championship Challenge Cups for
competition on May 5th at Manchester.*

Mr. J. Henry Iles (Director), The Officials and Adjudicators at Crystal Palace, 1934. Back row, left to right: A. Mackler, A. Sharpe, W. Nuttall. Second row: A. W. Trilsbach, D. Aspinall, G. Mercer, J. Eaton. Third row: Clifton Jones, G. W. Cave, H. C. Hind, J. Brier, J. Oliver, George R. Marshall. Front row: Frank Wright, Dr. T. Keighley, Miss F. Bantin, Mr. J. Henry Iles, Mr. S. Cope, W. Reynolds, F. Slevin. (Messrs. Geehl and Bennett were unavoidably absent when the photograph was taken.)

Jubilant Winners. This photo shows members of Foden's band cheering after being declared winners.

Mr. Henry Geehl whose works for brass band have achieved such great popularity. He has adjudicated in the championship section at Crystal Palace on seven occasions.

Festival 1934

Foden's Motor Works band, conducted by Mr. F. Mortimer, which created a record by winning for the third time in succession, playing the testpiece Overture "Comedy" in the Concert Room.

Left: Mr. W. Lowes, Conductor of Harton Colliery band, third prize-winners in the championship section.

Mr. Herbert Bennett who has done such good work in Scottish band circles as Band Editor of "The Glasgow Daily Record." He adjudicated in the Grand Shield section.

Mr. J. H. Elliot who, as Northern Music-Critic of "The News-Chronicle" has shown keen interest in brass bands.

Opposite: The Great Ord
Hume is laid to rest at
Edmonton.

the contest by Fodens at Finsbury Park Empire where hundreds milled about outside desperate for tickets. Police reinforcements were called in to control the good-humoured crowd. The actual concert drew so many encores it was in danger of continuing until dawn.

Two days later Fodens returned home to a Sandbach in Cheshire which was festooned and bedecked with bunting. Dozens of gaily decorated motor cars and waggons met the band. Led by the fire engine, the triumphant band played rousing marches to head a huge procession to the Market Square where thousands of people had gathered to cheer again and again as tributes were paid by the civic dignitaries. Finally the band went to the Elworth War Memorial where amid scenes of great emotion, they played *Abide With Me* sung reverently by the vast crowd.

All this was faithfully reported, almost without exception in local, provincial and national newspapers. It brought a touch of magic to brass bands and led Sir Landon Ronald to write to the *News Chronicle* that people just did not realise there were 100,000 players in brass bands of which there could not be less than 5,000.

Harry Mortimer says it was this tremendous achievement by Fodens which gave a much needed boost to brass bands and the crisis which had faced the movement during the summer months was over. Mentioning Mr. Mortimer, one is reminded that he at one time was closely associated with the Luton Red Cross Band. It was this year the Government ordered the band to drop the words 'Red Cross' from its title as it was an infringement of the Geneva Convention. Old habits die hard and for some time *The British Bandsman* still gave the band its full title as did many programmes.

James Ord Hume Memorial
Edmonton (Middlesex) Cemetery

MEMORIAL COMMITTEE

Chairman :
Councillor T. J. Harington,
E.U.D.C.

—

Hon. Treasurer : Mr. S. Cope,
Editor " British Bandsman "

—

Hon Secretary : Mr. E. D. Cain,
I, Carterhatch Lane, Enfield
Highway

—

Mr. W. F. Pratt and Mr. H. Sayer,
Edmonton Military Band

—

Mr. Chas. Cook & Mr. Fredericks,
Edmonton Silver Band

—

Mr. F. W. Walker, Mr. O. C.
Powell and Mr. M. Garvery,
Gothic Military Band

(Headstone)

Sacred to the Memory of

JAMES ORD HUME

Composer and Bandmaster

—

Born 14th September, 1864
Died 27th November, 1932

AGED 68 YEARS

—

A FRIEND OF ALL BANDSMEN

—

" The years shall not outgo
Our thinking of thee "

—

This memorial was erected through
subscriptions from bandsmen and
other admirers in the British Empire

27 *Henry Iles is defended*

The years prior to the outbreak of the World War II saw a narrowing of the great divide between the poor and the more comfortably off sections of the community. It was still a wretched time for the unemployed as the statistics showed one in ten of the workforce was without work. There was a slow start on rearmament, which helped the desolate areas of the industrial North but it came too late to sweeten the bitterness which demonstrated the utter despair felt by the unemployed when thousands marched from these areas in the so-called 'hunger marches' to London, sustained on some of the way by brass bands.

Between 1935 and 1939 the country was ruled by three kings, two prime ministers and suffered an unprecedented constitutional crisis with the abdication of King Edward VIII. There was a growing upsurge in world trade and this helped to put a little more money in bandsmen's pockets. Despite cautious optimism, there was an awareness that all was not well with the world. Mussolini invaded Abyssinia, Japan invaded China, Germany annexed Bohemia, Moravia, Austria and Czechoslovakia and Spain plunged into civil war.

Until the fleet was mobilised and gas masks issued to the public in 1938, most of the bandsmen who had fought in World War I thought it inconceivable the country could be involved in yet another. When it was debated in the band rooms there was a feeling of 'It'll be alright on the night' and this was reinforced when the Prime Minister, Neville Chamberlain, returned from a meeting in Germany with Herr Hitler saying, 'there will be peace in our time.'

In 1935 all this could not have been imagined. Talk was about the budget increases on cigarettes and beer, and holidays. Billy Butlin had opened his first holiday camp and hundreds packed the cheap train excursions to the coast. 'We are turning the corner', cried the newspapers but people could not see what was around the bend.

The slump in trade was nowhere near its death-throes. One bandsman can recall vividly his mother pleading with a maiden aunt to give her a threepenny bit to buy a meal for herself, husband and two children. When they sat down to eat, it was scraps from the butcher and potatoes. The pawn shops were full of brass instruments. Ship-building, colliery and factory bands were still finding it difficult to survive and the movement of the population was beginning to swamp London and the South East taking bandsmen with it.

This is not to say all brass bands were in the doldrums. It was a scene without any set pattern. In some parts of the country, 'house full' signs were posted at concert halls and in others, brass band concerts were cancelled because of abysmal support. The richer bands intensified their efforts to poach players but did not have much success with the colliery bands which had a fierce loyalty to their villages. The financial success of privately-owned coal mines was patchy. Some were in good or fair production, some were run down and others were just existing waiting for the demand for coal to pick up.

This meant some colliery bands played with new instruments and were resplendent in braided uniforms, whilst others were shabbily dressed. Some bandsmen in the mines were laid off and spent their time on the street corners and prey to the 'mumblers' from the crack bands who were well aware of any star player kicking his heels all day with nothing to do. It is to the eternal credit of such bands as Snibstone Colliery, Higglescote and Elliston that all offers to join these better bands were steadfastly refused.

The League of Band Associations, whose aim was to secure co-operation between the various brass band associations, viewed with ever-increasing despondency the withdrawal of invitations by local authorities to play in municipal parks. Southend established a precedent by saying to the bands, 'If you do come, you come for nothing but we would have no objection to a collection being held by yourselves.' This was nothing new but, surprisingly, the council did not want a cover charge payable from the collection. Most councils demanded this as a contribution towards the wear and tear of the bandstand. The Southend Borough Police were not too happy with the idea of a collection and said so. On the first day policemen moved amongst the crowd to make sure the various regulations governing collection of money in public places were not infringed.

The British Bandsman

WEEKLY JOURNAL FOR BRASS BANDS

FOUNDED 1887

No. 1,751 [Registered at the General Post Office as a Newspaper]   SATURDAY, OCTOBER 5th, 1935.   PRICE 3d.

NATIONAL BAND FESTIVAL 193

SPECIAL NUMBER

Legislation was always hovering around brass bands. The recent Children's and Young Persons' Employment Act was interpreted by local government officials as an Act, which, *inter lia*, prevented boys of school age playing in brass bands. The Band League, which was backed to the hilt by *The British Bandsmen*, told the municipal associations that their attitude was gross interference with the joys of children to engage in music-making and used the words 'stuff and nonsense'. The Minister of Education was petitioned. It brought a woolly reply but after a month or two the Minister did allow some flexibility. Immediately the secretary of the Stanford-le-Hope Band in Essex told *The British Bandsman* he had 25 school children ready to join and appealed for second-hand instruments.

'It is encouraging to note', wrote the editor, 'that provincial papers are reporting an interest in brass band concerts at the seaside.' Dover, however, favoured jazz bands at the expense of brass bands. The editor stuck his neck out and said, 'Don't worry, jazz is only a passing phase'. Dover eventually relented because the Chamber of Commerce was alarmed as holiday-makers were going to Herne Bay where they could listen to brass bands on the town promenade, whereas the jazz bands in Dover attracted 'all the kittenish girls and their rowdy strangely-dressed men'.

King George V celebrated his silver jubilee and again the extraordinary sight of street celebration parties with over-laden tables, bunting and games was seen. Everywhere at these community get-togethers, brass bands gave their services freely. They dipped into their funds to provide cigarettes for the adults and balloons for the children.

It was the year of the cigarette. Consumption soared as pay packets grew. It was a time of low prices with little inflation and men bought packets of 20 rather than five. Silver cigarette cases, suitably engraved, were given to retiring bandsmen together with presentation boxes of 200 cigarettes. *The Daily Post* recorded one bandsman being given a box of 200 Turkish cigarettes, a silver case and 'a new flame lighter.'

Bandsmen at contests placed cigarettes at a strategic place by their seat ready for a puff or two in between and at the end of playing a piece. At the Reading contest it got out of hand and the promoters banned all smoking on the stage. Slowly, stage discipline was tightened and at the Belle Vue contest the deportment of the bands on stage contributed to the sense of occasion as hundreds of players massed to play the *National Anthem* conducted by Henry Iles.

Opposite: The British Bandsman's first special issue.

The vast crowd of men and women, many of whom only the year before had listened sympathetically to seditious speeches and the playing of *The Red Flag*, sang with great emotion. The press, which always gave Belle Vue extensive coverage, made great play of this. One Manchester paper said, 'No one is more loyal than the working man'. Another referring to this 'inspiring spectacle' said, 'The brass bandsman is the result of an amazing and vigorous growth of a hitherto specialist type of music. It is now no more specialist.'

There is no doubt whatsoever that this growth of the brass band demanded diligent dedication. Time off for banding was often refused but it is refreshing (or alarming) to read that many players did risk the sack. At Belle Vue a player arrived with the Besses o' th' Barn Band. He had worked all night down the mine at the coal face and had no sleep. His enthusiasm was too much for his physical resources but he hung on by the skin of his teeth until his solo flugel horn part had been played. Then he slumped unconscious in his chair, his instrument clattering away across the stage.

Belle Vue was an outstanding patriotic success, and although Henry Iles was not a man to preen, he did savour to the full the applause that rippled around in the press, 'this great man' and 'the saviour of the brass band' were some of the headlines. Inevitably the pendulum swung the other way and the whisper of self-interest became louder. It was said, wherever the bandsmen met, that Henry Iles would not bother with brass bands if there was nothing in it for him. Many thought he made hundreds of pounds out of Belle Vue and the Crystal Palace contests and concerts.

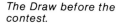

The Draw before the contest.

Sam Cope, knowing the truth, came to the rescue of his friend and wrote in *The British Bandsman*, 'Do not the readers know that if were not for Mr. Iles, the National Brass Band Club and the League of Band Associations would be in difficulties. He contributes £100 per year to each of them to further their cause. He has given £600 in trust to the Worshipful Company of Musicians. Perhaps these facts will enlighten people's minds.'

The *Guildhall Student* followed with, 'Henry Iles is a man of great intellect, robust in health and the father of the brass band movement.' The national press highlighted the huge amount of money now being received by the Performing Rights Society. The Society had 400,000 programmes under analysis and over two million others under its control and had just received £96,000 from the BBC. No matter how Henry Iles protested that he was not connected with the Society, there were vociferous doubters. Mr. Mackler, who worked closely with Mr. Iles at that time, says the allegations were entirely without foundation.

It was no coincidence that before 1935 was out, pen pictures and praiseworthy profiles of Mr. Iles appeared in many newspapers and magazines. Someone, somewhere was exerting influence.

28 *Success and disaster*

If the contributions from correspondents are taken out of *The British Bandsman* of 1936, it would be similar in style to what it is today. Alfred Mackler, editor in all but name, had introduced newsy, entertaining features supplemented with photographs. It was attractively laid out with little wasted space and modern print.

He was a young man, full of energy and quite capable of taking the twin responsibilities of the magazine and the Crystal Palace in his stride. It was important for him to travel around to listen to as many bands as possible, mainly because he was still responsible for the grading of the bands. If there is a place in the record book for someone who has heard more bands than any other person, then *he* can certainly stake his claim.

Mack, as everyone called him, brought to *The British Bandsman* the qualities of good journalism, good public relations work and musically, he was on equal terms with the composers of his day. He was the first person to publish a special edition to coincide with the Crystal Palace Contest and Festival and it was sold out on the day of publication.

As he sat back for a week or two before he began to think about the 1937 contest, disaster struck. On the night of November 30, 1936, the Crystal Palace was destroyed by fire. This mecca for bandsmen lay gutted with only the well-known twin towers still standing sorrowfully in the twisted girders, broken glass and carpet of ash. Such a calamity was fully reported in the press and included much background information regarding its use. The story of the brass band contest figured prominently together with the role of Henry Iles.

Readers of the press, unaware of his connection with the Crystal Palace and brass bands, began to take an interest in this extraordinary man. An editorial in *The Caernafon Herald* said: 'It is time Henry Iles was honoured as a public benefactor'.

Bad news as the destruction of the Crystal Palace was, it could have been worse. At least it gave long notice for another venue to be found. The offices of *The British Bandsman* hummed with activity. Messrs Cope, Mackler, Sharpe and the indefatigable Miss Frances Bantin, private secretary to Mr. Iles, were in almost constant session reviewing the situation and, with Henry Iles supplying almost unlimited funds, the Alexandra Palace in North London was chosen to carry on the tradition.

Memories of the Crystal Palace are still indelible in the minds of many bandsmen and it is spoken of reverently wherever older bandsmen meet. It was a surprise when the new venue was announced because it was believed 'Champagne Charlie', as Mr. Iles was nicknamed by some, would transfer it to Belle Vue. He had spent thousands of pounds improving this place. The grounds and the zoo had been enlarged, a sunken garden, the pride of the North, had been constructed and the facilities and amenities were now the envy of its continental equivalents.

But there was no way the National Festival was going to leave the capital. Sam Cope *et al* were determined it should remain even if it was held in Battersea Power Station. It is interesting to note that whilst many residents of Sydenham had complained to the police about the once-a-year disruption to their lives, it is surprising how many of them made their way to North London to attend Alexandra Palace. It had become a date in their calendar like the Boat Race and the football Cup Final.

King George V died and, as always, events connected with royalty meant a fillip for brass bands. They were in great demand at memorial and civic services. Football clubs hurriedly re-engaged them to play the *National Anthem* and solemn melodies at league matches.

Hardly had these echoes faded and the mourning become less acute than *The British Bandsman* was advising bands to think positively of the Coronation Year ahead. Uniform manufacturers were tempting bands with discount offers and advertised, 'the time of the Coronation is the time to look the part'.

Some bands accepted engagements to lead the marches of Sir Oswald Moseley and his political party, known as 'blackshirts', but not for long. They had initially thought it was just the same as leading a miner's gala but very soon cancelled them as the purpose of the marches became clear. The editor thundered, 'Have nothing to do with these people.'

Yet again 1936 was hailed by the popular newspapers as the year the slump would end. It would not end this year, next year or the year after. Stanley Baldwin resigned as Prime Minister and Neville Chamberlain took his place. There was a small surge in the economy prompted by an equally small surge in the production of arms as the government foresaw a potential threat to world peace by Adolf Hitler.

Not that there was any hint of this in *The British Bandsman*. Bands still played for mayoral cheer funds, for funds for the unemployed, the under-privileged, for outings to the seaside, for war memorial and cottage hospitals and food parcels 'for the poor and hungry at Christmas time'. This charitable activity did not go unnoticed. *The Glasgow Herald* told its readers of the tremendous goodwill generated by brass bands within its own class and wrote, 'We must have the welfare of brass bands at heart.'

The welfare to which it referred did not extend, apparently, to the various celebration committees set up throughout the land. The bands were either expected to play for nothing at coronation festivities or engage in a marathon for a pittance. The Waddesdon and District Coronation Committee asked the editor to name a band to take part in the local festivities. He was quite shocked to read what would be required of it. The terms were for the band to take part in the procession, play on the bandstand all afternoon and play for dancing in the village hall from 8.00 pm until 1.00 am. However, it was one of the few committees prepared to pay for the services of the band.

Other committees were decidedly autocratic and never offered payment. Bandmasters were arbitrarily summoned to attend these committees when they were told what was expected of the band. *The British Bandsman* was inundated with complaints. Several bands wrote to say that if they asked for payment they were accused of a lack of patriotism and disloyalty to the Throne. One bandmaster who asked for a few pounds to defray expenses was told by a committee chairman that he should hang his head in shame.

The editor came to the rescue and published a sample letter which should be sent to these dictatorial bodies. It read: 'Much as we would wish, we deeply regret that we find it impracticable to place £1,000 worth of property, with the necessary skilled attendance, and the subsequent risk of damage, at your disposal for the day, without a contract specifying suitable remuneration for the service rendered and the risk of our property necessarily encountered'.

It helped considerably but still some councils were saying in effect, 'if you persist in this disloyalty to the King then we do not want you.' A Colonel J.C.O. White was reported as saying, 'We ought not to deal with these mercenary brass bands. Leave it to me. I'll get a band from the barracks'. When he rang up under the 'old pals act' he found to his horror there was none available. Eventually it came to his notice that the brass band contained eight army reservists. He attended the bandroom and reminded them of their duty and, of course, the band played for nothing. Unfortunately the name of the band was not given, but it was from the Colchester area.

Where there were no brass bands, some district councils gave a grant from the rates for one to be formed. In Surrey, all the brass bands were fully booked for the celebrations. Knaphill Village, jealous of its neighbours, decided not to be outdone and somehow formed their own. An anonymous donor paid for the Malvern Imperial Silver Band to have a new set of instruments. A public meeting was called in Theale, Berkshire, specifically to form a brass band and it received overwhelming support.

Henry Iles pulled out all stops for the Belle Vue Coronation Year contest which ended with the 'Great Coronation Fireworks Spectacular'. The beer flowed freely but the editor had counselled to 'beware of too much hospitality on the great day of rejoicing' and the day went well. Brass bands were in great demand for the rest of the year. *The British Bandsman* thought this was a happy year because brass bands could be heard broadcasting on all regions. Perhaps, more truthfully, it was because its circulation had increased and it could now publish 20 pages.

In a couple of months *The Sunday Times* wrote, 'Brass Bands are vanishing. Are the days of the brass bands for three quarters of a century now numbered? Until recent years no village considered its life complete without one. The increasing competition of jazz, however, is giving the brass bands a struggle for existence. Musicians who have trained in the village bands are deserting them to take up more lucrative posts with dance bands. Unable to maintain their playing strength, some brass bands have gone out of existence. Others have suspended their activities until they can train new players.'

The Sunday Dispatch said the passing of brass bands will be regretted. 'A great change has taken place. Players no longer play for fame but play for guineas in the dance bands.' *The Daily Express, Huddersfield Examiner* and Scottish papers all printed doleful news. The Bradshaw Prize Brass Band had to disband because 30 members had deserted it in the past six years.

The editor said all this comment was balderdash and said: 'We advise the Jeremiahs to read the virile reports of the doings of our bands which are chronicled in our paper week by week.' And he had a point. On 3 July, 20,000 people attended the Romford Brass Band Festival and a fortnight later the Fairfield Festival was a sell-out. He had to admit, however, that the introduction of 'carnival bands' in the North Midlands had accellerated a decline in that area of brass band activity.

Newspapers had to eat their words when the first Alexandra Palace National Contest took place. 'House-full' notices were put up and for the first time cinema news-reel cameras were present and shown all over the country. Audiences were amazed at the scenes. Some thought it a semi-religious affair because this year the audience in Alexandra Palace stood to sing *Through All The Changing Scenes of Life, Now Thank We All Our God* and finally *Lead Kindly Light*. *The Muswell Hill Record* wrote, 'there is not much wrong with the British nation if these hymns can appeal to the heart and sentiment of men and women'.

Henry Iles was very impressed with the cinema coverage of his beloved Festival and saw the cinematograph industry as one of growth. He had witnessed the enormous success of Alexander Korda's London Films, the film studios springing up around the country and the building of large and ornate cinemas in every city. When the opportunity arose for him to invest in this industry he risked all, but unfortunately lost the lot. In 1938 he was made bankrupt.

It did not make any visible difference to his energy and ambition. He still mixed as an equal with the good and the great. His friends rallied around him and wherever he appeared on the stage he was loudly cheered. The rank-and-file of the movement could scarcely believe it. Was it really true that this man, who was larger than life, was really broke?

Alas it was true. All his assets were cobbled together but they were insufficient to satisfy his creditors. Although this was a terrible blow to his life style, it never affected his love of brass bands.

His first task, and to which he devoted much of his time, was to discharge the bankruptcy. He did not spend his days bewailing his fate but worked out a priority of aims. He was determined to play his debts in full. It took time but he held his head high and eventually achieved his goal. *The Daily Herald* called him 'A hero amongst men.'

With a tightening of the belt *The British Bandsman* survived the crisis and was soon well into the silly season of the year. *The Manchester Dispatch* said, 'Brass bands are disappearing because they play music meant for light orchestras'. Its sister paper, *The Manchester Evening Chronicle*, wrote that the whole of the brass band movement was in 'dissolution'. *The Glasgow Daily Herald* said, 'This decline is due to bandsmen behaving like schoolboys inasmuch as a weak bandmaster is like a weak headmaster and so the bandsmen play truant from rehearsals'. *The Eastbourne Gazette*, calling brass bands 'industrial bands', bade farewell to the bands because they were unable to play the new swing music. *The Southport Weekly* drew attention to the fact that only a year ago bands were engaged to play ten times in the council parks, now it was only five times and next year there would be a strong possibility that brass bands would not appear at all. It was left to *The Courier* to sum it all up. 'Goodbye brass bands, we shall never see your like again.'

All good rollicking stuff but unfortunately the BBC believed it and reappraised its policy towards the broadcast time given to brass band music. As a result of this there were no evening brass band broadcasts. The editor tried hard to persuade the programme controllers that all this newspaper talk was grossly exaggerated. The BBC relented and Soham Comrades Band was given a 30-minute slot but only on the London region programme.

The National Band Festival, 1938 with J. Henry Iles conducting the massed bands at the evening concert in the Alexandra Palace.

1938 deepened into pessimism and gloom as Hitler made ominous noises for more territory to satisfy his expansionist demands. *The British Bandsman* called the autumn one of 'anxious times'. War seemed imminent. Brass bands played at outdoor meetings where crowds were asked to join the Air Raid Precautions organisation which local councils were hurriedly trying to expand. *The Sheffield Independent* said, 'As an antidote to these situation nerves the brass bands should take to the streets.'

No wonder the Alexandra Palace contest that year reverberated to thousands of voices singing *Oh God Our Help in Ages Past* and the *National Anthem*. It brought headlines such as, 'A most moving occasion', 'First class patriotism' and 'Our pride is our Anchor'. Not everyone was happy with the agreement between His Majesty's Government and the Chancellor of Germany over the vexed question of Czechoslovakia. It won a year's respite but no more.

No one, however, could say the country was not behind the King in these perilous times. A good example was when the Arsenal Football Club won the league championship. When the final whistle blew, the capacity crowd invaded the pitch, their exuberance too much for the stewards to contain. Children were in grave danger of being engulfed and downtrodden. The Arsenal brass band immediately struck up with *God Save the King*. The excited, galloping, whooping crowd suddenly stopped as one man, removed their caps and sang the words with remarkable fervour.

29 *World War II*

1939 began full of hope and people looked forward to a year in which they could enjoy their leisure time without the awful shadow of war darkening their lives. A staggering figure of two million people listened to the bands playing in the London parks during the summer months. With a little more money available for luxuries, thousands flocked to the seaside but, by the time they returned, there was a nagging fear that peace was about to be shattered.

Hitler had marched contemptuously into Czechoslovakia and had laid claim to the port of Danzig in Poland. The country held its breath as it had done less than a year before. On 3 September, 1939 we were at war with Germany. Unlike the outbreak of war in 1914, it came as no surprise to the editor. He and Henry Iles had made contingency plans for it to be printed elsewhere if necessary and to reduce its publication to once a month.

The expected air raids did not happen for some time and to most people it was uncannily normal. Henry Iles appealed to the bands to carry on as usual. It was not too difficult to manage; a few reservists and young conscripts departed but for most of the time, bands played with a full complement. There was none of the jingoistic language employed by the editor and proprietor in the last war, only a mood of profound sadness that the country had once more to take up the challenge of Germany.

Henry Iles wrote: 'May God bless you all in this great trial. We will win and crush to dust these arch enemies whose despotism, wickedness and brutality are as bad as anything in the known history of the world. Again, God bless you and yours and bring us all together, and pray it will be soon, to our National Band Festival.'

For the next six months contests continued locally and although much reduced carried on for the rest of the war. Bands were able to present a full complement of players except where the twin problems of reservists and those of conscription age monopolised the band. Stavely Brass Band for example lost over a third of its players because of this. So unusual was the atmosphere in the early months that *The British Bandsman* only gave the war a passing reference or two. The magazine was reduced to eight pages and produced on inferior paper but all the trade firms continued to advertise.

The necessary imposition of the 'black-out' posed problems. Rehearsals suffered and contests and concerts were mostly over before nightfall. It was at these gatherings that news of departed bandsmen was swopped. There was no shortage of letters from France or, for that matter, from the rest of Northern Europe until the fateful blitzkrieg by the Germans. One of the last letters out of Holland was from a subscriber to *The British Bandsman* and gave no hint of disaster.

In May and June the sweet bitterness of the evacuation of Dunkirk kept the British people spellbound. Brass bands squared their shoulders and made sure that none of the dishevelled, bewildered troops disembarking at the Channel ports went without entertainment in the hastily-prepared rest and rehabilitation camps. It has to be realised that if it were not for these brass bands there would have been no bands at all. Military bands had been disbanded rather hastily on the outbreak of war and those which had survived the axe had lost stands, instruments and music during the rapid advance of the German army across France.

It was during the Battle of Britain that brass bands excelled themselves. They played in the streets, parks, factories, mines and dockyards only too pleased to be part of the national pride now manifesting itself as Great Britain, and the Commonwealth stood alone to fight. This pride showed itself in many little ways as the court trumpeter at Liverpool was to demonstrate. When the Assize judge made his solemn way in procession to the courtroom it was always a traditional practice for a trumpeter to sound a fanfare. It brought smiles to the faces when he played instead *There'll always be an England.* This tremendous contribution to public morale did not go unnoticed by the national newspapers and in July 1940, the War Office re-appraised its policy and, as a result, military bands were restored to their regiments.

Alfred Mackler joined the army and Albert Sharpe went to the War Office. Henry Iles and Sam Cope, now in his eighties, delegated more and more work to Miss Frances Bantin. Her work during the war years went largely unnoticed but she, more than anyone, was responsible for the continuing publication of the magazine often under indescribable conditions.

The 'blitz' raged against this country mainly from September 1940 to May 1941 and was directed at the big cities and ports. It was designed to savage our war effort and to cower the civilian population into submission. Brass bands and Salvation Army bands stood shoulder to shoulder playing amidst the rubble in all weathers. Older members have vivid memories of these bands moving from one blackened smouldering street to another stricken area to bring succour and cheer to the stunned survivors and, in doing so, renewing faith in themselves and their country.

Small villages and towns did not escape serious damage as many lost bombers unloaded their cargo indiscriminately. Wherever there was considerable damage, these bands emerged without being asked, maybe just half-a-dozen or so to play the songs of the day amongst the destruction and sadness of war. The Severn Tunnel Band played in a ruined part of Newport and a minute's silence was observed for the many dead. There were few dry eyes as the band followed this with the playing of *Aberystwyth*.

The offices of *The British Bandsman* in the heart of London were almost twice blasted out of existence. It narrowly escaped complete destruction during the intense bombing on the night of 11/12 January, 1941 when hundreds of enemy bombers criss-crossed over the capital.

The staff of the magazine, in common with all other workers throughout the country, somehow made their way to work. The morning of the 12th January was not the Central London they had left the night before. In the immediate vicinity of *The British Bandsman* office, army engineers were blowing up dangerous buildings. Fractured water mains and damaged gas pipes placed the offices out of bounds. Firemen were still dampening down the large fires and worse, the stench of sewage was everywhere. Frances Bantin eventually reached the office. It had no windows, the ceilings had collapsed burying the desks, there was no electricity, no water, no heat and no telephone. The chaos was heartbreaking. Hundreds of sheets of music, documents, memoranda, books and diaries were lost, all of which would have been invaluable to a researcher, but the magazine was published on time.

It was physically impossible for Sam Cope to come in every day and Henry Iles and Miss Bantin edited the paper. The small staff sat all day in the offices with their overcoats and gloves on, writing, editing and posting by the light of candles and hurricane lamps. The postal service was unreliable and the staff were often tired out from walking to and from work as the transport system buckled and nearly died. When the telephone was restored, horrific news reached them of the casualties suffered by bandsmen in Liverpool, Hull, Plymouth, Bristol, Manchester and Coventry whose brass band was practically wiped out overnight.

Badly blitzed areas were visited by politicians and service chiefs to stiffen the backs of the bomb-weary people. All, of course, highly commendable but *The Liverpool Post* wrote: 'A good brass band is worth a spate of speeches where morale is concerned' and the editor of *The Western Mercury* said, 'If a bright spot is needed in these dreary times send for a brass band'. *The Bristol Evening World* summed it up, 'Brass bands revive the spirit of the people'.

And contesting continued throughout. The Clydebank Burgh Band mustered its members and entered the Edinburgh Charities Band Association contest. It marched down historic Princes Street and into the enclosure in the castle gardens, heads held high and a swing to their stride a guardsman would have been proud to follow. Nothing Hitler could throw at them would stop these bands contesting. Those who saw this sight still remember having 'goose pimples all over' as the band marched proudly to the march *Slaidburn*. *The British Bandsman* wrote that it made the dark clouds less formidable.

Hundreds of brass bands were formed by other bands as players were drafted into the war effort. There were Auxiliary Fire Service, National Fire Service, Special Constabulary, Civil Defence and Air Raid Wardens' Bands, British Legion, Ambulance, Air Training Corps, Munition Workers and Church and Bible Class bands. Home Guard bands were established by existing bands. The Great Central and Metropolitan Railway Brass Band for instance, became the band of the Home Guard (12th Middlesex Regiment).

Home guard bands were just about tolerated by the War Office because they were excused duty in the majority of regiments and this time was used for rehearsal. Despite this lack of interest, Home Guard bands and others, played in fund-raising activities which brought thousands of people on to the streets. Sometimes processions marched two or three miles with often 12 bands taking part. They played for War Weapons Weeks, Spitfire Weeks, Naval Launch and Tank Weeks. They played indoors and outdoors for Anglo-Soviet Weeks, Mrs. Churchill's Russian Fund, British Prisoner-of-War and Red Cross Parcel Funds.

They were the toast of the fund raisers because they never refused any request. Yet these bandsmen were working all day and half the night on the war effort production lines. The players in the Morris Motors Band did not take kindly to the clumsy statement issued by Lord Nuffield that work in his factories must come first. It was soon pointed out to him that all rehearsals and performances were in the players' own time. Colliery bandsmen had to swallow hard when the various managers told them they were getting out and about too much and if work suffered then 'woe betide them'. All very understandable in the straining of every sinew to equip the war machine.

Nevertheless, miners came straight off shifts to play in their bands to give concerts for the troops stationed in the most bleak and desolate parts of the North. Bedlington Collieries Band became quite famous as a show band. Henry Iles, with full support from other stalwarts in the brass band world, promoted stupendous massed band concerts. In 1942, Besses o'th' Barn, Fodens and Black Dyke brass bands played at the Royal Albert Hall, London and Belle Vue, Manchester to packed houses. The daily papers were enraptured and *The Times* said the concerts recalled the great days of the Crystal Palace and headlines such as 'Brass band patriotism blazes forth' appeared.

This year Great Britain was bursting at the seams with troops of the allied forces and often were entertained by brass bands at concerts. As a tribute to the Russians it was not unusual for concerts to end with the *Internationale* as well as *God Save the King*. Bands went out of their way to obtain copies of various national anthems. At one concert, there were in the audience about 50 members of a battalion of the Free French Forces. At the end of the concert the band played the *Marseillaise* instead of our own anthem. The French troops immediately sprang to attention and sang the stirring words amid emotional scenes and great applause. What makes this report interesting is that one can detect the hidden hand of the censor. The band was not named, except it was a brass band; the theatre was not named and the concert took place somewhere on the south coast.

The budget requirements of the Chancellor of the Exchequer could never be satisfied and the Chancellor, Sir Kingsley Wood, imposed purchase tax upon all musical instruments. Henry Iles, now styled as Editor-in-Chief, lambasted the Chancellor, 'It is stupid and an audacity and I have told him so'. All to no avail; although George Bernard Shaw, the celebrated music critic, urged all brass bands to march *en masse* upon the Houses of Parliament and blow the walls of Jericho down. The press were on the side of the music makers and called the imposition of the tax 'heathenish, insensitive and a backward step'.

But the bands lived with it as they had lived and coped with all the other stringent restrictions and nuisances which total war effort demanded. They had coped and thrived in spite of petrol rationing, clothing coupons for uniforms, bombed band rooms smashed instruments, depleted membership and, it must always be remembered, existing on a monotonous diet of rationed food, the calorie content of which had been fixed at just an acceptable level and no more.

There was never any reference in the magazine to this 'glorious war' as had been the case in 1914-1918 and, in fact, it was seldom mentioned. Henry Iles did permit himself in *The British Bandsman* to say the battle of El Alamein was the turning point of the war and bands should now prepare for peace in 1943. At no time was a list of casualties published and no exhortations for bandsmen to volunteer. Even when the war ended it was greeted by the editor with subdued relief.

The last years of the war found *The British Bandsman* almost unable to pay its way. The money which seemed to have come from a bottomless pit was all but gone and Henry Iles produced his magazine on a very tight budget. Coupled with a circulation figure fixed by Government Decree, advertising was inadequate to help the finances. Consequently Mr. Iles and Miss Bantin were forced to print contributions from outside correspondents, using pseudonyms, without too much supervision and this, from time to time, caused a few eyebrows to be raised. As Geoffrey Brand said when he became editor, 'what people write anonymously is totally different to that which they write under their own names'. The poor old Salvation Army bands were still pilloried in print. It was asked why Salvation Army bandsmen could play in the bands of the Brigade of Guards but were barred by The Salvation Army from playing in the Home Guard bands.

In 1943, a momentous decision was taken by Harry Mortimer when he was music advisor to the BBC. He and Henry Iles decided the time was ripe to test public reaction to massed band concerts conducted by famous names in the orchestral world. Using *The British Bandsman* to spread the gospel, these concerts caught the imagination of the public with a vengeance. Sir Malcolm Sargent went to Belle Vue, Sir John Barbirolli to the Royal Albert Hall and Sir Adrian Boult travelled to Wolverhampton, Birmingham, Huddersfield and every other major city which had a concert hall.

Millions heard these amazing concerts on the radio and the ground was thoroughly prepared for the popularity massed band concerts enjoy today. A measure of this popularity can be gauged by press reaction. The *News Chronicle* wrote: 'There is something distinctly British about these massed band concerts'. *The Sunday Times* said, 'An orchestra would have found it difficult to equal the performance of these brass bands'. *The Birmingham*

No. 37 Area Fire Force band formed in 1940. All saw active service. After disbandment in 1945 renamed North Kent Silver Band.

Post wrote, 'Absolutely incredible, unbelievable, a wonderful life-lasting memory'.

In 1944, the editor, Henry Iles received the Order of the British Empire in the King's Birthday Home Front Honours List. Someone said it was good to see him once again smoking an outsize cigar. Hardly had this excitement died down when he narrowly escaped death in a serious railway accident. He tumbled around in his compartment before being thrown clear of the tangled debris. He was badly bruised and suffered multiple cuts. Almost his first words were, 'Well, I've survived the blitz and the flying bombs only to be injured by a railway train'.

His office in London suffered blast damage from the assault on the capital by the flying bombs. More than a thousand of these exploded killing 60,000 civilians and the production of *The British Bandsman* was hazardous. The staff had to evacuate the premises every time the telling rhythm of the bomb motor was heard. Throughout the war the building which housed the offices of the magazine was badly damaged eight times by enemy action.

As the allied armies advanced across France, the flying bomb launching pads were captured; the South East and London relaxed. The Home Guard was stood down and many of their bands reverted to their original names. The refreshing feeling of

The band of the 6th Bn. Essex Home Guard 1944. It contained many brass bandsmen and a fair sprinkling of Salvation Army musicians despite the prevailing S.A. rules. Most of the men in this photograph learned to play as children picking up their art without any formal training.

no longer being in the front line meant a more leisurely approach to living and people began to reflect on the future and what the final peace would bring in its wake.

Henry Iles pondered on the future of the National Festival and Contest. Already bands were asking him about its revival and he desperately wanted it to continue when the war ended. He also knew that he had no money to finance it.

Although his standing in the City of London was such that he could have borrowed the money he steadfastly set his face against the loans which friendship could have made available. He had no one to turn to for advice for most of his friends had died and Sam Cope was nearly 90 years old. Miss Bantin declared he was 'as broody as a hen'. It was she who suggested he turn to his influential friends outside the city life and approach friends in politics, music, the law and newspapers.

He turned to the newspaper barons. Through these contacts he received a whisper that *The Daily Herald* management was casting around for somewhere to hang its banner in the circulation war to come when printing restrictions were relaxed. As as result of this he had talks with *The Daily Herald* promotions department and secured its interest in the Belle Vue festival. This ear the festival was quite a remarkable success with over 20,000 applications for tickets.

This so impressed *The Daily Herald* that the newspaper promptly organised a massed band concert in Newcastle and engaged Harry Mortimer to conduct. This, too, was an eye-opener for the management as hundreds had to be turned away at the door.

Henry Iles sat back and waited. He had done everything possible to interest the commercial managers of the paper. He had attended several meetings, opened his books and given the financial director everything for which he had been asked. He could do no more. If his efforts failed the National Contest would fail and it would have a domino effect on contesting in the country. Miss Bantin said it was a harrowing, miserable time.

Again and again he enquired if any decision had been made to take over the National but always *The Daily Herald* was non-committal, mainly because it was entering unknown promotional territory. Weeks went by. Henry Iles was resigned to the National being lost and probably taking *The British Bandsman* with it. One day, 'a joyful day', Miss Bantin said, he was summoned to the newspaper offices and was told in the most cordial manner that the management had agreed to take it over almost in its entirety. The result of the meeting was to remain secret until a release formula was agreed. It was decided the first public announcement of the agreement would be made in *The British Bandsman*.

When it appeared it was nothing less than a bombshell. Henry Iles and the National had been indivisible for four decades. Bandsmen could not or would not believe the news. Henry Iles told them *The Daily Herald* would not only underwrite the National but would review the method of grading bands, the rules at present governing the National and the conditions under which bands would be allowed to enter. Eventually, he said, *The Daily Herald* would become the sole owner of the National Brass Band Contest and Festival.

On January 27, 1945 *The Daily Herald* published the following statement:

The Daily Herald *has decided to organise and sponsor a series of area contests in which every part of Great Britain will participate. Handsome cash prizes and trophies will be provided for contests in each district and any profits therefrom will be devoted to charity.*

To say Henry Iles was quite overcome that the future of the National was secure is an understatement. He wrote, 'I shall be able to start my last journey to one's eternal rest feeling happy that the future prosperity and progress of our bands will be in safe keeping. May the good God's blessing rest on all our effort to attain this end. Long live *The Daily Herald*.'

Everyone kept their fingers crossed as gradings were agreed and the first area contests approached. There was no precedent and therefore no judgement value. Henry Iles gave all his energy to make them a success but alternated between optimism and pessimism. He wrote that the great honour was to be given to the new Midland area. On Easter Monday, 1945 the new untried area contest began and the telephone wires hummed between *The British Bandsman* and *The Daily Herald*. It was a great success and tickets were sold on the black market.

Coincidence or not, but since *The Daily Herald* became responsible for the National, news of brass bands activities, contests and concerts disappeared overnight from the rest of the national press and this did not go unnoticed by bandsmen. Some brass band associations said the involvement of *The Daily Herald* was a retrograde step and Henry Iles received some abusive telephone calls. People, including famous names in the brass band movement, were anxious that 'this labour paper' did not extend its interest to the Belle Vue and other prestigious contests. These questions were asked: 'Are they going to run all contests?' 'We must make sure *The Daily Herald* does not get too big for its boots' and 'Are we but pawns in the battle for circulation?'

There were calls to boycott the area contests and a rebellion looked likely. *The Daily Herald* protested to Henry Iles whose patience finally snapped. He wrote in *The British Bandsman* 'if *The Daily Herald* had not come along when it did, then believe me, the great National Brass Band Festival would have been no more and, despite what you say, you have neither the organisation nor the finance to run it yourselves.' He repeated this at meetings of associations up and down the country and always ended these words by pulling out the empty linings of his trouser pockets to demonstrate quite dramatically that he was still broke.

Not that all the bands were his enemies; far from it. They saw the enormous first prize of 200 guineas as something well worth having a go for. Those which knew in their heart of hearts they did not stand much of a chance of winning this large sum of money said this would end the friendly rivalry between bands and lower section bands. The latter thought the Championship Section should now be classed as the 'Professional' section.

The contest was a success but it is surprising how many, who should have known better, dubbed it all as 'a flash-in-the-pan. What this sum of money did was to redouble rehearsal time and renew dedication to banding. Henry Iles wanted the new National to be a huge success and told bands to beg, borrow but not steal clothing coupons 'for new uniforms will attract the flashing eyes of the opposite sex'.

The last year of the war ended on a curious note. Something happened which would have been totally unthinkable a couple of years previously. Eric Ball was appointed music director of *The British Bandsman*. He had been the popular and most learned bandmaster of The Salvation Army International Staff Band for 19 months when, in 1944, he suddenly resigned. Readers looked in vain in the magazine for the reason leading to his departure but it only warranted a passing mention.*

One thing is for certain; this appointment was going to have a profound effect on every aspect of the brass band movement in the future.

*The full story is given in a book by Brindley Boon called *The Story of the International Staff Band* published by Record Greetings Ltd. 1985.

30   *The Daily Herald has second thoughts*

The demobilisation of brass bandsmen after the war was more gradual and more efficiently carried out than in 1918. Again their colleagues welcomed them back with open arms and proved the word 'brotherhood' was no cliché.

They returned to the austerity measures announced by Sir Stafford Cripps, The Chancellor of the Exchequer, whose efforts to improve the conditions of the people were well nigh impossible. The country had insufficient dollars to purchase American goods and the gold reserves were falling at an alarming rate. Drastic cuts were made, imports of food curtailed and the rationing of many items continued. Bands called emergency meetings to discuss their future as money was scarce. They struggled through 1946 on a shoestring hoping, as did *The British Bandsman's* New Year message, that 1947 would be a better year.

It got off to a bad start. Its winter was the worst since 1881 with a depth of snow affecting mobility for several weeks. There was a chronic shortage of fuel and by Government decree, made under the State of Emergency Regulations to conserve electricity, periodicals could not be published. In consequence of this *The British Bandsman* failed to appear for two weeks. The harsh climate delayed the recovery of brass bands to the level of activity they enjoyed before the war. The New Year also heralded an increase in the number of unemployed. Nearly two and a half million people were out of work and it was only because of the sheer love of banding and perseverance against the economic odds that some survived.

Once the winter was over, the bands peeped out and soon famous bands began to tour the country. Would there be a return to normality, asked *The British Bandsman*? Certainly Henry Iles was soon his old campaigning self, harrassing the Chancellor to reduce the crippling purchase tax he had imposed on all musical instruments. As the bands became more adventurous, and the available places for contests were filled, disturbing news reached the news desk. Some bandsmen had 'kicked over the traces', drinking too much and engaging in horseplay as contest results were announced.

The Yorkshire Area Contest was held in Easterbrook Hall, a place of worship. The church circuit stewards, mindful of the sense of the Holy, placed 'No Smoking' signs all around the hall. As the contest progressed the air was soon thick with cigarette smoke and the floor was littered with spent ends, bits of sandwiches, biscuit papers and cigarette packets. A member of the trustees attended and protested but was told in the most foul manner to get out. The Area Committee severely reprimanded the guilty and said this outrageous behaviour would result in ostracism by the whole of the music world.

At the Usher Hall, Edinburgh, the behaviour of one band was so bad that people left the hall in disgust. The Scottish Brass Band Association acted quickly and the offending band was suspended for one year. Compared with the hooliganism of the 1900s these were only pin-pricks but *The British Bandsman* campaigned to keep it under control.

The Luton Band rehearse for a broadcast in 1946 with Albert Coupe, conductor and Harry Mortimer, adviser Brass and Military bands, B.B.C. (lower left) giving a helping hand.

Eric Ball goes through the test piece, 'Salute to Freedom', written by him, with members of the Brighouse and Rastrick Band before the Open Championship 1946. Note the army style haircuts.

The problem of borrowed players surfaced again and one player was registered with three separate bands under three different names. Players were openly poached, officials were found with their hands in the till and it did seem as if the scene was well on course to 'normality'.

During 1947, the character of the magazine began to change. Henry Iles, now in his seventies, became quite nostalgic and no issue of *The British Bandsman* seemed complete without his contributions referring to his early days. Area correspondents were much too predictable in their approach to news and their writing was more descriptive than technical which made the content somewhat uninspiring.

Then, as so often happened in the history of the magazine, three contributors were welcomed to its columns who revitalised its contents. Eric Ball, a composer of note, wrote a discerning and sometimes provocative column. Mr. E. Vaughan Morris, writing under the name of David Nielson, gave all the news and gossip about the National Festival. He was the man responsible to *The Daily Herald* for running this event and, in later years, was to own the sole rights for its promotion. Harry Mortimer, already an international *force majeur* in the brass band world, found time to write for the magazine and gradually circulation increased from its all-time low of 1946.

On November 14, 1947, Sam Cope died aged 92 years. He had written for the magazine he founded 60 years ago well into his 90th year and the older bandsmen mourned his passing. No wonder the staff of the magazine dubbed this year one of the most dismal they had experienced. Brass bands were coping but the standard of living suffered because of the many unofficial strikes. Miss Bantin said later in her life, 'It was a very sad state of affairs but we kept going'. To rub salt into the wounds, the offices of the magazine were ransacked and valuable historical documents destroyed by frustrated burglars unable to find anything of value.

By and large, because there were some 'teething troubles', bands settled down to the new national contest structure which, with refinements, has stood the test of time. Henry Iles, now no longer responsible for the National, sat back and enjoyed all the congratulations which were heaped upon him at various band dinners to which he was invited as honoured guest.

At the beginning of the 1950s there were 27,000 names in the National Brass Band Registry and over 400 bands always clamouring to enter the fourth section of the National contest. Five million regularly listened to live excerpts broadcast from the National contest at the Royal Albert Hall. This exceptional interest in brass bands was further increased when the Morris Motors Brass Band became the first band to be televised. More importantly, these years noted a subtle change in the actual contesting season. For years the months of January, February, March and to some extent, April had been a sleepy time for bands but now the area qualifying championships were held in these months and, soon, other contest promoters followed suit. Bands, it seems, were rehearsing for something or other 52 weeks a year.

On May 29, 1951 Henry Iles, or to give him his full name, John Henry Iles, OBE JP, died and the entire band world was saddened. The messages of condolence which flooded into the office were all aptly summed up in the funeral tribute. 'We shall not see the likes of him again. The ageless godfather of brass bands is no more'. His death prompted changes at *The British Bandsman*. His son, Eric, became chairman of the company which owned the magazine, Miss Frances Bantin was appointed the

BRITISH BANDSMAN— JUNE 2, 1951

The British Bandsman

WEEKLY JOURNAL FOR BRASS BANDS

FOUNDED 1887

No. 2,570 (Registered at the General Post Office as a Newspaper)   SATURDAY, JUNE 2, 1951   Price 4

J. HENRY ILES, Esq., O.B.E.

It is my sad duty to announce to our readers the death of Mr. J. Henry Iles, O.B.E. He has been ill for some months, and passed to his rest on Tuesday, the 29th May.

Words cannot adequately express what his absence from the brass band world will mean. Everyone will agree that it has been his influence and work which have brought our brass bands to their present position. Since he first took an interest in them in 1898 it has been a labour of love to him to do everything he could for their advancement. His wonderful personality was acknowledged by everyone with whom he came into contact, and when one imagines contests at Belle Vue and the Royal Albert Hall without his genial presence, words fail one ; and in our brass band world at least, " we shall not see his like again."

Of my own feelings I can say little. I can claim to have been more closely associated with him than anyone outside his family, for many years. There will be a big void in my life, for Mr. Iles was not just my Chief, but a real personal friend. Many tributes will be paid to him, but none will be more sincere than that of

FRANCES E. BANTIN.

managing director and Eric Ball was invited to become the editor.

He had hardly sat down in the famous chair when rumours began to circulate that *The Daily Herald* was to make drastic changes in the structure of the National championships. Vaughan Morris, the efficient and popular administrator of this contest and festival, did his best but he was unable to prevent the change published in the following announcement.

When The Daily Herald, *with all its resources of a great national daily newspaper, began in 1945 its work for the welfare and development of the British Brass Band Movement, it was inspired by the thought of rebuilding the movement after the war years.* The Daily Herald's *contribution in organisation, presentation and enterprise has, as every bandsman knows, been carried out with vigour, enthusiasm and high regard for the traditions of the movement.*

Through The Daily Herald's *interest and active support the movement has witnessed the elimination of the borrowed player menace, the introduction of fair-for-all contesting rules and the bringing into effect the huge National Register, making it possible to keep a firm check and true picture of brass band personnel.*

It could not be expected that a national daily newspaper could carry on this work for the movement in perpertuity but in order that all it has done shall not be lost to the movement, contests will be carried on through the various organisations and associations and the national registry will be handed on.

The Daily Herald *is still interested in the welfare of the movement. It will sponsor the National Brass Band Championship Festival of Great Britain at the Royal Albert Hall to determine the Champion Band of Great Britain.*

The key sentence was 'contests will be carried on through the various organisations and associations.' It really meant that area committees found themselves trying to run the qualifying contests but with help from *The Daily Herald* if needed. It began a time when bands were under two separate masters but, by trial and error, the system worked; the indefatigable Vaughan Morris made sure it did.

Partly because of this, the general contesting scene did not produce a firm pattern. Some contests were abandoned but others took their place. The summer months became the doldrums whilst bands awaited the announcement of the test pieces to be played at the National and Open contests. As always, some bands made money but the poor struggled.

Help was at hand in 1951, the 'Festival of Britain Year', as councils needed the bands to add lustre to the celebration events. In 1952 the funds were stopped abruptly only to surface again in 1953, the year of the coronation of HM Queen Elizabeth II.

Fairford Silver Band at the armistice service in 1954 with some young beginners.

The same band in 1906 showing the influence of military style uniforms.

The press made much of the involvement of brass bands with the celebrations and, briefly, the bands enjoyed greater media coverage especially in the provincial press. All this coincided with the press tag, 'The Dawn of the new Elizabethan Era', and it gave everyone a feeling of optimism for the future because the early fifties were sombre indeed.

The seriousness of the 'uneven depression', as it was described by an economist, caused the editor to refer to these times as all very dispiriting and the pages of the magazine made for gloomy reading. One letter said, 'Please find room for lighter material.' In these years unemployment increased and some collieries were closed with their bands either disappearing with them or so depleted they could not contest. History was repeating itself and Eric Ball found himself using almost the same words as Sam Cope some 20 years previously when the rallying cry was, 'Stick together lads'. The press said that unpalatable changes were taking place in the industrial areas.

This time, however, there was no talk of the brass band scene disintegrating as there was in the 1930s; the movement was too

As soon as money became more available so did bands begin to buy new uniforms and move away from the military style. Bandsmen were more than happy to forget the last war. This picture shows Jack Atherton (left) with members of CWS (Manchester) Band, celebrating a success at Belle Vue.

Harry Mortimer with the BBC in 1959 and responsible for the broadcast of the National from the Royal Albert Hall.

resilient. The editor interpreted the pressures very well and wrote many excellent morale-boosting articles. In his editorial comment he explained again and again the Christian way, urging his readers to have faith in the future. Some of those bandsmen who lived through these years have said they did not often refer to his comments when in the bandroom but, in the quiet of their own homes found 'his little talks' a great comfort.

As *The British Bandsman* went into the sixties it reported an upsurge in brass band activity. Bands began to promote concerts and these multiplied as word spread of the profit which would be made. The industrialists were reporting better production figures, the amount of money in wage packets increased, television sets could be purchased and there was more money available for pleasure. Contests were well attended and the music trade was bouyant. So was the magazine. Eric Ball was now fully supported by Harry Mortimer, Vaughan Morris and a host of others including Alfred Ashpole and Dr. Harold Hind.

The genius of Eric Ball was in great demand throughout the world and he found himself unable to devote the time necessary to give of his best to the magazine. After 12 years he left. 'It was', he said, 'a most enjoyable period and I made many friends. the work of an editor is very demanding and I relied very heavily on my good friend Francis Bantin. I left to give more time for other musical pursuits.' He remained on the side-lines as music adviser.

Sir Arthur Bliss, Frank Wright, Denis Wright and Eric Ball who all conducted at the National Brass Band Festival, Royal Albert Hall 1959.

31 *Three exceptional editors and one wife*

Although Alfred Mackler had become, amongst other things, the brass band correspondent for *The Daily Herald, The British Bandsman* was his first love. He was still much sought after by various administrators in the band movement because of his great experience and, in April 1963, Mack, returned as editor of the magazine.

His qualifications were quite unique. Besides his editorial involvement with *The Daily Herald* and Odhams Press, he was the press officer for the National contest, a respected journalist and an excellent public relations officer. A rare bird indeed because he was also a musicologist and soon it all began to come together in the pages of *The British Bandsman*.

He revolutionised the format and the three wide columns gave way to four per page. This gave more space for headlines which he used somewhat in the style favoured by newspapers; they were lively, enterprising and to the point. Print was varied and photographs placed to complement the stories.

Since 1887 the true circulation figure had never been disclosed but the shake-out he gave to the magazine did attract more subscribers. The outgoing editor, Eric Ball, liked what he saw and commented it was a most welcome wind of change. Mack remained for just one year but, during his short period, he travelled extensively and got amongst the bands. In doing so the image of the magazine was improved.

He thought, quite properly, the editor should get involved in contests and concerts, a practice carried on to this day. It was a year in which he saw another change of direction by bands. His year co-incided with the burgeoning 'swinging sixties' to which brass bands were making a significant contribution. It was not long before they were playing arrangements of the songs of Paul

McCartney and John Lennon and the popular melodies of the famous 1960 groups. Many of these arrangements were written by talent within the brass bands and bands have proved adaptable to the changing mood of 'pop' ever since.

Mack moved on to bigger things and Eric Iles, the son of Henry Iles, asked Eric Ball to return. Eric Iles took a great interest in *The British Bandsman* although his ownership of the magazine was a very minor part of his business empire. Mr. Ball inherited a magazine which he has said since could not really be improved

A typical message from the editor, Eric Ball, to welcome 1960.

Comment

THERE are some occasions when it is almost impossible, and certainly not necessary to try to express ourselves in a new way, and in this the first issue of *The British Bandsman* for 1960 we cannot do better than wish our readers, simply and sincerely, A Happy New Year.

We are conscious of the fact that we depend upon a large number of well-wishers for our continued success, and we are particularly grateful to the many contributors to these columns who so willingly help us in our task.

As we move into the 1960's we shall hope to continue our crusade for increasingly high standards of music-making, believing that the cheap and meretricious brings no real satisfaction to mind and spirit, and has no lasting value; and that in the Brass Band Movement there are enough sincere lovers of the art to " leaven the whole lump " if only they will faithfully pursue their ideals.

We wish you all courage, gaiety of spirit, peace of heart and a quiet mind, and much happiness in your music-making.

EDITOR

upon. This was just as well because his troubles began immediately he came back.

Sadly, Miss Bantin died on April 5, 1964, after 34 years with the magazine. Her best epitaph was summed up in an after-dinner speech given by Henry Iles shortly before he died. He said, 'She is my continuity girl. People come and people go, bands change, contributors change and sometimes all is chaos but there, standing in the middle of it all, is my Miss Bantin, imperturbable, knowledgeable and without an ounce of panic within her'. Bandsmen all over the brass band world missed her.

A printing dispute closed the magazine for two weeks and when it reappeared it was reduced to only four pages. Fleet Street found itself at odds with itself, various unions and owners were

The first lady of the Brass Band Movement. Joined as secretary to Henry Iles in 1921. Photo taken in 1959 when she was General Manager of the 'B.B.'.

protecting their own interests as newspapers battled for readers and it was obvious there would be some casualties. Nevertheless it was a surprise to the majority of bandsmen when *The Daily Herald* ceased publication and, oddly, it was a genuine regret when one recalls the hostility towards it when it took over the National from Henry Iles.

The property in the National passed immediately to another Odhams Press newspaper, *The Sunday People*, with Mr. Vaughan Morris still fortunately in charge as administrator and producer of the National contest. There followed an extraordinary episode when the new owners, rightly or wrongly, restructured the path of competing bands to the ultimate finals at the Royal Albert Hall.

The management called a special meeting of the National Contesting Council, a body set up by the previous management, and gave it a simple brief. It was to review the changed atmosphere of brass band contests. It was the word 'atmosphere' which puzzled the bands, some of which even thought it might refer to the horseplay that sometimes accompanied the announcement of results. However, it meant something entirely different and, in its way, something quite serious.

When *The Sunday People* agreed to sponsor what it called 'the great music contest of the working man' and wanting to be worthy of the trust now invested in its name, the newspaper lavished all its attention and money on its new promotion project. It was, however, very disappointed, and this is why. Contests had proliferated and in many cases, due to local conditions and the authority of band associations, had different rules from those which governed the area qualifying contests and the National. Whether this was a reason or not, the fact remained that bands were flocking to these other contests and neglecting the National.

The Contesting Council announced its findings and shocked the brass bands. The report condemned out of hand the way in which the general contesting scene had developed and it said contests now had neither cohesiveness or objective purpose. It castigated bands, as the intolerable figure of one in five bands were withdrawing from the National contest.

'Enough is enough and it will not be allowed to continue', said *The Sunday People.* Then came the bombshell; bands were told that all area qualifying contests for the National would finish after the October final of 1965 and, to rub salt into the wound, the Contesting Council and the National Registry of Brass Bandsmen would be abolished at the same time.

In 1963 The Fairey Band completed a remarkable hat-trick of first-prize wins at Belle Vue, Manchester. Our photograph shows the conductor, Mr. Leonard Lamb, receiving the premier award from Mr. H. F. B. Iles, Chairman of Belle Vue. In the background can be seen Mr. Jack Fearnley, Belle Vue's popular Contest Manager.
Mr. Iles also presented to Leonard Lamb the Silver Medal of the Worshipful Company of Musicians, awarded annually to conductors of outstanding distinction in the brass band movement.

When the news sunk in, a groundswell of indignation arose. *The British Bandsman* was flooded with telephone calls and letters and the magazine called the report the most momentous, appalling and disastrous blow the movement had ever experienced. Eric Ball wrote, 'What *The People* has done has made a sad day for brass bands'. He chose his words carefully telling bands it was no use wringing their hands in despair. It was not the end of the road and wrote, 'Consider carefully the implications and let us all help each other'.

Meetings were held between Vaughan Morris and the various committees, and Eric Ball sounded out interested individuals. The outcome of this extensive lobbying was the decision of some committees to organise their own area qualifying contests rather than bands appearing by invitation only. It was a frustrating time and bands were in a turmoil.

Mr. Ball and other stalwarts knew the National Registry, which kept a tight rein on the names of bandsmen *bona fide* registered as playing members of a named band, was most important to the continued success of all contests. If it were discontinued there would be a return to the fraud, corruption and Machiavellianism of the old days. The mere thought of this made many shudder. In time, Jack Fearnley of Belle Vue Gardens, Manchester, with financial help from the bands, assumed responsibility for the Registry and kept it in being.

Eric Ball said, 'My first year of my second period as editor was one of shock upon shock. I had an unending stream of enquiries from people anxious to know if area contests were to continue under the area contesting committees. I just did not know. Some seemed enthusiastic, others were resigned to the demise, not only the area contests, but of the National itself. All I could say was, "have faith".'

The next sensation was the announcement of the retirement of Mr. Vaughan Morris from the International Publishing Company, publishers of *The Sunday People*. Rumours were rife that cash was haemorrhaging from the paper at an alarming rate. The National was to be sacrificed in the interests of economy and Vaughan Morris was getting out whilst the going was good. All poppycock, of course, and the bands gave a collective sigh of relief when *The British Bandsman* printed the news that the newspaper had invited Mr. Vaughan Morris to stay on and produce the whole of the National on a freelance basis.*

Straight away area contests found the strength to have a go and organise the first of the area contests. It was a bit of a mixed success. The Yorkshire area was quick off the mark but it was not an easy thing to do and the Midland area was a good example of the work-load which they had to undertake. The Midland Committee awarded its own prizes, fixed entry fees, printed the programmes, decided on admission prices and hired the hall. It appointed its own adjudicators (in this first effort, Eric Ball, Frank Wright and Walter Hargreaves) and decided which test piece would be played. A formidable task but the movement produced the ladies and gentlemen to do it. On April 22, 1966 the contest went ahead and a precedent had been set for years to come. The bands had found leaders and they knew they would survive.

Mr. Vaughan Morris was here, there and everywhere, cajoling, enthusing and organising, making sure the infra-structure would not collapse, when the good news broke that *The Sunday People* had announced it has passed its corporate responsibility for the National, lock, stock and barrel, to Vaughan Morris. The news was received enthusiastically by all bands and James Abbott, President of the Scottish Amateur Band Association, spoke for all when he wrote, 'Mr. Vaughan Morris has given the brass band business procedure, presentation and organisation. He has emerged as a natural leader'.

This good news was tempered by bad news and bands were learning about inflation the hard way. Harrassed on all sides by the advertising ploys of 'sensational offers', a band scraped together enough money for the deposit on instruments only to find that it was insufficient at the time of payment. The Horncastle Silver Band, for example raised £400 towards a new set of instruments but found in the meantime there had been two quick rises of five per cent in the price. The bandmaster, Mr. E. J. Kemp, said it was an uphill task to raise money at a rate greater than the rise in prices due to inflation. This was a bitter pill for older bandsmen to swallow. They had experienced little or no inflation during the wars. A good example of this was the cost of the Crystal Palace National Contest programme; it was six old pennies in 1922 and the same 13 years later.

Eric Ball left *The British Bandsman* at his own request on March 31, 1967. He paid a generous tribute to two ladies at the magazine who had made his task as editor, possible. Had it not been for Connie Clark, who shouldered heavy editorial and business responsibilities, and Muriel Jakeway, with specialist knowledge of music catalogues and kindred matters, his job, as he said, would have been 'onerous to say the least'. The last three years were, he went on, 'the most rewarding in a long life'. He was awarded the Order of the British Empire in 1969.

Geoffrey Brand, a highly qualified musician, assumed editorial responsibility for the magazine and a wealth of experience with brass bands from which he could draw. Born into a well-known Salvationist family in Gloucester, his talent for music soon revealed itself. It led him to the Band of the Royal Army Service Corps and the Royal College of Music. As a trumpet player with the Royal Philharmonic Orchestra he toured the world and eventually played with the Royal Opera Orchestra at Covent Garden. In 1955 he joined the BBC as producer of music programmes.

With this varied background he was well placed to sustain the best traditions of the magazine and it was not long before he broadened its scope and appeal begun by Mr. Mackler. Out went the long columns of news and personal comment provided by area correspondents using pseudonyms to disguise their true identity. In came the same contributions but under the true name. This new departure increased circulation and, to quicken its pace, Mr. Brand soon embarked on a series of promotional ideas.

Amongst those which received some support were short story competitions, prizes for the best record sleeve and one which caused a lot of comment, 'My heart stopping moment'. He also inaugurated a 'Public Awareness Year' to stimulate interest by the general public. It was not a glittering success but it did give a little fillip to the bands.

Every editor had his problems. In the case of Geoffrey Brand it was the relentless increase in inflation which affected his business and altered the social life enjoyed by brass bandsmen. More and more wives were going out to work to supplement the family income, the value of which was diminishing, it seemed, month by month despite an out-of-pocket supplement given by the Government to counter the extra cost of living. With hindsight, this was counter productive. The press was quick to prophesy

Walter Hargreaves conducting Brighouse and Rastrick at the 1969 National Festival Concert.

that the traditional male breadwinner would soon see his authority eroded.

No longer could a player return from his work, grab a bite to eat and go off to rehearsals, two, three, four or more evenings a week. Now he had to give and take. It was surprising how vivid this memory is in the minds of some bandsmen.

Like Mr. Mackler and Mr. Ball before him, Geoffrey Brand found he was unable to cope adequately as editor because of his many international commitments. He was lucky because his wife, Violet, became editor in all but name, and the magazine reflected her cheerful outlook on life.

*All the facts are in a booklet called *The Story of the National* written by Violet Brand and published in October 1971.

32 *The National returns but escapes*

Toward the end of 1970, Mr. Vaughan Morris realised the time was fast approaching for an appraisal of his involvement in the National contest. His interest in its survival and long term security was no less than that of Henry Iles. He held talks with Geoffrey Brand and Ray Dutfield – a former Salvation Army bandsman and life-long friend of Geoffrey – the owners of *The British Bandsman*, the outcome of which was a painless and amicable sale of all rights and property on the contest to the magazine. To accommodate the National, a new company, called Band Promotions Limited, was formed, and for the first time since 1939 the magazine and the National were together again. One can almost sense Henry Iles smiling benevolently in the wings.

Vaughan Morris bowed out with grace and dignity immediately after the National contest in 1971 amid glowing tributes from the whole of the movement. It was he who had to use all his guile, his friendships and administrative ability to keep the contest in being during the ups and downs of the previous years. His name joined that of Henry Iles to be illuminated in the history of brass bands. But just as Henry Iles had his enemies, so did he. He had been forced into unpopular decisions and had ruthlessly pruned the cost of staging the contest. This resulted in an initial unhappy relationship with some but, within time, the loyalty of area committees was never in doubt.

His last National was a particularly happy one. He stood by the narrow door back-stage at the Royal Albert Hall to shake hands with individual members of the contesting band as they moved along the short corridor (known to all bandsmen as 'the bull run') to enter the vast circular auditorium filled to capacity. A daunting moment — a nervous moment — for them. But one of pride.

The test piece was *Le Roi D'ys,* the melodies of which were hummed and whistled around the public corridors. At the end of the contest he said to his loyal helpers, 'The basic fact is that without you ladies and gentlemen of the various committees who come and work here for nowt, the National Brass Band Festival, this great contest, could not take place, and I was ever mindful of this and the thanks that you never received from the grass roots'. With a voice, subdued with emotion, he said goodbye, shook hands and was gone.

He was quite right. The National Contest, or any other, could not take place if the two dozen or so helpers were paid; the profit was just not sufficient to provide the incentive to undertake such a big enterprise. They came because they loved the movement, the atmosphere of contesting and the chance to exchange banter with the elders of the scene.

Now that Geoffrey Brand was responsible for the National, he cast around for a new organiser. He was determined to employ someone to further the great tradition. He wanted almost too much for he saw the person as a player, a conductor, an administrator and, above all, a diplomat. He remembered he had met such a man briefly in Scotland. His name was Peter Wilson, then 35, and he was invited to take over.

It was a big step to take. The roots of his family were in Scotland, he had never worked outside his native country and London was a long way off but he seized the opportunity and moved. The South did not exactly welcome him with open arms for some committees were still loyal to the memory of Vaughan Morris. 'VM', as everyone called him. They hoped, as had been

A photographer's glimpse back-stage at the Royal Albert Hall, showing the draw being taken for Championship Section. Organising secretary, Peter Wilson, was shortly to be appointed editor of The British Bandsman.

the case with Henry Iles, that he might have continued his interest in the events which had occupied him so fully. This, however, did not conform to the wishes of the incoming promoters and he resigned all his committee offices.

Peter Wilson found himself under some scrutiny. He travelled hundreds of miles throughout the country to introduce himself to committees and outline to these autocratic bodies his approach to his new job. Some treated him with indifference and others with open hostility but he quietly set out his stall and sought their co-operation. It was not long before this young foreign intruder

Peter Wilson, current editor of The British Bandsman.

was accepted. For the next five years the National ran like clockwork despite the inevitable troubles that always seemed to beset any newcomer into the National administration.

Within a couple of years, *The British Bandsman* experienced the effects of serious industrial trouble. The National Union of Mineworkers called the miners out on strike. The Government declared a state of emergency as power cuts hit the country. Colliery bands were, as usual throughout their history, very supportive to the strike and played their hearts out at gatherings, marches and entertainment concerts.

The Government rationalised the production and availability of electric power in industry by introducing a three-day working week with sometimes a consequent loss of earnings. Lights went out almost at a whim, although this inconvenience was tempered sometimes by publishing the times people could expect their area to be darkened. Concerts, contests and rehearsals were cancelled or the bandsmen took pot luck.

Harry Mortimer was conducting a massed band concert when the lights went out; fortunately the emergency lighting came on. Where there was no alternative lighting, bands had to cope the best they could. The Telford Band used bulldog clips and candles, others had torches and hurricane lamps but they were not ideal. One casualty was the important contest organised by the Council of Brass Band Associations to take the place of the famous WD and HO Wills Contest, now defunct through loss of the sponsorship.

No promoter could plan and no band could guarantee an audience because if the lights failed then central heating failed and people stayed at home and went to bed. The papers were full of advertisements selling candles and generators but, generally, social life came to a standstill. The band trade just about coped. Boosey & Hawkes offered interest-free loans to get its stocks moving, a brave move especially as inflation was edging towards the roof.

The British Bandsman attracted many advertisements, it being the chief shop-window for traders. Boosey & Hawkes became the first company to place a colour advertisement. The magazine was dispatched to 19 countries world-wide and found its way into famous orchestras, school, wind and military bands. It was still only eight pages but by increasing the page size by nine square inches it carried more news.

The movement sat back to see how well the new partnership of Geoffrey Brand and Peter Wilson would cope with running the National. Human nature being what it is, there were some secretly hoping they would make a hash of it. It was an amazing, oversubscribed success with the press and radio stations from Europe much in evidence. As the day approached the demand for tickets was phenomenal and the Royal Albert Hall could have been filled three times over. Ticket touts outside the hall were selling tickets at 20 times the original price. An interesting side note is that at Wimbledon Tennis Championships that year, the tickets only sold at ten times face value.

To satisfy the demand for the evening concert, two concerts, one at 5.00 pm and one at 8.00 pm, were staged but, even so, ticket applications poured in. It was astounding how bandsman and women found the cash to spend three days in London, pay hotel fees, travelling expenses and the high cost of tickets and

Geoffrey Brand, the editor of the 'B.B.' conducting Black Dyke to victory in the National of 1972.

programmes. 1972 and the next few years were considered good years but the trend of unemployment was upward. Credit buying was coming to the rescue and credit cards issued by the banks were helping to spread the cost of what one Cheshire bandsman called 'the knees-up in London'.

Then came what was thought to be a body blow. Value Added Tax came into operation as a direct result of Great Britain joining the Common Market. Some secretaries to bands thought the cost of instruments was now beyond the ability of bands to pay. It took a bit of persuading by the Government, the Confederation of British Industry and, of course, the band trade, to convince the public everything was in fact cheaper. VAT replaced Purchase Tax, which was then running at 25 per cent and was a tax on wholesale prices, whereas the new tax was 10 per cent on retail prices. But the doleful pessimistic mutterings continued.

Before rumours of another change of ownership of *The British Bandsman* begun to circulate, the famous BBC newsreader and commentator, Frank Phillips, retired from compèring the National Contest; it was a happy performance to which everyone looked forward. His place was taken by another popular BBC man, John Dunn, who in turn has become part of the tradition.

The National Brass Band Club, once a mainstay of the movement, was now a poor reflection of its past glory. Bill

Elgar Howarth conducting Grimethorpe Colliery brass band in 1975 National Championship at The Royal Albert Hall, London. (Courtesy F. L. Phillips).

Sir Charles Groves, C.B.E. conducting the evening concert given by the massed bands at the Royal Albert Hall on 5 October 1974. (Courtesy Robert Irons).

England, its secretary, tried to increase its statesmanlike authority but watched the membership drift away. He called a meeting to discuss its closure and only 16 turned up. Mr. England could do no more and resigned. His place was taken by Evelyn Bray who through sheer perseverance was able to make the Club a recognisable feature of the movement. Her efforts were rewarded with the award of Member of the British Empire in the Queens Birthday Honours List of 1979.

In 1975, Band Promotions was sold by Geoffrey Brand to Robert D. Alexander, a man variously described at the time, as

an impresario, an entrepreneur and with extensive business interests.

Many asked who was he? Was he a bandsman, musician or conductor? Where did he come from and where was his office? It was revealed the office was a private house.

Geoffrey Brand and, more importantly, his wife Violet, bequeathed a magazine with a healthy circulation. Both had managed *The British Bandsman* well and sustained its finest traditions. It was a force to be reckoned with when it went into the hands of the new owner and immediately some startling changes were made which certainly raised a few eyebrows.

The magazine did not appear until September 6, 1975 after a period of 14 days. Its price was increased by one third from nine pence to 12 pence and it was to be published once a fortnight. It had undergone a drastic facelift with a colourful red masthead which, although eye-catching, commanded a lot of space. It was certainly readable and had good clear print on first-class paper.

The editorial said, 'We all have a great sense of pride in being entrusted with the paper's future and regard it, not only as a challenge, but a grave responsibility. And we can promise we will face the tasks ahead without fear.' The brass bandsman is a canny fellow and one remarked, 'Time will tell', echoing the thoughts of others. After a few months it was considered a good read but some said it was 'brash, flamboyant and too clever by half'.

Robert Alexander had surrounded himself with proven writers and presenters; Norman Parkinson, news editor, and Ron Massey, an established journalist on an influential Yorkshire paper. He called upon three musicians and composers of note as reviewers; Edward Gregson, George Thompson and Albert Jakeway. Correspondents were of the calibre of James Abbott who wrote about the scene in Scotland.

Mrs. Evelyn Bray handing to the sponsors of the Trans-Pennie Contest, the Sydney Pogson Trophy, which she presented for the second section of the contest held in May 1972. The fanfare was provided by children from the primary school of which Mrs. Bray was headmistress.

91-year-old Mr. Edward Tadd and his 61-year-old son, Mr. Eric Tadd, between them represent 124 years' service with one band – Chichester City. A celebration concert was given during 1972 to mark Mr. Tadd senior's 75 years with the band.

This somewhat cultural shock had just subsided when, on 20 September, Geoffrey Brand announced his company would no longer be responsible for the National Contest and the company was now owned by Robert D. Alexander who would present the National in future. He was happy to say Peter Wilson would remain as organising secretary.

It all seemed to be going from strength to strength and, in 1976, Mr Alexander unveiled grandiose plans to launch a European Brass Band Championship at the Royal Albert Hall with an outstanding first prize of £1,000. The band movement settled back. All was well. It was in good hands and there was money to back it. 'Good old Bob', people said as *The British Bandsman* reverted to a weekly publication.

No one seemed to detect anything untoward as Norman Parkinson left and Robert Alexander became 'Chairman and Managing Editor'. He brought back Eric Ball as a columnist. The magazine was still a good buy at 12p and 12 pages. Peter Wilson was showing his flair as a writer and *The British Bandsman* had the appearance of a good solid investment, with the *International*

Bandsman, a short lived monthly, covering bands overseas and marching bands.

1976 was a year of concern for brass bands. There was a pessimistic outlook because of a marked falling-off of bandstand and park concert engagements. Some schedules had been curtailed or cancelled altogether even in the areas which were traditional brass band strongholds. Fees offered to bands to play in municipal parks were, in the words of *The British Bandsman*, 'quite disgusting'. Such was the necessity for bands to get money that many bands accepted these ridiculous fees which only led some councils to think they could engage bands for nothing.

David Neilson, writing in the magazine, thought 1976 held heavy in the hearts of bandsmen and went on, 'Unless we reshape our relationships, I can see no prospect of our getting out of the muddy rut we secretly know we are in. The future cannot be and must not be, an extension of the past. A radical rethinking of the whole system is needed.'

But it never was and never will be. Bandsmen seem to enjoy the loosely knit movement it is. There is no move to make it less of an abstract idea and more of a material reality with a central authority to speak for it with vested and final sovereignty.

33 *A rough ride*

The New Year message of 1977 from the editor included the words, 'Remember in particular that, as bands, we cannot prosper and progress where harmony and goodwill are wanting'. But it was to be a year in which the words meant little as far as the staff of *The British Bandsman* was concerned. There was an atmosphere of uncertainty. The magazine was not the force it once was, and worse, Peter Wilson was disappointed with the way the National Contest was going.

He gave in his notice as organising secretary and, in a press statement, Robert Alexander said, 'This is not a sudden decision as Mr. Wilson had for some time been considering a new challenge in a wider field'. Diplomatic words indeed, but poppycock. Peter Wilson left because he was fed up!

I had the opportunity to speak to Robert Alexander at the Bugle, Cornwall, brass band contest in 1985. He told me that despite all his so-called troubles at that time, he was determined the National Contest should prosper. He went on, 'I knew I was entrusted with a great tradition and, believe you me, I knew there was no way I could or would break this trust. I suppose, with hindsight, *The Bandsman* and the National were too much for one man.' I asked him why he sold the magazine and he replied, 'Well, for the money — but it made me very sad. I loved every minute of owning and editing it.'

He was delighted when Trevor Austin showed an interest in ownership and negotiations began to purchase the magazine. On 16 July 1977, Mr. Alexander issued a press statement which stated he had sold *The British Bandsman* to Messrs Austin Catelinet of Beaconsfield, Buckinghamshire. The biggest surprise to the brass band world was the appointment of Peter Wilson as editor of the magazine and, a little later, a shareholder in the ownership. It was a popular choice, a measure of which was the number of people who came to his office in Beaconsfield to wish him well on his first day.

The sale of the magazine secured a better financial future for the National which was badly needed. Robert Alexander gave his reasons for the sale in the magazine, 'I am very anxious to extend my interest in contesting and concert promotion and allied affairs within the brass band scene, including recording.' His plans, his vision of bigger and better festivals and contests never materialised although he did promote a contest at the Wembley Conference Centre.

He told me he was really up against it during this period and agreed with me he had two priceless strokes of luck. The first was employing a lady called Angela Lynskey. She had no experience of brass bands but was well equipped with know-how and business acumen which came just in time to inject a sense of purpose into the National Festival and contest. In next to no time she became an efficient contest co-ordinator and administrator and had a feel for the movement which she never ever contemplated as she walked into the office of Mr. Alexander for the first time.

The second stroke of luck happened when James Abbott, the popular chairman of the Scottish Brass Band Association, accepted the post of Contest and Festival Controller. His proven record over many years in brass band contesting and administration stood him, the contest and the fortunate Robert Alexander in good stead.

The magazine was ticking over when it was handed over to Peter Wilson but it had failed to satisfy the market; the readership and consequently its circulation was ailing. The new editor slipped into the chair to the manner born. It was ironical that he was to watch the near demise of the National in a few brief years. He was well out of it all.

Gradually the circulation of *The British Bandsman* increased. The editor soon found his bearings and analysed the strengths and weaknesses of the magazine. In one sense he went back to the stated aims of Sam Cope. He returned to the traditional responsibilities of an editor, guiding, cajoling, enthusing and commenting on the issues of the day. He did not shy from controversial subjects and some of these were soon upon him.

Mr. Alexander, now in sole charge of the National somewhat arbitrarily re-organised the system of grading for bands in the various sections of the National Championship. The new rules for this were accepted by some area committees, under protest by others and refused by the Welsh Area Committee. This meant no Welsh bands would go to London to participate in the National finals.

This was a particularly unhappy blow to the movement and left Robert Alexander's reputation badly bruised. *The British Bandsman* put forward a peace proposal which led to Mr. Alexander seeking peace with the Welsh area and in 1980 the *impasse* was resolved.

In 1980, his company, Band Promotions Limited, walked a financial tight-rope, just hanging on by its finger tips. The European Championship, which it organised following the day of the National at the Royal Albert Hall each year, needed cash and quickly. The dilemma coincided with the appointment of Bill Martin of Messrs Boosey & Hawkes as Special Projects Director. Mr. Martin was given a free hand to strengthen the firm's contacts with brass bands here and abroad.

The dire financial straits of the 'European' were well known and Messrs Boosey & Hawkes stepped in with sponsorship. Not only did it put up the cash but Mr. Martin, an ex-brass player, took an active part in its promotion. However, the organisation, presentation and cash flow was left to Mr. Alexander.

Once he had secured a sponsorship for the European then he cast around for a sponsor for the National and he was successful in interesting the second largest bank in America to inject a large amount of cash.

Two important contests in the South had been cancelled by other promoters because of the lack of funds and strong rumours were circulating that Band Promotions Ltd. was in difficulties. All this did nothing to improve the morale of the bands, especially at a time when unemployment was soaring to horrifying levels. Nevertheless they were able to plan for the future as the inflation rate was beginning to fall.

What did bemuse the various band committees was the spectacle of band suppliers 'cutting each others throats' in a discounting free-for-all in the climate of the deepening recession. Yet, although the summer months had been a period of uncertainty and bewilderment, James Abbott and his helpers made a great success of all the preliminary work put in by Angela Lynskey for the 1980 National. Those of us close to the management knew in our heart of hearts that all was far from well. Some people, including me, were asked to put up money to save it from extinction. Nobody did.

Robert Alexander seemed to draw more and more into himself leaving Angela Lynskey to shoulder the pressing and often abusive demands for immediate payment of debts. Rumours abounded that the winning bands had not been paid their prize money. Accusations of maladministration and mounting debts were reaching the national press which caused *The Yorkshire Post* and *The Huddersfield Examiner* to speculate on the future of the

contest and of Robert Alexander himself. Ron Massey, still a weekly contributor to *The British Bandsman* and a journalist with his finger firmly on the pulse of the movement, reported an air of resignation had befallen the bands.

After this Angela Lynskey telephoned me. She was at the end of her tether. There was a queue of creditors and she was unable to coax Mr. Alexander into any definite plans for the future. Nothing had been done, it was all drifting away. There had been no forward planning for the 1981 National although the resilient area committees were going ahead with the regional qualifying contests. I told her to telephone Peter Wilson. He took her out to lunch and listened to the full sorry story of an empty kitty and horrendous debts.

One of the most unusual incidents in Harry Mortimer's long and glorious reign as promoter of the Open Championship (which many say is the most prestigious contest of them all). The picture was taken in 1978 when the King's Hall, Belle Vue, Manchester was evacuated because of a bomb threat. The police ordered the premises to be evacuated immediately, which meant the judges were removed from their enclosure and kept in an isolated place of safety until the resumption of the contest.

The photograph shows members of Stanshawe, CWS (Manchester) and other bands waiting for the all clear.

34 *A happy ending*

A curious episode followed. Information reached *The British Bandsman* that Boosey & Hawkes were openly talking of stepping in to save the day, presumably by paying the massive outstanding debts of which £11,000 was due to prize winning bands of the National. Negotiations were opened between Robert Alexander and Boosey & Hawkes and rapidly entered the final stage which would have meant the latter acquiring all rights to the National, European and World Contests. Then came the news which rocked Boosey & Hawkes. It was this.

The firm learned to its horror that what it was doing was quite illegal. It was informed that a contract was in existence, drawn up and properly signed, legally binding Robert Alexander to offer all the titles to the owners of *The British Bandsman* in the event of his desire to sell. In other words *The British Bandsman* was lawfully the rightful heir and must be given first refusal. It had not been. It had not even been consulted.

A new formula had to be hurriedly agreed between the firm and Mr. Alexander. To obviate any legal repercussions, the negotiations reopened to *present* the National by Boosey and Hawkes. This new wording would, presumably, allow the firm to settle the outstanding debts with Mr. Alexander still clinging to his tottering company. It was a confusing situation.

On 17 January 1981 *The British Bandsman* printed the following statement from the new presenters:

In view of much rumoured doubts about the future of the National Brass Band Championships, Boosey & Hawkes has undertaken to stage brass band championships at the Royal Albert Hall on 3rd October 1981 and in successive years.

In doing this, as in restoring the Royal Opera House after the war, the company is moved by the need to maintain a British musical institution as the acknowledged leader in its field. Boosey & Hawkes believes that any

*such championships should be non-profit-making and that representatives of
the band movement should be given a voice in their organisation.*

With this in mind the firm called a meeting in London to
which all regional secretaries and members of the National Brass
Band Advisory Committee were invited.

At 4 pm on the evening before the meeting, Michael Boxford,
the chief executive of Boosey & Hawkes, and his sales director
met with Peter Wilson and Trevor Austin at Heathrow Hotel.
Questions came by the dozen. To the eventual question as to
whether or not he would be prepared to consider an invitation to
join an 'advisory panel' Peter Wilson said, 'No'. He felt that the
independence of *The British Bandsman* was his first priority. The
answer to the next question, 'What would it cost to buy *The British
Bandsman?*' The answer was as firm as it was short. *The British
Bandsman* wasn't for sale!

At the meeting the following day plans were revealed by
Boosey & Hawkes to form a company known as Boosey &
Hawkes Band Festivals Limited which would run a national
contest similar to the one owned by Robert Alexander. The
representatives gave their unanimous support to this idea and
severed all connections with Robert Alexander.

It was a most unreal situation as Mr. Alexander adamantly
refused to relinquish his right to the title and, of course, the
owners of *The British Bandsman* were still very much aware of its
legal rights. It is apparent that the formation of this new company
neatly sidestepped the vexed problem of the Alexander contract.
Bill Martin of Boosey & Hawkes was appointed managing
director of the new company which Angela Lynskey joined as
contest controller. Soon Robert Alexander, now in ill health,
gave up his control of the National title.

A period which had both appalled and fascinated the brass
band fraternity had come to an end. *The British Bandsman* was still
the vigorous independent magazine it had always been and said:
'The new administration will be judged by the way in which
matters are tackled and solved. For the future of brass band
contesting, as well as the reputation of the Boosey & Hawkes
company, it cannot afford to fail'.

Epilogue

After the year-long strike called in 1984 by the National Union of Mineworkers which seriously affected colliery bands, the movement settled down into what it is today. Sponsors come and go. The trade is still in fearful competition and the movement can still produce the man for the moment.

In the issue of 26th December, 1903, Sam Cope wrote the following:

"A RETROSPECT

It has been suggested to me that a few words on the establishment of *The British Bandsman* would be of interest to the present readers.

The question occurred to me one day whilst reading the pages of a musical paper devoted to the string department of the orchestra. "Why not a paper for the wind section?" I there and then determined to "feel the pulse" of those who I thought would give me valuable advice. The replies came readily, and in every instance the idea was approved and encouraged. Foremost amongst those who promised support were the late Lieut. Dan Godfrey , Lieut. Chas. Godfrey, Lieut. G. Miller, Mr. Chas. Cousins, Mr. Kappey, the brass instrument manufacturers, and some well-known conductors.

At this time I had not seen any paper of a similar character, but Lieut. Chas. Godfrey drew my attention to a newspaper devoted to the interests of contesting brass bands. I did not look on this as a serious rival, as I intended my venture to be a high-class magazine, but a curious coincidence happened about the same time, for in going through Wych Street (now demolished) to order a musical directory I was thunderstruck in seeing in a window a magazine entitled "The Military and Brass Band Gazette," published monthly, price 1d. Needless to say I purchased it, and scanned the contents with feverish haste, and was considerably relieved to find that although it was an excellent little paper, it was not my ideal. Mr. Chas. Cousins was at this time the principal of Kneller Hall, and I well remember his observation when I remarked to him that the magazine, of course, would be of no personal value to him, but it might appeal to him as of use to the students. He replied in an impressive way, "Don't make that mistake, Mr. Cope. The older I get, and the more knowledge I acquire, the more I realise how ignorant I am."

This is, or should be, I think, true of us all; but how many have the courage to confess it?

As the "B.B." then appealed to the military band as well as the brass, I was advised by Mr. Cousins to enlist the assistance of Mr. Waterson as editor, which I did; but Mr. W. was at that time in very poor health, and unable to work in real earnest; consequently the burden of the whole undertaking fell on my own shoulders.

I was editor, publisher, canvasser, manager and general factotum. Mr. Waterson continued his advice for the first three or four months, and then fell out of it.

The first issue was 1,500, but I had to have a reprint. The second month ran into 2,000 copies, and the third, 2,500; but I was never able to exceed this, as my time was occupied very considerably in other directions.

The magazine was published from my private residence, and large bundles of copies were distributed monthly to an agent I had appointed in each large town. I took these parcels direct to the railway termini myself to make sure there would be no delay at this end, there having been so many complaints.

I kept going in this way for some fifteen months, with the assistance, during the latter part of this time, of my brother, who undertook the clerical work, he being a band enthusiast. About this time two gentlemen associated with the printing works, who had decided to start "on their own," approached me with a proposal to undertake the publication, but I bargained with them to take over the whole business part, which they did, I having bound myself to continue the editorial work.

Owing to circumstances having no connection with the magazine, these gentlemen decided to sell the copyright, and the Rev. R. Viney, a musical enthusiast, became the owner. This gentleman gave the greater part of his time, energy and fortune to the establishment of a musical institute (the Cecilia), but it was not a success, and Mr. Viney, partly on this account and partly because of ill-health, retired into country. As I had other work which monopolised my time, I retired from the editorial chair. Mr. J. A. Browne, who had so ably assisted me from time to time, succeeded as editor, and I resumed duties again at the time Mr. J.

H. Iles assumed ownership, and continued for a period until indeed I found it impossible to give the attention to it that it really required. About this time those excellent music supplements from the "Champion" Journal were introduced.

Of its conversion into a weekly paper I need say nothing, except that almost everyone thought it a suicidal act. Mr. Iles had, however, the courage of his own conviction, and launched it; and now it floats in triumph, bearing good things to all parts of the globe.

As to its contemporaries, the "Military and Brass Band Gazette" is dead; "The Instrumental Journal," which followed it, has also departed; the "British Bandmaster," which was started ostensibly in opposition, soon died a natural death; and the "Musical Enterprise" (H. J. Metcalfe's paper) is no more.

The early numbers of the "British Bandsman" contain some splendid articles of the greatest practical value to bandsmen, and I sincerely hope they may be reprinted for the advantage of the present readers. Amongst the contributors were Dr. E. H. Turpin (formerly of the Robin Hood Band), the late Lieut. Griffiths, and Messrs. Chas. Cousins, J. Waterson, Hamilton Clarke, V. C. Mahillon, D. J. Blakeley, A. A. Clappe, R. Smith, and other well-known writers.

If anyone were to ask me what, in the first instance, was the principal inducement to establish the magazine, I should unhesitatingly reply, "Because, first, I wanted to raise the status of bandsmen and to see the merits of this deserving class duly recognised; and, secondly, because I wanted to effect an improvement in the instrumentation of brass bands, so that there would be more variety of tone colour. No doubt I am still premature in the last desire, but I prophesy the time will come when our best brass bands will possess saxophones, trumpets, and French horns, which I have so long advocated.

As regards the first object, is it not *au fait accompli?* For this we have to be grateful to our esteemed principal—Mr. J. H. Iles (who was, by the way, dubbed by Madame Besson "the Napoleon of the Band World"). All my readers will, I am sure, join with me in wishing him long life, good health, and continued interest in our bands' welfare. In conclusion, permit me to wish all readers of the "B.B." a Happy Christmas and a Prosperous New Year.

S. COPE."

The richness and variety of brass bands has co-existed with *The British Bandsman* for one hundred years during which time the various editors have been outspoken, sympathetic and encouraging

whilst maintaining total independence with no outside interference or proprietorial control.

It is the consistency of its readership which makes for a sense of
community. It is this that has sustained *The British Bandsman* for so
long.

The British Bandsman:

A Monthly Magazine

For Bandmasters and Members of Military and Brass Bands.

Vol. I. No. 1.   September, 1887.

The British Bandsman

AND ORCHESTRAL TIMES:

A Monthly Illustrated Magazine

FOR WIND INSTRUMENTALISTS.

Vol. I. No. 10.   June 15th, 1888.

The British Bandsman

AND ORCHESTRAL TIMES:

A Monthly Illustrated Magazine

FOR INSTRUMENTALISTS.

Vol. II. No. 13.   October 1st, 1888.

The British Bandsman

AND ORCHESTRAL TIMES:

A Monthly Illustrated Magazine for Instrumentalists.

Vol. III. No. 25.   October, 1889.

The Orchestral Times & Bandsman.

A Monthly Magazine devoted to the interests of Band and Chamber Music, and of Solo Instrumentalists.

VOL. IV.   No. 1.   January, 1891.

The British Musician.

An Illustrated Monthly Magazine devoted to the interests of Band and Chamber Music, and of Solo Instrumentalists.

VOL. X.   No. 113.   February, 1897.

The British Bandsman.

An Illustrated Monthly Magazine devoted to the interests of Brass, Reed, and String Bandsmen, and the Trade.

VOL. XII.   No. 136.   January 1st, 1899.   PRICE THREEPENCE.

VOL. XIV.   No 161.   January 12th, 1901.   Price **3d.**

A WEEKLY NEWSPAPER DEVOTED ENTIRELY TO BRASS BANDS.

No. 9. Vol. XV.   MAY 3, 1902.   PRICE ONE PENNY.

The British Bandsman.

[REGISTERED AT THE GENERAL POST OFFICE AS A NEWSPAPER.]

No. 218.   Vol. XIX.   MAY 5, 1906.   PRICE ONE PENNY.

The BRITISH BANDSMAN

A WEEKLY NEWSPAPER DEVOTED ENTIRELY TO MUSIC.
[REGISTERED AT THE GENERAL POST OFFICE AS A NEWSPAPER.]

No. 305. Vol. XXI.   JANUARY 4, 1908.   PRICE TWOPENCE.

THE
BRITISH
BANDSMAN

No. 528. Vol. XXX.   APRIL 13, 1912.   PRICE TWOPENCE.

The
British Bandsman.

No. 644.   JULY 4, 1914.   PRICE TWOPENCE
All communications for this paper should be addressed to "The British Bandsman," 210, Strand, London.

Special Number   *for the New Year*

British Bandsman
WEEKLY JOURNAL FOR BRASS BANDS
FOUNDED   1887

No. 1,660. [Registered at the General Post Office as a Newspaper]   SATURDAY, JANUARY 6th, 1934.   PRICE 3d.

THE
BRITISH
BANDSMAN

No. 3,545   Price 8d.
Saturday, February 21, 1970   Registered at the General Post Office as a Newspaper

265

THE *BRITISH* *BANDSMAN*

Sponsors of the National Brass Band Championships of Great Britain

No. 3,827   Price 9p

Saturday, August 2, 1975   Registered at the General Post Office as a Newspaper

Getzen Clinic to be conducted by Carole Dawn Reinhart at 29 Exhibition Road, Kensington, 7.30 p.m. Friday 10th October (Contest Eve), tickets 75p each from —
Rosehill Instruments,
London End, Beaconsfield,
telephone 71717.

NATIONAL CHAMPIONSHIPS

No. 3,831   Registered at the General Post Office as a Newspaper   Saturday September 6, 1975

No. 3833   Published Fortnightly   Saturday October 4, 1975

No. 3856   Published Fortnightly   Saturday, August 21st 1976

ISSUE No. 4160   Registered at the General Post Office as a Newspaper   SATURDAY 10 JULY 1982

ISSUE No. 4161   Registered at the General Post Office as a Newspaper   SATURDAY 17 JULY 1982

For Instruments
and
Accessories
Rosehill Instruments
Tel: 04946 71717

ISSUE No. 4418   Registered at the General Post Office as a Newspaper   SATURDAY 20 JUNE 1987   PRICE 28p

IS YOUR INSTRUMENT CLEAN INSIDE AS WELL AS OUT?
MOUTHPIPE CLEANLINESS IS MORE IMPORTANT THAN EVER.

Detergent Cleaner	£2.00
Long Brush	£1.25
Valve Brush	£1.25
Mouthpiece Brush	£0.36

CASH WITH ORDER £5 POSTAGE PAID
Rosehill Instruments
64 London End, Beaconsfield HP9 2JD

271